"Harper is best known as the first man to step onto the summit of Denali during Stuck's famous 1913 expedition. But as Ehrlander shows, there was much more to Harper's tragically short life. . . . [Ehrlander] offers a much more nuanced and balanced assessment of the role Christianity played in this era than many modern writers understand and provides rousing descriptions of weeks-long dogsled trips in the depths of winter."

—DAVID JAMES, *Daily News-Miner* (Fairbanks)

"A fascinating glimpse into a pivotal moment in Alaskan history through the story of the short life of Walter Harper, a protégé of the redoubtable missionary Hudson Stuck. The men and women of Alaska were tough and hearty souls."

—STEVE THOMAS, author and host of *This Old House* and *Renovation Nation* and grandson of the Reverend William A. Thomas, a contemporary of Walter Harper

"A concise picture of Walter Harper's character and personality. This is a historical account of a courageous Athabascan leader whom we all should learn about."

—WALTER CARLO, chair of the board of Doyon, Limited, the Alaska Native Claims Settlement Act corporation for the Athabascans of Alaska's Interior

"A fine biography of a young man of talent and energy who successfully coped with two cultures during a time of rapid change in Alaska. Mary Ehrlander has employed crisp and enlightening prose to illuminate both the era and the history of the Yukon region."

—JOHN R. BOCKSTOCE, Arctic historian and archaeologist

"Mary Ehrlander's assiduous scholarship combined with a delightful storytelling style make *Walter Harper, Alaska Native Son* both easy to read and available for multiple fields of academic interest."
    —PHYLLIS FAST, professor of anthropology emeritus at the University of Alaska Anchorage and great-niece of Walter Harper

"Not only a fine work of history but a rousing adventure tale and a love story. This is a great book."
    —TERRENCE M. COLE, professor of history at the University of Alaska Fairbanks

"Ehrlander's portrait is of a remarkable young man who lived life to the fullest. An inspiring example of resilience, character, faith, service, and loving-kindness, Walter Harper's legacy is a testament to the Native peoples of Alaska, the indomitable human spirit, and the selflessness of those who work as missionaries in the Church in the harshest and remotest of places."
    —JASON VANBORRSUM, *Anglican and Episcopal History*

Walter Harper
ALASKA NATIVE SON

MARY F. EHRLANDER

University of Nebraska Press

LINCOLN

The University of Nebraska Press is part of a land-grant institution with campuses and programs on the past, present, and future homelands of the Pawnee, Ponca, Otoe-Missouria, Omaha, Dakota, Lakota, Kaw, Cheyenne, and Arapaho Peoples, as well as those of the relocated Ho-Chunk, Sac and Fox, and Iowa Peoples.

First Nebraska paperback printing: 2023
Library of Congress Cataloging-in-Publication Data
Names: Ehrlander, Mary F., author.
Title: Walter Harper, Alaska native son / Mary F. Ehrlander.
Description: Lincoln: University of Nebraska Press, [2017] | Includes bibliographical references and index. |
Identifiers: LCCN 2017005537 (print)
LCCN 2017020905 (ebook)
ISBN 9780803295902 (cloth: alk. paper)
ISBN 9781496236906 (paperback)
ISBN 9781496204042 (epub)
ISBN 9781496204059 (mobi)
ISBN 9781496204066 (pdf)
Subjects: LCSH: Harper, Walter, 1892–1918. | Athapascan Indians—Biography. | Mountaineers—Alaska—Biography. | Stuck, Hudson, 1863–1920—Friends and associates. | Mountaineering—Alaska—Denali, Mount. | Denali, Mount (Alaska)—Description and travel. | Irish-Americans—Alaska—Biography. | Racially mixed people—Alaska—Biography. | Missionaries—Alaska—Biography. | Frontier and pioneer life—Alaska.
Classification: LCC E99.A86 (ebook) | LCC E99.A86 E57 2017 (print) | DDC 978.004/9720092 [B]—dc23
LC record available at https://lccn.loc.gov/2017005537

Set in Scala OT by Rachel Gould.

To Lars

Contents

Illustrations

Maps

Preface

MANY ALASKANS FIRST learned of Walter Harper during the centennial celebration of the 1913 pioneer ascent of Denali. Harper, who was of Irish and Athabascan descent, had been the first to stand atop North America's tallest peak. A legacy climb by descendants and relatives of the pioneer ascent team aimed to give long overdue credit to co-leader Harry Karstens and team member Walter Harper. Attention given Hudson Stuck, an Episcopal archdeacon who was the organizer of the expedition, had overshadowed Karstens's and Harper's crucial roles in the triumph.

I had learned of Walter Harper a few years earlier when I opened Hudson Stuck's *A Winter Circuit of Our Arctic Coast*. The moving dedication had piqued my interest:

IN LOVING MEMORY OF

WALTER HARPER

COMPANION OF THIS AND MANY OTHER JOURNEYS

STRONG, GENTLE, BRAVE, AND CLEAN

WHO WAS DROWNED IN THE LYNN CANAL

WHEN THE "PRINCESS SOPHIA" FOUNDERED

WITH HER ENTIRE COMPANY

25TH OCTOBER, 1918[1]

The sinking of the *Princess Sophia* remains the worst disaster in Alaska's maritime history. Walter Harper and his bride of seven weeks, Frances Wells Harper, were among the more than 350 souls who perished after the steamer ran aground in a blinding snowstorm. So ended Harper's plan to attend medical school and return to his homeland as a medical missionary.

Walter Harper had been Archdeacon Stuck's riverboat pilot and winter trail guide since 1910, when he was seventeen years old. Stuck had relied heavily on resourceful young Alaska Native assistants since he assumed his position as a traveling missionary in Alaska's vast Interior in 1905. Harper soon became the "best boy" Stuck ever had. Eventually he became the son Stuck never had. As I read the engrossing account of their final winter circuit, I resolved to uncover and publish the little-known story of this remarkable man's life. The journey has been the most challenging and rewarding of my academic career.

I became increasingly convinced of the interest his biography would generate as I grew to know Walter Harper. His thrilling adventures in Alaska's expansive wilderness and his heroic qualities provided the perfect ingredients for a gripping saga. Harper's thorough integration in both his mother's Athabascan lifeways and his father's Western culture made him a terrific role model for individuals with mixed heritage the world over. In particular he serves as a beacon to Alaska Native and other Indigenous youth as they prepare for the future in a globalized world. Harper's tragic early death infuses the story with a poignancy that heightens its appeal, rather than diminishing its value.

Hudson Stuck's many published accounts of his travels in Alaska led me into Harper's world. Stuck's diaries offered further insight into Walter's development and character. Additional archival and published materials both validated and complicated the portrait of Harper within Stuck's narratives. A delightful trove of Frances Wells Harper's letters that I discovered on a family website proved to be a windfall. Her depictions of Walter, her accounts of their adventures, and her reports of their plans deepened my understanding of him. The letters shed light on her character and personality, which also spoke to the man she married.

My quest to know Walter Harper also led me to Northfield Mount Hermon, today a coeducational preparatory school in western Massachusetts; Walter attended the Mount Hermon School for three years in the 1910s. Walking the grounds, touring his dormitory, surveying the dining hall, and visiting the chapel helped me imagine his boarding school years. America's largest boarding school in the early twentieth century, it differed strikingly from the government-sponsored industrial boarding schools of the era that aimed to assimilate Native Americans. Mount Hermon's founder, the well-known evangelist Dwight Moody, established the school to provide a sound, Christian-based education to boys with high aims and limited means. By the time Harper entered Mount Hermon, the school had developed a strong reputation for educating Native Americans for careers in teaching, medicine, law, and other professions.[2] School policies neither denigrated Native cultures nor forbid the speaking of students' native languages. The school aimed to produce Native American leaders who would return to their communities and serve their people. Letters Harper wrote to his sisters and to Hudson Stuck during his three years at Mount Hermon revealed his impressions of the boarding school experience. They also illustrated his character traits, his affection for his sisters and for Stuck, and various other sentiments. These letters and the journal he kept while on Denali provided the most reliable indications of Harper's own impressions of his experiences. The comparative dearth of such accounts in Harper's hand hindered my ability to discern his own perspectives on his life.

Stuck's copious narratives were therefore both a boon and a curse as I sought to know and understand Harper. In the absence of other evidence I have relied heavily on Stuck's depictions of their travels and their relationship. More of Harper's impressions would have balanced Stuck's perceptions and enriched my comprehension of Harper's experience and his attachment to Stuck. I also longed for more insight into Harper's Christian faith from his own perspective. Stuck wrote that Harper lived his faith, rather than espousing it. The sparse references to his faith in Harper's surviving journal and letters support Stuck's impression. Absent further evidence, a more nuanced assessment of his faith is not possible.

I was also unable to discover how much Stuck compensated Harper for his labor, though I know Stuck paid him. The question pertains to broader concerns about the nature of Stuck and

Harper's relationship. Did Harper's wages and other benefits reward his labor appropriately? In addition to wages Stuck paid all of Harper's expenses, beginning in the summer of 1910 when Walter first worked for him. Those expenses included the cost of his travels in the continental United States and visits to landmarks and amusement parks. Stuck tutored Harper when they were together. He arranged payment of Harper's tuition at Mount Hermon, and he sent him spending money from time to time. He also paid for Harper's music lessons at Mount Hermon. He secured a scholarship for Harper's college education and planned to pay his medical school tuition with royalties from his book sales.

Stuck clarified in a letter to his friend John Wood that covering Harper's tuition would repay a debt. He had compensated Harper for his labor over the years, but not for the full value of his faithfulness. The balance lay "heavily against" him, he explained, for Harper constituted Stuck's "indomitability, my courage, my ready-made information of native matters, my tirelessness, my strength, my resource." Harper had become the "other part" of him, Stuck concluded.[3] Not only was Harper the source of Stuck's strength and inspiration, he would also further his mentor's legacy. Harper would bring to fruition Stuck's vision of a resilient Athabascan people long after Stuck was gone, he imagined. Thus Harper's service to Stuck could not be compensated in wages. In return for Harper's labor and faithfulness Stuck invested his time, energy, and resources in Harper's development, anticipating the benefits to future generations of Alaskans. Their relationship reflects reciprocal faithfulness and the capacity for human interaction to maximize the individual's potential.

Introduction

STANDING ATOP DENALI marked a stunning achievement for Walter Harper, a twenty-year-old of Irish and Athabascan descent. He was the youngest member of the climbing party, led by Hudson Stuck and Harry Karstens, that made history in 1913 by scaling North America's tallest mountain.[1] He had stepped onto the summit first, a fitting honor. This master of wilderness skills, with the physical condition of an elite athlete, had fared the best of the team members during the ascent. His energy, self-restraint, and positive attitude had moved the team forward while defusing tension and lifting spirits. The expedition might have concluded quite differently without him.

Hudson Stuck, an Episcopal archdeacon, had initiated the expedition, but at forty-nine years old he could not perform the most physically challenging tasks on the ascent. In fact he barely managed to reach the summit. Harry Karstens, the tactical team leader, had extensive wilderness experience and displayed herculean strength in carving steps through the ice on the mountain. But his quick temper and impatience with Stuck's domineering personality increased tension among the men. Anger, along with digestive problems, led to his taking "days off" in camp. Robert Tatum, just a year older than Harper at twenty-one years of age, was least prepared physically and emotionally for the climb. At higher elevations he frequently remained inside the tent, overwhelmed by anxiety and depression. Harper alone displayed truly exceptional stamina while maintaining complete self-composure.

Harper's extraordinary promise renders his life story even more

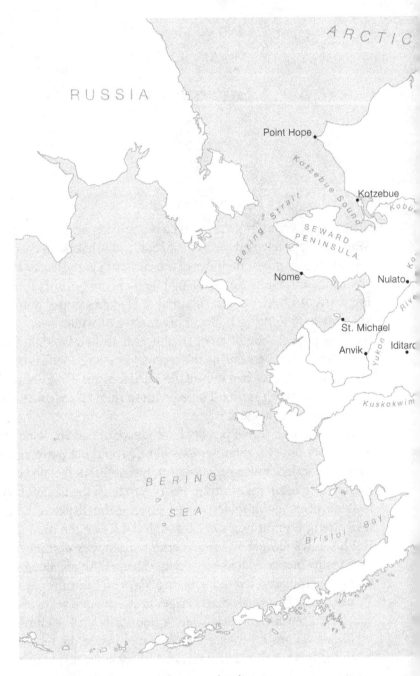

MAP 1. Map of Alaska. Dixon Jones, graphic designer,
Rasmuson Library, University of Alaska Fairbanks.

compelling than the singular feat of climbing Denali. His splendid complement of physical, mental, and emotional assets ensured his emergence as a great leader in twentieth-century Alaska. This era in Interior Alaska's history demanded competent leadership more than any before or since. Harper's tragic death at the age of twenty-five therefore lends the narrative an exquisite poignancy, the lost potential incalculable.

Walter Harper was the youngest child of an Athabascan woman, Jenny Albert, and the well-known prospector and trader Arthur Harper. Following his parents' separation, Walter's mother raised him in the Athabascan tradition. He developed a drive to excel at wilderness arts at a young age. His introduction to Western culture began at sixteen, when he arrived at St. Mark's Mission in Nenana in 1909. The following year he accepted a position as Archdeacon Stuck's traveling companion, riverboat pilot, and winter trail guide.

Living up to Archdeacon Stuck's expectations was not easy. Walter likely found his new way of life bewildering and taxing at times. Mainstream American social norms were not intuitive to an Athabascan youth, and he missed the freedom to hunt and fish as he pleased. No doubt Walter occasionally chafed at the archdeacon's demands. Many people bristled at Stuck's intensity and sometimes abrasive demeanor. Yet, Walter saw through these exterior traits into the heart of the man. His rapid growth as Stuck's pilot and guide was empowering. His English-language skills expanded quickly, and reading opened his mind to a world outside his direct experience.

Walter's striking good looks, charismatic personality, and remarkable place-based skill set won him many admirers. His soft-spoken manner heightened his appeal. Those who came to know him recognized the sense of honor that grounded the young man. His spirit seems to have been immune to corruption or dishonesty, though he engaged in boyish mischief. As he matured, self-knowledge bred stoicism and graciousness in him. Challenges overcome bolstered his self-confidence. Regular praise from Stuck and others affirmed his competence and highlighted the benefits of his employment.[2]

It is no mystery that Stuck found Walter an ideal assistant. Walter embodied Stuck's vision of Alaska Native people embracing Christianity's message and adapting to Western civilization while maintaining their traditional lifeways. Walter's expertise and assistance allowed Stuck to spread his message. As an intermediary he fostered trust between Stuck and the Athabascan people. His translation of Stuck's words effectively endorsed Stuck's views and gave them credence among Athabascans. Walter thereby enhanced Stuck's reputation in Interior Alaska, in Episcopal Church circles, and in the general public.

Exactly how much agency Walter exerted in his relationship with Hudson Stuck and in his furtherance of mission goals is impossible to know. The totality of the evidence suggests that the increasing responsibility he assumed as Stuck's riverboat pilot, trail guide, and translator allowed Walter to progress toward what the psychologist Abraham Maslow described as self-actualization. He enjoyed profound personal fulfillment as he developed his physical and intellectual potential. His solid foundation in his birth culture deepened, even as Stuck guided his introduction to Western culture. His stature among the people of Interior Alaska steadily grew. With his evolving identity as a resourceful, principled man of Athabascan and European ancestry, Walter's capacity to serve as a bridge between Native and Western peoples emerged. Eventually he settled on a career path through which he could contribute to the health and well-being of his people, while remaining immersed in the culture and homeland he loved. He planned to become a medical missionary.

During their final winter circuit, in 1917–18, Harper and Stuck grew closer than ever. Paradoxically Walter made decisions that marked his independence during this last odyssey. He resolved to join the Air Corps to serve the Allied cause in the Great War. After the war he would resume his educational path. He also decided to marry the missionary nurse with whom he had fallen in love. Both of these choices deviated from his and Stuck's carefully conceived plan to enter college, attend medical school, and return to Alaska as a medical missionary. Harper told Stuck of his change in thinking late in the journey. The disclosure signaled a departure from their earlier pattern of making decisions about his future together. Harper had made these choices without consulting Stuck. He sought Stuck's support rather than asking his permission. He was ready to chart his own course. Before long Stuck accepted Walter's decisions, gave the couple his blessing, and married them himself. Such is the time-honored tradition. Each generation matures, separates from parents, and finds its own way.

Walter Harper would have become an expert hunter and fisherman under any circumstances. He may well have become a leader among his people. The intersection of his life with Stuck's raised the possibility of his having a much more profound impact in Alaska's Interior. His remarkable record of accomplishment during his short lifetime suggests that he would have achieved his dream of becoming a medical missionary had he lived longer. Multiple generations of Alaskans would have known and respected him. Young people would have admired his abilities and his quiet self-confidence. As a physician and missionary Harper would have led and served his people physically and spiritually. His principled and charitable bearing would have acted as a lodestar. In his senior years Alaskans from all walks of life would have turned to this intelligent, accomplished, devout Elder for his wisdom.

Walter Harper's tragic early death denied him the legacy of a respected Elder. Yet, his life history of just one-quarter century presents an inspiring model of a life well lived. Harper approached each day with energy and purpose. His raw talent and persistence led to proficiency in wilderness arts. His curiosity and keen intelligence produced brilliant results in all things mechanical. He integrated into Western culture without forfeiting an ounce of his Athabascan heritage. His immersion in both cultures allowed him to bridge the two and to ease communication and understanding between Natives and non-Natives. Self-respect, integrity, faith, and a benevolent spirit guided Harper's social interactions. The man had the makings of a moral giant. His excellence is as noteworthy today as it was during his lifetime.

Walter Harper, Alaska Native Son

1

Childhood and Adolescence

WHEN WALTER HARPER arrived in the world in December 1892 at Nuchelawoya, his parents, Jenny Albert and Arthur Harper, had been married eighteen years.[1] She had borne seven other children—five boys followed by two girls. The family had traveled extensively along the middle and upper Yukon River, establishing trading posts at sites near gold discoveries. Jenny and Arthur's relationship bore the strains of many separations during his long prospecting journeys. Jenny and the children suffered separations from one another as well. Arthur sent each child Outside, as Alaskans called the continental United States, to boarding school in Ross, California, at the age of six or seven, against Jenny's objections.[2] She wanted her children at home with her. The couple separated just a few years after Walter's birth, and Jenny returned to her native region at Nuchelawoya to raise her youngest child in the Athabascan tradition.

Seentaána, as Jenny's Koyukon Athabascan people knew her, may have been part Kobuk River Iñupiaq. Oral histories told of Athabascans on the Koyukuk River raiding the encampments of Kobuk River Iñupiat to the north for wives and vice versa.[3] Some said Jenny's heritage was thus mixed.[4] However, she grew up according to Koyukon Athabascan tradition, learning to cut, dry, and smoke fish, snare rabbits, and gather berries.

The Irish potato famine had driven twelve-year-old Arthur Harper to emigrate in 1847.[5] Harper lived with an uncle's family in Brooklyn, New York, for several years.[6] He then made his way to California at the age of twenty and prospected for minerals in the American West, eventually migrating northward into British Columbia.[7] In 1872 Harper began an odyssey that would define the final decades of his life in Alaska and the Yukon Territory, Canada. He became a legendary figure, credited as the first to recognize the region's potential for gold mining.

Harper traveled more than two thousand miles, living off the land with three other men. Starting near the head of the Peace River at Munson Creek, they followed the Liard, Mackenzie, Peel, and Porcupine Rivers to Alaska. No non-Natives, except for Hudson Bay Company (HBC) traders, had yet entered much of the land they crossed. The men arrived at Fort Yukon, Alaska, a former HBC trading post where the Porcupine entered the Yukon River, in July 1873.[8] Harper later told William Ogilvie, who was a surveyor and the commissioner of the Yukon Territory, that they had seen gold in many locations. On the Yukon River they had found "prospects everywhere."[9]

A month after Harper reached Fort Yukon, Jack McQuesten and Alfred Mayo arrived there, having followed some of the route Harper had taken. Harper, McQuesten, and Mayo formed a decades-long partnership as traders in Alaska and the Yukon. Always maintaining his interest in prospecting, Harper spent much of his time in the last three decades of the nineteenth century scouting for signs of gold.

In the summer of 1874 just thirty-two white persons lived along the Yukon River and its tributaries, including Harper at Nuchelawoya.[10] In the Athabascan language that place-name meant "where the rivers meet," referring to the confluence of the Tanana and Yukon Rivers. Alaska Natives came from far up the Tanana River, from the upper and lower Yukon River, and from the upper Kuskokwim River to trade goods and furs at Nuchelawoya.[11] Later the community where Walter was born became known as Tanana.

On one of Harper, McQuesten, and Mayo's first excursions down the Yukon River in 1874 a fall freezeup trapped their boat. Unable to proceed downriver they inquired in the area about eligible marriage partners. According to family history, residents at Koyukuk Station chose three "deficient" women for the men.[12] The residents considered Seentaána deficient because she was tall. Her

CHILDHOOD AND ADOLESCENCE

cousin Margaret, who married Al Mayo, was said to have inadequate sewing skills.[13] Arthur Harper was thirty-nine and Seentaána,
or Jenny, was fourteen when they met that fall.[14] Euro-American
migrants to Alaska and the Yukon often entered into common-law
or legal marriages with Indigenous women, and children often
were born of these unions. During the gold rush era many men
abandoned their Native partners and children when they left the
north country, regardless of whether they were legally married.[15]
Jenny and Arthur Harper's marriage endured much longer than
most, despite their incompatibilities. Al and Margaret Mayo's
marriage was much more harmonious. It produced eleven children, ten of whom survived to adulthood, and lasted until 1924,
when he passed away.[16]

The summer after they were married Jenny and Arthur poled
up the Yukon River 1,050 miles to Fort Selkirk, well within Canada.[17] They moved often as Harper established and operated trading
posts at various locations in Alaska and the Yukon. Sites included
Fort Selkirk, Eagle, Nuchelawoya/Tanana, the mouths of the Stewart, Fortymile, and Sixtymile Rivers, and Fort Reliance.[18] Harper
developed a reputation as a trusted and honorable trader who provided miners with supplies according to need and regardless of
whether they could pay for the goods.[19] Natives and non-Natives
alike respected him.

Although Arthur Harper's activities are rather well documented,
almost no written records shed light on Arthur and Jenny's relationship. The successive separations from her children no doubt
caused Jenny anxiety, as well as loneliness, especially considering
Arthur's frequent absences. Jenny's cousin Margaret reportedly
adapted well to Western lifeways. She and her husband, Al, sent
their children Outside, to boarding schools in Wisconsin and Bux-
ton Mission, Ontario, with Margaret's approval. After they settled
in Rampart at the turn of the twentieth century she served as a
liaison between Native and non-Native residents.[20] The great age
difference between Jenny and Arthur Harper may have contributed to their discord.

Jenny's Koyukon Athabascan people and other Athabascan tribes
had inhabited interior Alaska for thousands of years. The Brooks

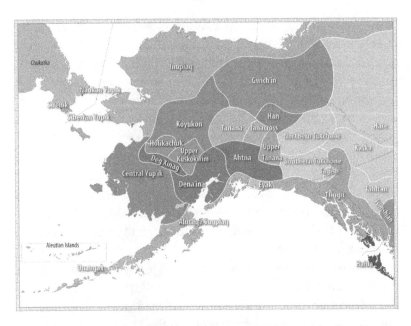

MAP 2. Indigenous peoples and languages of Alaska. Michael Krauss, Gary Holton, Jim Kerr, and Colin T. West. 2011. Indigenous Peoples and Languages of Alaska. Fairbanks and Anchorage: Alaska Native Language Center and UAA Institute of Social and Economic Research. http://www.uaf.edu/anla/map.

Range to the north and the Alaska Range to the south bordered their traditional region in the forested Interior. The Yukon River united Athabascans on either side of the Alaska-Canada border, which Russia and Great Britain settled at the 141st meridian in 1825. Beyond the Athabascan homeland lived Alaska's several other Indigenous peoples. The various Athabascan tribes, dispersed over Alaska's vast Interior, spoke one of more than ten languages.

The Interior landscape varied dramatically. For instance, in the broad flat area at the Arctic Circle known as the Yukon Flats, the Yukon River separated into a complex web of streams. To the west, as the terrain rose toward the Ray Mountains, the multiple channels rejoined, and the Yukon flowed through towering ramparts.[21]

Bands of a few Athabascan families moved in seasonal rounds to harvest the nutrient-rich foods that nature provided. In the Tanana region, Walter Harper's homeland, the people relied heavily on

CHILDHOOD AND ADOLESCENCE

fish, primarily salmon, whitefish, and grayling, or Arctic trout. They caught large numbers during the summer and dried and smoked them for use throughout the winter. They also hunted moose, caribou, and smaller mammals and birds, but fish sustained the people and their dogs more reliably. Various commodities, including guns, ammunition, axes, files, knives, needles, pails, pipes, tobacco, snuff, and beads, had entered Alaska's Interior through trade routes from the east and west before white explorers and settlers entered the region.[22] Athabascans incorporated these items into their daily routines and pursuits.

In addition to supplying fish, rivers formed travel routes in Alaska's Interior region, in both summer and winter. Rivers connected villages, allowing people, goods, and supplies to be transported in and people and goods to travel out. Athabascans traveled in birch-bark canoes, sharp at both ends and sometimes decorated with beads or porcupine quills. The canoes were so light that a man could carry one with one hand.[23]

Millennia after Alaska's Indigenous peoples settled in the region Russian explorers and fur traders arrived. Alaska's Russian era began in 1741 with Aleksey Chirikov's sighting of Prince of Wales Island and with Vitus Bering's arrival at Kayak Island. Subsequently Russian fur hunters exploited Alaska's waters and Native peoples, especially the Aleut, Alutiiq, and Tlingit.[24] In 1799 Emperor Paul I granted a monopoly on the Alaska fur trade to the Russian American Company (RAC).[25] The RAC established a fort at Nulato on the lower Yukon River in 1839, and a Russian explorer traveled upriver into the heart of Athabascan country as far as the Tanana River.[26] But Russians exerted no control over Athabascans in the Interior.

In 1847 the Hudson Bay Company built a trading post at Fort Yukon, on the Arctic Circle, well within Alaska's eastern boundary, and HBC employees traveled down the Yukon River to buy furs.[27] At Nuchelawoya they met RAC traders. But the RAC seems not to have been troubled by the HBC's activity in Alaska. Because Russian traders and later administrators generally ignored Alaska's Interior, Athabascan lifeways remained largely unchanged during the Russian era.

By the mid-nineteenth century Russia's American holdings were losing their appeal. Harvests of sea mammals had declined, and the far-off territory became more of a burden than an asset to Russia. Preferring to focus on internal modernization, Tsar Alexander II decided to sell Alaska.[28] The United States was in an expansionist era following the Civil War, and Americans saw potential in the region's natural resources. In 1867 the two countries settled on a sale price of $7.2 million. Following the transfer of the territory, merchants established several trading posts in the Nuchelawoya area. By 1870 the Alaska Commercial Company had come to dominate trade in Alaska.[29]

Soon after the United States purchased Alaska, surveyors discovered that the HBC post at Fort Yukon lay within American territory.[30] The Alaska Commercial Company therefore bought the post.[31] Before long, steamships regularly plied the Yukon's waters during summers, carrying people and trade goods upriver and returning with people and furs.[32] This economic activity opened some wage-labor opportunities to Iñupiat in the coastal region and Athabascans in the Interior. Alaska Natives worked as pilots, firemen, assistant engineers, and wood choppers on the steamers.[33] Athabascans supplied beaver, fox, marten, wolverine, bear, and wolf skins to traders in return for tea, flour, cotton cloth, and other sought-after household items.[34] As river traffic increased, interaction with migrants and the habits they introduced dramatically altered traditional lifeways along the Yukon.

By the late 1800s the preferred means of travel in winter was by dogsled. Dogs reportedly outnumbered people in some villages.[35] The U.S. government provided mail service throughout Alaska, in summer by boat and in winter by dogsled. Arthur and Jenny Harper at one time owned forty to fifty "Eskimo dogs," a husky-malamute mix, which they kept at Nuchelawoya and used for winter transportation. Each dog ate a chum salmon a day, when they were available. The Harpers and other dog owners typically fished intensively during summers and dried the salmon to use during the winter. Feeding dogs through the winter was burdensome; owners sometimes had to destroy the hungry animals when it was impossible to feed both their families and the dogs.[36]

CHILDHOOD AND ADOLESCENCE

Eventually Arthur Harper and Jack McQuesten reported their gold discoveries to the officers of the Alaska Commercial Company's steamer, the *St. Paul*. The news spread to San Francisco, and several prospectors arrived in the St. Michael district in western Alaska in 1882.[37] Both Harper and McQuesten also reported the discoveries in letters to miner friends in southern Alaska. These letters lured miners into the Interior via the Chilkoot Pass.[38] Harper's widespread prospecting, numerous discoveries, and communication to outsiders about the area's gold prospects won him recognition as the discoverer of gold in the region.[39] Yukon commissioner William Ogilvie credited Harper with being the first to consider the Alaska-Yukon region as a "mining field."[40] By the time tens of thousands rushed to the Klondike in 1898 Harper and others had done much to ease the journey and support the mining process.

Meanwhile in 1884 Congress created Alaska's first civil government. It was a bare-bones system, with a weak appointed governor and no elected legislature.[41] Prospectors hailed from nearly every country in the world. They tended to be hardy characters, and many were rough around the edges. More than a few were "wanted" by the law elsewhere.[42] With no formal law enforcement in the Interior, people relied on direct democracy, or "miners' meetings," to promote order and solve crimes. Miners in a given region would gather to consider the evidence surrounding a crime. They would then vote on the guilt or innocence of the accused and impose a punishment. Depending on the severity of the crime, the penalty might be banishment, restitution, or, in the case of murder, death by hanging.[43]

Norms centered on the golden rule, officially adopted as the emblem of the Yukon Order of Pioneers. The Canadian historian Pierre Berton described the code in *The Klondike Fever*. Anyone who discovered gold shared the good news with others. Any miner could use an empty cabin he found, but he was expected to replenish the wood supply before leaving. And no miners went hungry. Harper, McQuesten, and Mayo grubstaked, or supplied, miners regardless of whether they could pay for the items.[44]

The 1886 discovery of coarse gold on the Fortymile River, just inside the Alaska border, sparked the first gold rush into Alaska's Interior. Harper, McQuesten, and Mayo built a trading post at the mouth of the Fortymile River, on the Canadian side of the border, and a settlement sprang up there.[45] In 1889 Arthur and Jenny Harper established a new trading post at the mouth of the Pelly River, well within the Yukon territory. The geologist Israel Russell met the Harpers and their "several interesting children," as they traveled to the new trading post site opposite old Fort Selkirk.[46] He described Harper as "one of the most genial and best informed men that I met in Central Alaska."[47] In the early 1890s a settlement grew around the Fort Selkirk trading post, and the Anglican Church built a mission there.[48]

By 1893, when Walter Harper was born, Circle City, Alaska, was the largest settlement and supply point on the Yukon, with a population of five hundred. A sawmill at Circle City, and another at Fortymile, owned by Arthur Harper and Joe Ladue, provided lumber to those who could purchase it.[49] However, many miners personally sawed the boards for their cabins and their sluice boxes, the standard device miners used to separate gold from other earthen matter. The miners shoveled promising gravel and soil, or pay dirt, into the long wooden boxes with slats, or riffles, in the bottom. As they flushed water over the dirt, the lighter contents washed away, while the riffles caught the gold.

By this time Tanana had become a bustling trade and transfer point for freight and passengers traveling along Interior rivers. Steamships regularly supplied trading posts that served both Natives and miners. Just one government official was stationed along the length of the Yukon River in Alaska; he was the tax collector at Circle City. But because most of the miners in the region were American, thoroughly American and democratic communities developed in the mining camps on the upper Yukon.[50]

In 1895, when Walter Harper was not yet three years old, Arthur and Jenny Harper separated.[51] She returned with Walter to Tanana, where she raised him in the Athabascan tradition and he spoke the Koyukon Athabascan language.[52] He became adept at hunting and other subsistence activities well before beginning his Western education and acculturation. In stark contrast his brothers,

1. Harper & Ladue Mill Company, Dawson, Yukon, with Arthur Harper in
doorway on right. Wickersham State Historic Sites Photo Collection,
P277-001-098, Alaska State Library, Juneau.

after spending their formative years Outside at boarding school,
had to readjust to their mother's culture during adolescence. They
returned home when their father could no longer pay their tuition, in the mid- to late 1890s. The boys found their homecoming as disorienting as their arrival at boarding school had been.
They had forgotten their mother's language and had grown accustomed to indoor plumbing and electricity. They disliked the odors
of the animal hides and tanning solutions that permeated Jenny's
crowded cabin. The disruptions of their childhood years left the
older Harper brothers stranded between Native and non-Native
cultures. Discrimination against mixed-race individuals deepened
their sense of alienation. Walter's sisters, Marianne (known as
Jessie) and Margaret, continued their studies in California. They
eventually graduated from San Francisco Teachers College.[53] Having marketable skills eased their homecoming.

In August 1896 George Carmack and his Indigenous companions Skookum Jim and Tagish Charlie found gold on Bonanza

Creek in the Yukon territory. The creek flowed into a river the local Natives called Tron Deg, which non-Natives mispronounced as "Klondike."[54] Word of the gold strike spread quickly. In early September Harper and Joe Ladue built a trading post and saw-mill at the mouth of the Klondike River that provided them a good income.[55] The business partners established a town site there and named it Dawson.[56]

As word of the Klondike discovery reached other mining camps in Alaska, their populations dropped as miners rushed to the new strike. When news of the stunning discovery reached the world, the Klondike gold rush began in earnest. About one hundred thousand people set out for the Klondike. Thirty thousand to forty thousand of them reached Dawson. The rush peaked in 1898. According to Pierre Berton, a few hundred became rich in the Klondike, but only a small number retained their wealth.[57] With the 1900 gold discovery at Nome, Alaska, most miners vacated Dawson.

Arthur Harper left the Yukon for Arizona in August 1897, hav-ing been taken ill with tuberculosis. The Alaska Commercial Com-pany, for which he had worked for many years, paid his passage Outside.[58] He died that November at the age of sixty-two.[59] His confidence in the Yukon-Alaska region as a gold field had proved correct, but Harper benefited little from the major discovery in the Klondike. He had few assets at his death.[60] Mount Harper in the Ogilvie Mountains, north of Dawson, was named in honor of Arthur Harper.

Walter Harper never knew his father personally. However, owing to Arthur Harper's celebrated reputation, the youngster grew up with a strong sense of his father's role in the developing terri-tory. In part Walter's cheerful disposition and resourcefulness may have been an inheritance from the father he knew only by reputation. His solid foundation in his Native culture gave him a strong sense of identity, and the freedom he enjoyed fostered resourcefulness and self-confidence.

The tens of thousands of gold seekers and others who entered Alaska's Interior in the 1890s caused great disruption to Native lifeways. Most destructive were the epidemics of influenza, small-pox, and measles that killed thousands of Alaska Natives. Year

CHILDHOOD AND ADOLESCENCE

2. Arthur Harper. From Ogilvie, *Early Days on the Yukon*.

after year tuberculosis plagued the people. Cramped living conditions and lack of awareness of how the disease spread increased the death rates.[61] Several diseases blinded people, including syphilis, scrofula (a form of tuberculosis), and trachoma, a highly infectious eye disease.[62]

Alaska governors urged the U.S. government to provide medical care for the Native population, but little changed. In 1886 Governor A. P. Swineford reported that diseases threatened Alaska Natives with "complete extinction." He requested provision of a hospital to treat Alaska Natives as soon as possible.[63]

In 1914 Governor J. F. A. Strong reported in detail the alarming health conditions among Alaska Natives, declaring, "Medical relief is necessary and urgent."[64] Three years later Governor Strong wrote in frustration that if Congress was not willing to meet Alaska Natives' health needs, then it might as well "do nothing at all and allow the race to die out as quickly as possible."[65]

Europeans and European Americans had long recognized a connection between unclean conditions, foul water, and illness.[66] In the 1880s scientists discovered just how germs cause infectious disease. Remarkable advances in prevention and treatment followed. However, Alaska Natives had no access to this information. They did not know that coughing and sneezing spread disease or that blood from a diseased person could infect another.[67] Missionaries and other teachers arriving in Alaska at the turn of the twentieth century knew that disease spread through contaminated water, fecal matter, and body fluids. Unsanitary conditions in communities, in homes, and on the soiled faces and hands of the children alarmed them. They stressed hygiene and strongly urged sanitation measures in Native villages.[68]

Along with infectious diseases, migrants brought alcohol to Alaska, and their abusive drinking habits "infected" many Alaska Natives. Congress forbid alcohol importation, as it did on reservations elsewhere in the United States. But scant law enforcement allowed liquor to enter the territory through numerous ports. It could be bought in all mining towns.[69] Missionaries tried to bar alcohol from Native villages, but doing so became increasingly futile as migrants streamed into the territory.

With the beginning of the Klondike gold rush so many people and so much liquor poured into Alaska that prohibition of alcohol was impossible. Therefore Congress approved liquor sales in licensed saloons.[70] The ban on sale or trade of alcohol to Alaska Natives continued, but its widespread availability, along with increased wage-earning opportunities, allowed Natives easier access to liquor. Alcohol abuse rose most dramatically in com-

CHILDHOOD AND ADOLESCENCE

munities along the heavily trafficked Yukon River. Fort Gibbon's location near Walter's home village of Tanana heightened the alcohol-fueled turmoil there. Because whole families typically lived in one-room dwellings, children witnessed and suffered from violence and neglect.

Walter spent his early childhood years with his family at St. James Episcopal Mission at Fort Adams. The community was just downriver from where the village of Tanana grew. Sometime after separating from Arthur Harper, Jenny married Chief Alexander William of Tanana. Jenny Albert and Chief Alexander had a child, Robert, whom she reportedly spoiled "to pieces."[71] Keeping Robert at her side must have delighted her, after her first husband had sent seven of their eight children away to boarding school at tender ages. Alexander was a kind and indulgent stepfather to Walter. His mother disciplined him from time to time, but she let him roam and play freely, in the Athabascan tradition. Sliding down the riverbank was a favorite winter pastime when he was young.[72]

Chief Alexander was one of the chiefs who gathered in Fairbanks for the historic July 1915 meeting of the fourteen Tanana chiefs with Judge James Wickersham. The chiefs asked Wickersham, who was Alaska's delegate to Congress, about the implications of the railroad that was being built into the Interior. They expressed concern for their lands and subsistence rights. They also told Wickersham they wanted industrial schools for their children and equal opportunities for railroad construction jobs and other employment.[73]

In 1900 the Episcopal Church rebuilt the Mission of Our Savior at the confluence of the Tanana and Yukon Rivers, near present-day Tanana. Walter's family and other families moved there to be close to the mission. One of his earliest memories illustrated the freedom he and other children had to wander. He would walk to Fort Gibbon to play with the children there. One day one of the children fell off the seesaw. The child wailed so hysterically that Walter feared the child's father, an officer, would punish him. He dashed to the riverbank, dropped to the river, and ran, his head bent down, the full three miles back to the mission.[74]

The lively and mischievous boy loved pulling pranks on oth-

3. Jenny Harper and Chief Alexander William. Yvonne Mozée Collection, #2002-98-20, Mozée Family Papers, APRCA, University of Alaska Fairbanks.

4. The 1915 gathering of the Tanana chiefs with Judge James Wickersham. Wickersham State Historic Sites Photo Collection, P277-001-098, Alaska State Library, Juneau.

ers. His favorite stunt was to startle people who were sleeping in open tents. He and his friends would tie a tough piece of dried fish to a strip of caribou sinew and slip the other end over the toe of the sleeper. Before long a dog would greedily swallow the fish and awaken the person, causing a commotion. Once Walter lingered too long at a tent, enjoying the ruckus, and the victim of his prank gave him a sound thrashing.[75]

The pleasure the youngster took in hunting and fishing led to an early drive to excel in these pursuits. Walter regularly traipsed through the wilderness and brought home the fruits of his hunting and fishing prowess. With nearly twenty-four hours of sunlight in June and July, night and day were indistinguishable. Oftentimes he would wander until three o'clock in the morning and sleep until noon.

In summer the family would migrate from their winter home to a choice fishing location. They spent one summer at a coal mine cabin up the Yukon River near Rampart. Walter and his mother fished while his older brothers earned cash by cutting wood for steamers.[76] Later the family settled at Rampart. Jenny's cousin Margaret and her husband, Al Mayo, lived in the mining town. After moving about from trading post to trading post, they had settled in Rampart about the time of the Klondike gold rush. Several of Jenny and Margaret's other relatives lived there as well, so Walter had plenty of cousins to play with.[77] He also benefited from the companionship and mentorship of male adults in pursuing subsistence activities. Alexander gave Walter a new hunting rifle when he was perhaps ten. One day while out hunting birds in early spring with Rampart Joe and James Pitka, Walter nearly drowned when he fell through rotten ice and was pulled under by the strong current. Rampart Joe's quick action saved the boy's life. He ran downstream, jumped into the icy, chest-deep water, and pulled Walter out.[78] The lad learned from such lessons. Each scrape he survived expanded his traditional ecological knowledge, increasing his self-confidence and reinforcing his identity as a capable outdoorsman.

Walter learned to avoid equally perilous social conditions that prevailed along the Yukon River. At the age of twelve or thirteen he took his first and last drink of alcohol. Upon returning from a successful moose hunt, Walter found visitors in the Alexander home. One of the guests put a bottle of liquor on the table and urged Walter to drink. After three swallows he felt ill. The next morning he awoke outside, miserable, and vomited. The incident left him with a lifelong aversion to alcohol.[79] And it cemented his resolve to reject such new habits and uphold his Native traditions.

Such a conscious choice eluded Walter's older brothers, who returned from California to a disorienting mixture of sociocultural conditions. Of his five older brothers, Andrew, Alfred, Frederick, Charles, and Samuel, Walter identified most with Sam, who was nine years older than he. Like the other Harper boys, Sam was good looking, charming, and popular with women.[80] In 1907 Sam married Louise Minook, who was of mixed Russian and Athabascan heritage. Sam supported his wife and children with subsistence activities and seasonal wage labor. During the summers he and Louise lived at various camps along the Yukon, catching fish

CHILDHOOD AND ADOLESCENCE

in their fish wheel. He also cut wood for the sternwheelers.[81] Sam and Charley Harper sometimes earned cash delivering mail by dog team. They typically made three-day to five-day runs, depending on conditions, earning twenty dollars per run. They would stay overnight at cabins and homes along the way. According to family lore, Sam's orienteering and sled-driving skills did not begin to match his younger brother Walter's.[82]

Walter's personality sparkled from a young age. He was his sister Margaret's favorite brother. "Ever since the 'Dawson' days," she later recalled, "when he was a lad in red flannel shirt, playing with me on the doorstep, I have longed to have him with me, but fate interfered." The girls' years Outside at school separated them from family, and when they returned, Walter was traveling with Archdeacon Stuck.[83]

Wherever he went, Walter's pleasing personality and good looks attracted girls' attention. Margaret recalled, "Walter had personality—scads of it. Everybody liked him. The girls were crazy about him."[84] However, the archdeacon's plans for Walter's education were well known, and they did not include marriage.[85]

Archdeacon Hudson Stuck's plan for Walter's schooling reflected his broader vision of resilient Alaska Native peoples flourishing in their homeland after the gold rush era subsided. Stuck's vision coincided with the aims of other progressives who sought to help those left in the wake of America's rapidly industrializing society. The concept of the social gospel developed in the late 1800s, as tumultuous social conditions coincided with rapid economic growth in America.[86] The movement called upon Christians to devote themselves to solving social problems in American society. Chiefly women spread the social gospel by providing health care, education, and economic aid to the less privileged.[87] In Interior Alaska, Episcopal women missionaries, in particular, devoted themselves to Alaska Natives' well-being when soldiers, gold seekers, and other adventurers swarmed into the region.[88]

The social gospel movement coincided with a change in federal policy, from relocation and concentration on reservations to allotment and assimilation of Native Americans into mainstream society. Recognizing the failure of reservations, where

Native Americans lived in misery and poverty, government officials and Christian "Friends of Indians" sought to improve the
conditions of Indigenous Americans. The Dawes Act divided reservations into allotments, or parcels of land, for individual families based on the belief that private land ownership would bring
Native Americans into mainstream American society.

A national system of boarding schools followed. It aimed to
"uplift" Native Americans by teaching them industrial skills and
assimilating them. The "Friends of Indians" truly wanted to help
Native Americans, in part by preparing them for the inevitable
change that was coming. They failed to recognize, however, the
long-term harm of coercing Native Americans into abandoning
their identity and heritage. The historian Francis Paul Prucha has
called the reformers' zealous confidence in their cause "ethnocentrism of frightening intensity."[89] Prucha's sharp assessment captures reformers' ardency and narrow-mindedness, but it glosses
over the variability in perceptions among these progressives. Catholic, Moravian, and Episcopal Church efforts during the late nineteenth and early twentieth centuries to document Alaska Native
cultures and language and perpetuate their use countered mainstream assimilation efforts.

By 1880 a number of Christian denominations had planted missions in Alaska. That year several Protestant churches came to an
understanding that assigned mission work in various regions of
the territory to specific Christian churches. The so-called Comity
Agreement sought to prevent harmful competition and to ensure
that the Native peoples throughout Alaska were served.[90] Owing
to the Anglican Church's well-established work along the Yukon,
the agreement assigned much of Alaska's Interior to its daughter
church, the Protestant Episcopal Church of America.[91]

Missionaries primarily aimed to spread Christianity among
Alaska Native peoples. Almost all missions also provided schooling, medical care, and hygiene awareness. Some missionaries
learned and documented Native languages. Prior to Alaska's purchase by the United States in 1867 the Russian Orthodox Church
had sought to convert Alaska Natives to Orthodoxy. The Russian
Orthodox priest Ivan Veniaminov had documented Aleut and

made it a written language by translating the Bible and other works into Aleut. Schools during the Russian era taught Aleut children in both Aleut and Russian. During the American era the Jesuit missionary Jules Jetté documented the Koyukon Athabascan language in an effort that was equally noteworthy. Beginning in the 1870s Catholic missionaries visited Nuchelawoya and taught Athabascans the Lord's Prayer, the Ten Commandments, and some Bible verses in their own language.[92]

Of the Protestant denominations in Alaska the Moravians in the southwest and the Anglicans or Episcopalians in the Interior showed the greatest appreciation of Indigenous languages and cultures. In the early 1860s the Anglican pastor Robert MacDonald spread Christianity along the upper Yukon and translated the Bible, the Hymnal, and the Book of Common Prayer into Kutchin Athabascan.[93] MacDonald established Kutchin Athabascan, now called Gwich'in, as a written language and thus had a long-term impact on its survival.[94]

The Anglican Church remained active in Alaska along the Yukon River for twenty years after Alaska's transfer to the United States.[95] In 1888 the Anglican missionary Thomas Canham and his wife established a mission at Nuchelawoya. Three years later the Episcopal missionary Jules Prevost arrived.[96] Canham and Prevost translated the Prayer Book, the baptismal and marriage ceremonies, the Morning Prayer, and some hymns into Upper Koyukon Athabascan. This work exemplified the Anglican/Episcopal Church's dedication to maintaining and preserving Native languages and culture.[97]

Nevertheless, introducing a new religion, with its corresponding worldview, had certain cascading effects on Athabascans and their culture. For instance, Christianity reoriented people's concerns toward an afterlife, undermined the authority of shamans, and urged legal marriage. Moreover the very act of suggesting a new idea implied its superiority, which simultaneously devalued the former belief system. However, this early contact did far less to destabilize Athabascan languages and lifeways than the waves of gold-seeking migrants and later official English-only language policies. Episcopal missionaries tended to urge Athabascans to shun the trappings of mainstream American culture and maintain their traditions.

The Presbyterian missionary Sheldon Jackson, as education agent in Alaska from 1885 to 1908, enforced federal assimilation policy in the territory. Fellow Presbyterian pastor S. Hall Young persuaded Jackson and the Presbyterian Mission Board to suppress Native languages, which in turn suppressed Native traditions and religion. Young, who in 1879 established Alaska's first Presbyterian church, in Wrangell, objected to translating the Bible and other religious materials into Tlingit. Instead he urged letting the "old tongues with their superstition and sin die—the sooner the better—and replac[ing] these languages with that of Christian civilization." He advised compelling Alaska Native schoolchildren "to talk English and *English only.*" This, he believed, would transform them into "an intelligent people who would be qualified to be Christian citizens."[98]

Eventually the adoption of English-only policies in schools throughout Alaska, as well as in regional boarding schools that removed Native children from their homes and communities, caused irreparable harm to Alaska Native languages and cultures. As the linguist and Alaska Native languages specialist Michael Krauss put it, "From about 1910 to about 1960 a deathly silence descend[ed] over the Alaska Native language scene."[99] Some denominations, such as the Moravians and Episcopalians, ignored and resisted the policy. For instance, in 1918 Iñupiaq children still spoke their native tongue in school at Point Hope, where the teacher was an Episcopal missionary. But eventually all Alaska schools operated under the English-only policy. This form of censure belittled not only the Native languages but the broader cultures and the people themselves.

Mistreatment of Alaska Native children in residential schools also has been well documented. Not all denominations or missionaries endorsed such policies, however, nor were all or even most missionaries guilty of abusive treatment of Alaska Native children. On the contrary, during a time when Alaska Natives suffered from high death rates and great social disruption, mission schools and orphanages took in many orphans and other children whose parents were unable to feed and clothe them. Without their efforts, death rates and exploitation of Alaska's Native peoples would have reached much higher levels.

Regardless of where missionaries fell on the spectrum—from those who actively suppressed Native languages and traditions to those who fostered language and cultural maintenance—missionaries engendered change. Even those who urged Alaska Natives to maintain traditional lifeways implicitly encouraged at least partial acculturation in mainstream American society. The Episcopal missionary Hudson Stuck fell in this class.

Stuck arrived in the territory in 1904. He would serve until 1920 as "Archdeacon of the Yukon [River] and of the Arctic regions to the north of the same," that is, archdeacon of Interior and northern Alaska.[100] The British-born Stuck had immigrated to the United States in 1885 at twenty-one years of age. He graduated from the University of the South's Episcopal seminary at Sewanee, Tennessee, in 1892. At Sewanee Stuck developed a reputation as an advocate for social causes. Later he was pastor and then dean of St. Matthew's Cathedral in Dallas for ten years. At St. Matthew's he devoted himself especially to youth. He fought for social reform in Dallas, focusing on women's and children's needs.[101] In his sixteen years as Episcopal archdeacon in Alaska, Stuck made many enemies in his efforts to shield Alaska Natives from harm. As his biographer David Dean has noted, "Most whites deplored his views on virtually every subject."[102] Yet Stuck persevered. In fact he took pride in his ability to ignore criticism.[103]

When Stuck arrived in Alaska, the future of the Indigenous peoples looked grim. Whalers, miners, and other migrants had brought infectious diseases that had killed tens of thousands in recent decades. Social problems, including alcohol abuse, had destroyed the social fabric of villages and had killed many people. Stuck believed that only the Church could save Alaska's Native peoples from extinction.[104] He saw their future in resilient Native youth who would lead their people, with the Church's guidance, after the current turmoil had run its course. Walter Harper would become the Athabascan lad in whom Hudson Stuck placed his greatest hope.

5. Episcopal archdeacon Hudson Stuck. From Stuck,
Alaskan Missions of the Episcopal Church.

Initially Stuck settled in Fairbanks, a booming mining town that arose after Felix Pedro discovered gold there in 1902. In 1905, when he assumed the role of archdeacon, Stuck began his years of travels by dogsled in winter and by river in summer, visiting missions and villages throughout Alaska's Interior. Stuck established his headquarters at Fort Yukon's mission.

Fort Yukon had remained quite isolated from direct outside influence, except for the Anglican mission, until the 1890s. The discovery of gold near Circle City in 1893, followed by the Klondike gold rush of 1897–99, brought a flood of problems to the village.[105] Despite the frequent social turmoil in the village, Stuck became deeply attached to the Native residents, and they came to love and respect him.[106] The Athabascan Elder and Episcopal deacon William Loola had a positive influence throughout the region.[107]

By 1907 Episcopal missions were operating at Anvik, Tanana, Rampart, Circle City, Fort Yukon, Eagle, and Fairbanks. Seven years later Allakaket, Nenana, Chena Village, Salchaket, Iditarod, Tanana Crossing, and Stevens Village also had missions. The majority of the earlier structures lay on the Yukon River. Most of the later missions lay on tributaries of the Yukon (the Tanana and the Koyukuk). These later mission sites encouraged Natives to remain in their traditional areas, away from negative Western influences. In this way Stuck and other missionaries hoped to slow the pace of inevitable change.[108]

Athabascans often settled near Episcopal missions, and the mission buildings became community centers.[109] Their influence spread far beyond the villages themselves, as personnel provided assistance to Natives and non-Natives in the vicinity. Missionaries offered medical care and provided hygiene instruction, school for the children, and English lessons for adults.[110] Native intermediaries, including William Loola, Arthur Wright, Walter Harper, Johnny Fredson, and Moses Cruikshank, eased communication between Natives and missionaries.

The work was discouraging at times, especially where Western influences were strongest, as they were at Tanana. Nine liquor shops in the town of Tanana did brisk business as about forty outsiders profited from selling liquor to Natives.[111] The ban against

6. Double interpretation at the Allakaket mission. From Stuck,
Ten Thousand Miles with a Dog Sled.

selling or trading alcohol with Natives had little effect, owing to
frontier attitudes, insufficient law enforcement, and lax juries.

Until 1913 conditions were worst along the Yukon River, with
boatloads of liquor coming downriver from Canada.[112] The 1913
discovery of gold on the Chisana, a tributary of the upper Tanana
River, increased Western influence at the village of Tanana and
all along the river.[113] Alcohol was not the only problem. Miners
depleted subsistence resources on the upper Tanana River. During
the winter of 1913 they shot an estimated two thousand mountain sheep, as well as caribou.[114]

St. John's-in-the-Wilderness at Allakaket and St. Mark's Mission at Nenana exemplified the Episcopal Church's efforts to reach
Alaska Natives in their traditional settings. Missionaries sometimes dramatically improved community members' health and
well-being.[115] Before St. John's-in-the-Wilderness was built about
half the children in the Allakaket region died in infancy. After the
mission's founding in 1907 infant mortality plummeted. Thirty-
one children were born in the area in the next three years, and
all but one survived.[116] Prior to the opening of the mission, Iñupiat on the north side of the river and Athabascans on the opposite side deeply distrusted one another. The mission encouraged

CHILDHOOD AND ADOLESCENCE

peace, trust, and friendship between the former enemies.[117] On Christmas Day 1909 about 150 people, both Kobuk River Iñupiat and Koyukon Athabascans, came from far and wide to celebrate.[118] Two interpreters, one Iñupiaq and one Athabascan, translated worship services.

Athabascans along the Tanana River had traditionally gathered seasonally at Nenana. By the early twentieth century many had settled nearby. The people of Nenana repeatedly requested a pastor.[119] Episcopal leadership recognized the need for a boarding school in central Interior Alaska as well. The closest mission school was several hundred miles away, at Anvik on the lower Yukon River. Interior parents hesitated to send their children so far away to school, to a place where the people spoke Ingalik, rather than the Tanana Athabascan spoken at Nenana.[120]

In the summer of 1907 Annie Farthing arrived at Nenana to establish a mission. When residents heard of her expected arrival, they built her a cabin.[121] The following summer, with government approval for a school and $5,000 donated by the Episcopal Church, community members built a large dormitory, which they named Tortella Hall.[122] A second teacher arrived, relieving Annie Farthing to manage the mission, treat the ill, and attend to the children outside of the school day. She stressed sanitation, hygiene, and cleanliness to combat disease.[123] By fall of 1908 Tortella Hall was housing twenty-six children. They attended classes, performed daily chores, learned Bible verses and hymns, and reportedly played and worked happily.[124]

Archdeacon Stuck regularly surveyed the Interior for children who might benefit from St. Mark's. In 1909, when Walter was sixteen years old, Stuck discovered him at a fish camp. With his mother's permission, he sent the boy to St. Mark's for schooling. Walter knew little English at the time and could neither read nor write, but he learned quickly. Other students admired his advanced subsistence skills.[125] In February 1910 Stuck visited the school and romped with the children in Tortella Hall. Walter had grown noticeably, and his schoolwork was progressing well. Stuck's confidence in the youth's potential grew.[126]

Annie Farthing's influence reached into the village of Nenana

7. Walter Harper (*standing*) at St. Mark's Mission, Nenana, winter 1909–10.
St. Mark's Mission Nenana Manuscript Collection, MS004-IIA-2,
Alaska State Library, Juneau.

and beyond. She urged the area's Athabascans, who had been living in tents all winter, to build cabins. In support of that advice the church established the Window and Door Fund, which provided two windows and a door for each cabin the people built. They cut the logs themselves.[127]

People from nearby villages who visited Nenana often stopped by the mission to chat or to ask for assistance. Visitors and residents looked forward to the mission's Monday night dances. Athabascans loved dancing. They would begin with singing in low tones, gradually raising their voices and becoming more animated. The evening would end with "dancing English," as the children called American popular dancing.[128]

Academic and industrial work, both inside and outdoors, filled the children's days. They farmed, cured fish, cared for the mission dogs, and gathered wood and water. The girls learned to make and mend moccasins and to sew. Each older girl took care of one younger child's clothing. Chores were not strictly assigned by gender. Boys laundered their own clothing, and girls sometimes sawed wood.[129]

Moses Cruikshank, who was nine years younger than Walter, arrived at St. Mark's in 1913. He later recalled the work the children did: "On Saturday . . . [we] went out with five-foot one-man saws and six footer saws and we had to cut our own wood, haul it in by ourselves. . . . Everybody had to pitch in and work."[130] The mission kept a large garden with all sorts of vegetables that the children tended. And two fish wheels caught enough fish to nourish the mission staff, children, and dogs. In the morning the children would take a boat across the river to check the fish wheel, sometimes returning with three hundred to four hundred fish. Then would begin the cutting and drying work. Native hunters in the region sometimes donated meat to the mission as well.[131]

Along with neatness and cleanliness, Farthing taught the children honesty, respect, and religious service. In the boys she encouraged a rather touching chivalry. Stuck and other mission personnel envisioned the children carrying these values and habits back to their villages, extending the influence of the mission schools broadly within the Indigenous population.[132] These efforts intentionally introduced many aspects of Western culture into Athabascan culture. But Episcopal missionaries simultaneously encouraged the Native people to maintain their traditional ways and withstand the negative socioeconomic and cultural changes influencing them.

In November 1910 a drunken, gun-wielding bootlegger arrived at St. Mark's and demanded to marry a young girl at the mission. Annie Farthing fended him off. Early the following morning she died of a stroke. She was buried on a bluff overlooking the mission.[133] In her three short years at St. Mark's Farthing had profoundly influenced the Athabascans of Alaska's Interior.[134] Ten years after her death Stuck wrote that her memory was still an inspiration at the school.[135] One of the boys whose lives she touched was Walter Harper.

In the summer of 1910, after Walter had been at St. Mark's less than a year, Archdeacon Stuck chose him as his riverboat pilot, winter trail guide, and interpreter. The archdeacon tutored Harper on the river, on the trail, and at his headquarters in Fort Yukon. Walter's reading and writing advanced quickly. In his travels with the archdeacon Walter left a positive impression wherever they went. As Stuck wrote in his book *Ten Thousand Miles with a Dog Sled*, "He spoke the naked truth, and was so gentle and unobtrusive in manner, that he was a welcome guest at the table of any mission we visited."[136] Harper quickly became, in Stuck's words, "the best boy I have ever had," and Stuck came to love the youth as a son.[137]

2

On the River and on the Trail
with Archdeacon Stuck

ALL THE BOYS at St. Mark's Mission wanted the job of assisting Archdeacon Hudson Stuck, but only the student who earned the best grades won it.[1] Since Stuck became a traveling missionary in Alaska, he had selected bright Native boys as trail guides. He mentored his assistants, and when the days' tasks were done he tutored them, emphasizing classical and British literature, history, and Bible studies. Walter became a valued assistant to Stuck, piloting the mission's riverboat, the *Pelican*, during the summer and driving his dogsled during his winter travels.[2] In time Walter became an avid student as well as a valued assistant to Stuck.

In 1906 Stuck had the *Pelican* custom built in New York City and shipped to Whitehorse in the Yukon Territory, where it was lowered into the Yukon River. In summer 1908 Stuck, along with his first Native assistant, Arthur Wright, and Dr. Grafton "Happy" Burke brought the launch down the Yukon River to Fort Yukon.[3]

Arthur Wright, a mixed-race youth, had been raised in the Episcopal mission at Tanana. Missionaries Jules and Louise Prevost had adopted him at a young age. When the Prevosts left Alaska in 1906, they sent Arthur to school in California. Two years later he returned to Tanana at the age of sixteen. Soon thereafter Stuck chose Arthur as his riverboat pilot and trail assistant.[4] Dr. Happy Burke had been Stuck's protégé at St. Matthew's Cathedral in Dallas. He had recently graduated from medical school and had followed Stuck to Alaska to assist him in the mission work.

That first summer on the *Pelican* Stuck established the pattern

8. The *Pelican* at Eagle, Alaska. Courtesy of the Archives
of the Episcopal Church, Austin, Texas.

he followed each year. Stuck, Burke, and their Native assistant traveled along the Yukon River and its tributaries, the Tanana and the Koyukuk, stopping at Native fish camps and villages, mining camps, and towns. Stuck held religious services, including sermons, weddings, baptisms, and funerals, while Burke attended to people's medical needs. Each day any number of crises might arise. Resourcefulness was perhaps the most essential survival skill at the time. That first year freezeup occurred earlier than usual as the *Pelican* traveled up the Koyukuk River, laden with supplies for St. John's-in-the-Wilderness at Allakaket. They had to beach the *Pelican* for the winter and build a sledge to hold the 250 pounds of cargo, which they pulled 125 miles along the river to the mission. Treacherous ice conditions threatened disaster at every moment. After ten days of torturous work, with a Native man and his sled dogs helping during the latter half of the trek, they arrived at the mission, exhausted.[5] Injury to Stuck's shoulder from pulling the sledge would torment him in later years.[6]

Soon after Walter joined Stuck in early summer 1910 the archdeacon described the lad as "a nice boy, quiet and courteous, with all the marks of Miss Farthing's training upon him." He apprenticed with Arthur Wright, who would be leaving for Mount Her-

ON THE RIVER AND ON THE TRAIL

mon School in Massachusetts that fall.[7] Interior rivers were laden with silt and often clogged with debris, especially at breakup time. The *Pelican* frequently broke down, ran aground, and battled rough waters, and its propeller often became entangled in willow fibers and branches.[8] Handling such difficulties and setbacks required problem-solving skills. Walter learned quickly to pilot the launch, to repair and maintain its four-cylinder engine, and to troubleshoot other mishaps.[9]

Accepting the position with the archdeacon immersed the adolescent in Episcopal mission activity in Alaska's Interior. As the archdeacon's assistant, Walter met and interacted with people from all walks of life, including dignitaries in church and civic arenas. Bishop Peter Trimble Rowe spent two months each summer traveling with the archdeacon on the *Pelican*. Shadowing the archdeacon and the bishop gave Walter new perspectives on the Church's work, on the challenges facing Athabascans, and on relations between Natives and non-Natives. He interpreted the archdeacon's and the bishop's words for the Athabascan people, wherever he knew the language spoken. Sometimes Walter took part in conversations with Stuck, Rowe, and others. On other occasions he tinkered with the *Pelican*'s engine, hunted, or read while the clerics talked "church business."[10] Remaining in his homeland and applying the skills he had honed since early childhood reinforced his Athabascan identity, even as he adjusted to Western lifeways and Episcopal Church norms and practices.

In late July 1910 Walter was confirmed in the Episcopal Church at Tanana and took his First Communion.[11] Just how he experienced this event is not clear, but it seems that Christian teachings reinforced his natural tendencies. Moreover he recognized the Church's dedication to the welfare of the Native people. According to Stuck, that winter Walter began speaking of dedicating his life to mission work.[12] Stuck later wrote that Walter lived his faith, rather than proclaiming it. He was not religious in a formal or pretentious way. Instead his Christian faith expressed itself in conscientiously fulfilling his duties and maintaining his self-respect. His reverence shone in his kindness and consideration toward others, in resisting temptation, and in his honorable bearing. Stuck concluded that the basis of Harper's character lay in "an intense self-respect."[13]

Edgar Loomis, another of Stuck's protégés from Texas, had become a physician, and he joined in the mission work that summer of 1910. He and Happy Burke, best friends since childhood, treated medical conditions of people they encountered along the river. Whenever a physician was aboard, the *Pelican*'s medical flag flew below the mission flag to signal the arrival of medical care.[14] Sometimes the doctors determined that critically ill or injured patients needed transport to a hospital. On occasion healthy people hopped aboard for a lift to the next village.

The *Pelican*'s crew delivered mail and carried messages and general news wherever they traveled. Folks living along the rivers looked forward to the *Pelican*'s visits, just as they eagerly awaited the arrivals of steamships. The *Pelican*'s light draft allowed it to ply many of the Yukon's tributaries that steamers could not navigate. Its access to some of the Interior's remotest locations inspired the Episcopal Church Periodical Club's program to distribute magazines to miners as the *Pelican* made its rounds. People throughout the United States sent publications to the distribution point in Fairbanks, where crew members loaded them onto the *Pelican* for delivery.[15]

On August 6, 1910, the *Pelican* arrived at St. John's-in-the-Wilderness for Dr. Happy Burke's marriage to missionary Clara Heintz. She had done mission work at Allakaket since 1907. Edgar Loomis served as best man. Athabascan and Iñupiaq choirboys at the mission sang hymns they had practiced for six months for the ceremony. Wedding guests arrived in their birch-bark canoes wearing their Sunday best, having traveled from nearby fish camps. Following a postwedding feast, Clara left Allakaket to join her husband at the Fort Yukon mission.[16]

Hap and Clara Burke served the medical and other needs of northern Interior Alaskans for three decades. He died in 1938, just weeks after he was ordained an Episcopal priest.[17] The Burkes made a home in their house for Stuck until his death in 1920. Clara was one of the few women whom Hudson Stuck truly loved. He often teased Happy, whom he loved like a son, that his own affection for Clara had nothing to do with him.[18] Walter too became part of the mission family at Fort Yukon.

In late August 1910 the *Pelican* docked at Iditarod City in Alaska's western Interior. The site was experiencing the peak of a gold rush following a strike there the previous winter. Three thousand non-Natives lived in and near Iditarod City in August 1910, including miners, doctors, lawyers, and other professionals and tradespeople. Bishop Rowe held well-attended worship services at the courthouse. The Episcopal Church began planning for a hospital in the town.[19]

Stuck and Harper crossed paths with many people they knew at the mining camps they visited. Some of the people Stuck most enjoyed seeing during his travels were "old-timers" with extensive knowledge of Alaska's history, Arctic exploration, and world events. Brothers Bill and Herman Yanert, who lived in the Yukon Flats area, were two of Stuck's most interesting friends.[20] Bill had emigrated from Germany at the age of seventeen. During the Klondike gold rush he participated in expeditions to map broad sections of Alaska's Interior.[21] He retired in 1903 and settled at a place he named Purgatory.[22] Yanert built a home there and lived out his life hunting and trapping for subsistence with his brother Herman. Bill carved, painted, and wrote poetry to amuse himself. The brothers operated a wood yard, and steamers regularly stopped at Purgatory to restock their fuel supplies.[23]

Of his close friends, Stuck likely admired the Jesuit, Jules Jetté, the most. Stuck and Walter visited Father Jetté at least once a summer at his quarters on the lower Yukon. Stuck described Jetté as a "fine flower of the Roman priesthood."[24] He especially prized Jetté's work in documenting the Tena Athabascan language.[25]

Given the regular movement of Athabascans in seasonal rounds and to find wage labor, Walter saw his brothers fairly regularly. In April 1911 he and Stuck stopped over at a cabin where Andrew Harper was staying. A week later at the wood yard near Stevens Village they met his brothers Fred and Sam, along with Sam's wife, Louise, and their daughter Flora Jane. The men were chopping wood for the steamers.[26] After Walter's sisters, Jessie and Margaret, returned from school in California and accepted teaching positions at Tanana, he visited them whenever he and Stuck stopped at the Tanana mission. Jessie and Margaret were just three and two years older than Walter. Of his siblings, they remained closest to him as he grew older.

By September of his first summer on the *Pelican* Walter was handling the boat skillfully, even in the dark of night. At season's end Stuck wrote in his diary, "Walter has proved on the whole very satisfactory and today especially he brought the boat along splendidly. I grow very much attached to the boy."[27] They had traveled more than five thousand miles that season.[28] Stuck found Harper's demeanor especially pleasing.[29] He remained calm and cheerful no matter how trying the circumstances. His sunny disposition and firm sense of identity allowed Walter to interact easily with both friends and strangers. In fact he was so utterly disarming that he drew people of all ages and walks of life to him. Once, after a French Canadian visitor to Fort Yukon had entertained a crowd with magic tricks, he took Walter into the mission house and revealed all of his techniques.[30]

As challenging as Alaska's waterways were in summer, winter posed greater risks to travelers. Temperatures could suddenly plummet to 60 degrees below zero or colder. In the best of circumstances, glare ice covered the rivers, with just enough ice crystals to give the dogs traction. Under such conditions Walter once skated ahead of Stuck and the dogsled for fifteen or sixteen miles. In some places the ice was so transparent that they could see clearly the sand and gravel on the river's bed.[31] But oftentimes rough and chunky ice hindered travel. And they always had to scan the river's surface for perilous overflow—water sitting atop the frozen river. At frigid temperatures wet feet could freeze in minutes, resulting in death or amputation.

Changeable and unpredictable weather required travelers to be prepared for the worst possible circumstances. Wind increased the chill factor and caused snow to drift, hampering navigation and possibly obscuring the trail. Sometimes the duo emerged from the woods into wide-open spaces with no hint of a trail or even a direction to travel. In one such case a pair of dogs rescued them. They had searched the wide-open landscape for some indication of the trail, with no luck. Finally Stuck saw in the distance two stray dogs that he sensed were returning from the roadhouse ahead. He and Walter followed the dogs' tracks until they saw the trail. Once in a while, in a whiteout, they were lucky enough to find that someone had staked the trail.[32]

In winter the cold itself was their worst enemy. Difficult conditions could slow their travel, forcing them to camp in the open, form a bed of spruce bows, and hang a tarp as a wind break. Such delays could deplete their grub supply. In cases of overflow they occasionally had to "corduroy" a path of logs over a stream so they could cross without drenching themselves, the dogs, and their cargo. Sometimes the river level dropped after freezeup, and later the ice would crack and drop to the river level. During his first winter on the trail Walter fell into such a crack. Stuck struggled mightily to pull him out.[33]

In warmer temperatures the chance of precipitation increased. The warmer the temperature, the heavier the snow became. Sometimes it was so wet that their clothing, including their footwear, became soaked. Then their only option was to stop, build a roaring fire, peel off their clothing, and dry it. On occasion blizzards forced the duo to turn back to a safe place to hole up until the weather cleared.[34]

Travel over freshly fallen snow was always taxing. Sometimes Stuck would forge ahead on snowshoes to break the trail, and Walter would follow with the cargo-laden sled. More often Stuck sent Walter ahead to break trail. He also sent Walter on side missions to purchase dogs or supplies. Walter continually expanded his subsistence skills on the trail. In early 1911 he worked one full day making a pair of snowshoes for Stuck.[35] Before long he became expert at making and repairing both snowshoes and dogsleds. Beginning with their first winter together, Stuck relied heavily on Walter's wilderness skills. He followed "the boy's" advice, especially on where they should stop to set up camp. In late spring when the snow was heavy and soft they sometimes camped during the day and traveled at night, when the ground surface was colder and more firm.

Under poor conditions the duo would travel fewer than eight miles a day.[36] Over smooth trails they could travel close to fifty miles in a day. The two found such circumstances—clear weather with smooth trails—most exhilarating. Regardless of the weather, Walter thrived out on the land. He relished the challenges, put his ingenuity to work, took setbacks in stride, and slept soundly at night.

The two set out on their first winter trek on November 17, 1910. They followed the Porcupine River to the Chandalar trail, running six hours with only one fifteen-minute stop for lunch. The first night out they stayed at a cabin, where they began their trail routine with Walter reading a book chapter following supper. Before bed the two always wrote in their diaries.[37]

During the first weeks they struggled to find their way over the rough terrain. Later on, warm, heavy snow fell, slowing their progress. After a long day on a "fearfully rough" trail Stuck recorded in his diary, "Walter does exceedingly well & is good humoured & pleasant."[38] In the days that followed the two ran into overflow and heavy snow drifts alternating with gravel trail. At seventeen Walter was still learning the ropes and sometimes made mistakes. Once he built a fire directly in front of the tent opening, and smoke filled the shelter. Another time he burned the dogs' supper so completely that it could not be salvaged. This was no small matter; the dog food was already dangerously low. But his sled-handling abilities and other skills were beyond reproach. Once he carved a new spruce axe handle when the original broke, and one morning he shot five spruce hens. Stuck cooked a stew of the birds, and they shared it with their hosts at the cabin where they overnighted.[39]

Two weeks after leaving Fort Yukon the pair arrived at Coldfoot, a mining camp. Stuck held worship services at Coldfoot and Wiseman. The Chandalar mining district had opened following the discovery of gold at Wiseman in 1902. A minor prospectors' rush into the region followed. Stuck and Walter found a miner at Wiseman suffering from severe edema. Stuck took charge of the matter, hiring a man and dog team to transport the patient, named Charley, to the hospital at Tanana, 250 miles away. Stuck and Walter bundled Charley up, and the two teams struck out together. When they reached the mission at Allakaket, the temperature was 65 degrees below zero, so they stayed over, waiting for the weather to break.[40] Just as they prepared to leave for Tanana, Stuck stepped on a nail. He therefore sent Charley ahead to Tanana in the care of two men he hired to transport him. The following day, with Stuck's foot wound improved, he and Walter departed for Tanana.[41] When they arrived five days later, the duo found Charley resting comfortably at Fort Gibbon's hospital. The ride from Allakaket had not been pleasant. He had been jostled over rough terrain and had tumbled down a riverbank while lashed to the sled. No worse for the wear, he laughed about his adventure as doctors removed more than two gallons of fluid from his body.[42]

In February 1911 Stuck and Harper struck out toward Iditarod City to check on conditions and hold religious services. Four hundred miles and twenty-four days later they reached their destination. The community now resembled a typical overgrown mining camp, with sky-high prices and miners disappointed at the gold prospects. Stuck held Sunday morning church services for several dozen people. In the afternoon the two traveled seven miles to Flat Creek, where another several dozen gathered for services. That evening back at Iditarod about 175 people attended the worship service Stuck led. The following day the two began their return journey to Tanana. A different trail brought them to their destination on March 31. Altogether they had run about 750 miles on the six-week excursion.[43]

During the winter Harper and Stuck usually traveled alone, but on occasion a missionary or an interpreter and/or guide traveled with them. Sometimes they stayed overnight at an occupied cabin. Fishers, miners, hunters, and trappers built log cabins, usually along rivers. When they moved on, the dwellings served as shelters for others migrating in and through the Interior. According to custom, users left the cabin tidy and restocked the wood supply so the next person in need could warm the cabin quickly. The practice had developed as more than common courtesy. A traveler might be hypothermic upon reaching the haven. Being able to build a fire within minutes could mean the difference between life and death.

On other occasions the duo stayed at roadhouses. Some were so wretched that Stuck preferred camping out. The high prices at such dives especially rankled him.[44] But sometimes they found pleasant accommodations. After two weeks on the trail in March 1911 they savored a delicious meal at a Northern Commercial Company trading post. They relished sleeping in comfort that night, a sharp cold spell having settled in.[45]

Along the trail the two enjoyed the company of wildlife. Camp robbers were so comfortable around people that Stuck nearly had them eating out of his hand.[46] They regularly saw ptarmigans, grouse, and spruce hens in winter.[47] Naturally Harper's familiarity with the wildlife in interior Alaska exceeded Stuck's. He once chuckled at the archdeacon when he mistook a moose's tracks for a man's.[48] By the winter of 1910–11 Stuck was deeply impressed not only with his protégé's wilderness skills but with his intelligence, gentleness, and faithfulness. Stuck wrote his friend John Wood that Walter was talking of devoting his life to mission work.[49] In the years that followed, as the two grew closer, they envisioned Harper becoming a medical missionary, perhaps at the Tanana hospital.

Their first winter on the trail ended April 23, 1911, more than five months after it began. They had traveled two thousand miles. Initially Harper showed more interest in physical activities than in his studies. In time his aptitude for academic work grew. Stuck noted that during their first winter on the trail the young man's reading ability improved markedly.[50]

It may have been his exposure to G. A. Henty's adventure stories that kindled Harper's interest in reading and history.[51] Henty was Great Britain's most prolific author of children's literature in the "muscular Christianity" genre in the late nineteenth century. The books championed the spread of Christianity and Western civilization. Henty's novels promoted such values as loyalty, honesty, resourcefulness, and especially gumption. The young hero of his stories, usually a teenage boy, would leave home to try his luck elsewhere. He would become embroiled in major world crises and encounter disasters, such as military battles and shipwrecks. In the end the boy hero always returned home safely, having become a man. Henty researched the historical settings and events in his novels thoroughly. The books were so popular that generations of schoolboys learned history through reading them.[52]

Walter read the books aloud to Stuck, who greatly admired Henty. They developed the habit of calling the boy hero in every story "Cedric." When Walter began a new novel, as the boy hero entered the scene, he would pronounce, "Here comes Cedric!" Later, when he was at Mount Hermon School, Walter told Stuck that Henty's stories sometimes helped him to understand the teacher's historical references, and he would often be the only student who did. Walter also read aloud for Stuck such classics as *Robinson Crusoe, Treasure Island,* and many of Shakespeare's works. Eventually he read most of the Bible aloud.[53]

Soon after they returned to Fort Yukon, Harper and Stuck began preparations for their summer tour on the *Pelican.* Walter attended school in the mornings, focusing on arithmetic. Stuck tutored him in literature, history, and Bible reading. In the afternoons they worked on the *Pelican,* tuning the engine, puttying, and scraping paint, inside and out. The work continued well into the evenings. The water in the Yukon was rising, and soon it would lift the *Pelican* from her mooring.[54] To keep an eye on the launch and the rising water, Walter and Johnny Fred slept on a barge beside the boat one night. Johnny was a Native boy who lived at the Fort Yukon mission and would follow in Walter's footsteps. In the morning the two boys slipped away to hunt wild game. They did not return until 2:00 p.m., much to Stuck's annoyance. Back at the mission Walter immediately resumed the repair work.[55]

On May 11 the ice went out. The water rose so high that when it fell, it left the launch high and dry. Breakup caused much anxiety along the Yukon, because the rising water and large ice chunks wrought havoc when they finally broke loose and rushed down-river. Ideally the water would rise just enough to lift the *Pelican* gently from its winter resting place. Then Walter could guide the launch to its mooring in front of the mission. But humans could not always control the process. In the spring of 1911 they had to drag the *Pelican,* using screw jacks, pulleys, and the boat's windlass, into the stream to moor it at the mission.[56] Following the ordeal Stuck had a skidway of logs built so the riverboat could be rolled out of the river in the fall. In spring after breakup the craft could be moved back down the skidway to the river. After sev-

eral days of intensive labor Harper, Stuck, and other men helping them finally had the skidway in place.[57]

The *Pelican* began its summer tour of 1911 on June 2, running upstream to Native camps and the towns of Circle City and
Eagle, near the Canadian border.[58] Circle City, which had been a
bustling mining camp of three thousand in the late nineteenth
century, now was home to only about thirty white residents. A
village of about forty to fifty Han Athabascans was nearby. The
proximity of the settlements to each other led to much misery
in the Native village.[59] A "gang" of white men, including Judge
Dodson, and the saloon owner, Tom Hauter, had run Circle City
for some years, ignoring the federal ban on selling alcohol to
Natives.[60] Stuck tried to discourage drunkenness and unseemly
behavior by refusing Holy Communion to individuals charged
with misconduct.[61] Such "meddling" caused many white Alaskans to loathe the archdeacon.

As they headed upriver toward Eagle, Walter's boyish exuber-
ance overpowered his judgment, leading to a regrettable incident.
When he spotted a moose, he grabbed his rifle, jumped on the
roof of the cabin, and began shooting. After the moose fell, he
and Stuck saw that a young calf was running alongside her. They
went ashore, located the animal, and bled and gutted her, hoping
that someone nearby could use the meat. One can imagine the
scolding Stuck gave Walter. Not only had he shot a cow moose,
but hunting season had not begun. Still, when word of the incident spread, Stuck contacted Judge Myers at Eagle, pleaded the
boy's case, and won the judge's forgiveness for Walter.[62]

Upon their return to Fort Yukon, Isaac Stringer, Anglican bishop
of the Yukon Territory, visited the mission. He and Stuck had
much to discuss, given the similar social climate in Alaska and
the Yukon.[63] Listening to the two wise men converse was just one
of the many educational opportunities Walter enjoyed during the
years he assisted the archdeacon. Later that summer Walter Clark,
the newly appointed governor, and his wife, Lucy, visited Fort Gibbon while Harper and Stuck were in Tanana. Stuck dined with
the couple on the *Schwatka*, a steamer. Later that evening Walter
took them aboard the *Pelican* and traveled to the mission, where

Stuck gave the Clarks a tour.[64] The archdeacon proudly introduced Walter to others, including dignitaries, wherever they traveled.

Blistering temperatures, an active fire season, and swarms of mosquitoes marked the summer of 1911 in Alaska's Interior. At Rampart for several days in late June the temperature reached 92 degrees. Thick smoke filled the air as the *Pelican* moved downstream past several forest fires.[65] The blazes were a natural part of the life cycle of the northern boreal forest. Even more bothersome than the heat and smoke that summer were the mosquitoes, which tormented people and animals alike.

Harper and Stuck celebrated July 4, 1911, at the Tanana mission. Stuck organized athletic competitions for children and adults. In the final event competitors raced across the river and back in canoes at midnight. Gunshots, rather than fireworks, marked the stroke of midnight in Alaska villages; fireworks' visual effects fell somewhat flat under the midnight sun.[66] Besides, ammunition was much more readily available. Rural Alaskans also celebrated the New Year with rifle shots.[67]

From Tanana the *Pelican* and its crew continued down the Yukon to the Chageluk Slough and toward Iditarod City. About fifteen miles from the mining town the river grew so shallow that the launch ran aground. Stuck boarded a flat-bottomed scow and continued to Iditarod, while Harper and Muk, Stuck's pet malamute, waited aboard the *Pelican* for the water to rise.[68] When Stuck arrived at Iditarod, he discovered that all mining activity had halted owing to drought conditions. Two weeks later rain finally fell, allowing mining to resume. The river rose, and Harper and Muk arrived. Stuck spent his days at the mining camp planning and fundraising for the hospital the Episcopal Church aimed to build there. He met with Harry Karstens, an experienced prospector and guide whose path Stuck had crossed many times before. The men shared a goal of climbing Denali.[69] Meanwhile Walter worked handling freight to earn cash.[70] In late August a telegram alerted Stuck of a smallpox outbreak on the Porcupine River, northeast of Fort Yukon.[71] The Episcopal Church network responded rapidly.

Stuck wired the Church Mission House in New York to rush supplies of vaccine to every mission along the Yukon.[72] He and

9. Iditarod City. From Stuck, *Ten Thousand Miles with a Dog Sled*.

Harper left Iditarod at once. Upon reaching deeper water and buying extra gasoline, they ran sixteen hours straight, using a searchlight to navigate in the darkness of night, shining the beacon on one riverbank and then the other. Walter's piloting skills were those of a seasoned professional by now.[73] At Anvik, on the lower Yukon, they intercepted Dr. Loomis, who was on his way Outside. They took him aboard and headed up the Yukon River, stopping at every village and camp to vaccinate the people.

Missionaries at Anvik, Allakaket, and Fairbanks vaccinated those living along the tributaries to the Yukon. Fear of the dreaded disease and trust in mission personnel spurred the people to queue up for injections. According to Stuck, not a single Alaska Native refused the protection. In just one summer Episcopal mission personnel vaccinated almost every Indigenous Alaskan in the Interior, from Eagle at the Canadian border to Holy Cross on the lower Yukon, and along all the Yukon's tributaries.[74]

In mid-September 1911 the *Pelican* and its crew pulled in at Fort Yukon with the boat's searchlight burning. The crew fired a red flare to announce the homecoming.[75] The *Pelican* had traveled more than three thousand miles that summer.[76]

Harper and Stuck spent the fall and Christmas season of 1911 in Fort Yukon. They began their winter journey in mid-January with five dogs—Argo, Jerry, Muk, Two Bits, and Snowball, Walter's

ON THE RIVER AND ON THE TRAIL

favorite—and one heavily loaded sled. Five days out they came upon heavy overflow on the Chandalar River. Trudging through water for up to one hundred yards at a stretch, they completely soaked their boots and pants. At Caro, a mining camp on the Chandalar, they found shelter in a miner's cabin and built a fire to warm up and dry out.[77] Further trail breaking brought them to Coldfoot, on the Middle Fork of the Koyukuk River, where they relished hot baths and comfortable beds at Hill's Roadhouse. After conducting church services for the miners at Wiseman, the two began the next leg of their trek, following the Koyukuk River southwest toward Allakaket.

On the trail they sometimes camped out and sometimes stayed in occupied or unoccupied cabins. Wherever people gathered, Stuck held religious services, with Harper interpreting.[78] Folks in these isolated communities appreciated the ritual and warmth of the seasonal services Stuck offered. Sometimes a year or more could pass between visits by clergy.

Following a few days' stay at St. John's-in-the-Wilderness, they continued on to Tanana. There they discovered that village residents had been drinking heavily during the Christmas season. Seven had been jailed at once for drunkenness, assault and battery, and other charges. Stuck's sense of doom and despair for the people of Tanana deepened with each year. The contrast with Allakaket could not have been starker.[79] No such troubles beset the isolated village.

After a short visit in Fairbanks, where Walter interpreted for Bishop Rowe during services for the Native community at St. Matthew's Church, the duo struck out toward Eagle. This northeastward journey took them through breathtaking mountainous country.[80] By now daytime temperatures rose well above freezing, slowing their pace. But the skies were often clear and the scenery spectacular. One day when drifting snow completely covered the trail the ever-resourceful Walter climbed a mountain to orient himself. Soon they traveled swiftly on glare ice on the Charley River, its winding banks rising to towering heights. Looking up, Walter caught sight of a band of mountain sheep, his first view of the majestic animals.[81] The following afternoon, as Stuck basked in the sun, Harper climbed another peak, hoping to see the Yukon River, which would lead them to Eagle. The river was not yet in sight, but the Yukon hills soon came into view. After eleven days on the trail, they arrived at Eagle early on Easter morning, April 7, 1912.

The following day the two began the last leg of their winter journey—the return to Fort Yukon. On this stretch a near catastrophe proved just how treacherous the winter trail could be. They traveled at night, when the trail was more firm. As Stuck led with the dogsled, he veered off the trail. Suddenly the hard snow collapsed under his feet, and he plunged into icy water up to his elbows. His feet unable to touch the riverbed, he felt the current pulling his legs. As he struggled to escape, the ice broke under his weight. Harper, who followed closely behind, seized the collar of Stuck's parka and pulled him out. In subzero conditions Stuck's clothing instantly stiffened. Hurriedly they replaced his frozen footwear with dry socks and rubber boots. With the rescue accomplished, finding a warm refuge now absorbed them. Racing toward the roadhouse a few miles ahead, they panicked, fearing they had missed it, and doubled back. Realizing their mistake, they turned back again, desperate to reach warmth and safety before hypothermia set in. At last they reached the roadhouse. Stuck's only injury was a raw heel where the rubber boot had chafed his skin. Four days later, after four months on the trail, the travelers pulled in at Fort Yukon.[82]

Shortly after their homecoming Walter began preparing the *Pelican* for the summer circuit. He and Stuck spent two hours each evening on his education, except when Walter went duck hunting. The *Pelican* began the summer rounds on May 27, traveling upstream toward Circle with a few passengers. Among them was young Moses Cruikshank, an Athabascan youth at the Fort Yukon mission whom Stuck had promised to take to Circle and back for the experience.[83]

At Circle, Bishop Rowe joined Stuck and Harper for the summer tour.[84] As usual Walter constantly wrestled with the *Pelican*'s mechanical and electrical problems. Shallows, narrow channels, and overhanging vegetation posed constant threats. At times the

Pelican became so mired in silt that Walter had to jump ashore and push the boat back into the stream with a pole. In late June as they traveled up the Tanana River the cast-iron bracket supporting the sparking mechanism in one of the engine's cylinders broke. Walter whittled a new bracket from the stock of a shotgun. Soon the engine purred again. Walter continued to tinker with the engine to keep it running until they were forced to turn back. During the wild ride downstream Walter stood at the wheel, his eyes on the water, carefully dodging sandbars and driftwood during the three-hour run to Chena, near Fairbanks. They had struggled upstream for eighteen hours.[85]

At Fairbanks, Stuck dined with Harry Karstens, and the two resumed their talk of climbing Denali. Karstens had resisted Stuck's suggestion that they tackle the mountain together, but now he came around to the idea.[86] The two began planning in earnest for a spring 1913 ascent. By the summer of 1912 Walter had aided Stuck for two years. He had proven himself physically fit and a resourceful outdoorsman. A Denali ascent would be the most arduous undertaking of Stuck's life. There was no question that he wanted Walter on the ascent team.

In early July the *Pelican* pulled in at Ruby, the newest mining camp in the Interior. It had mushroomed in the past year, as miners rushed in from other camps.[87] Two years before, thousands had rushed to Iditarod. Now just a few souls remained there. Iditarod miners had sold their claims to the Alaska Syndicate, which used dredges to recover the gold, thus slashing the need for human labor.[88] The social atmosphere in Alaska mining camps differed strikingly from that of isolated Native villages, regardless of whether they had missions. Mining camps had many more features of towns or small cities. On a Sunday at Ruby, Stuck sandwiched a worship service between a wrestling match and a picture show.[89]

The boom-bust cycle in mining camps sent shock waves through nearby Athabascan settlements. The short-term benefits of wage-labor opportunities lured some Alaska Natives from subsistence activities. The increased cash flow eased access to liquor and vice, which contributed to violence and domestic turmoil. When miners' luck ran out, they rushed to the next strike or left the territory.

In the wake of these exoduses Alaska Native families and communities struggled to reestablish their equilibrium. No town exhibited the social turmoil of the era more graphically than Walter's home village of Tanana. And each time Stuck and Harper visited the mission there, Stuck grew more despairing of the community's future.

During their August 2012 visit to Tanana, however, Walter provided a diversion from the grim social scene. He returned to the *Pelican* with three young foxes he had dug from a hole nearby; he planned to make a companion of the female. He must have thought it would be all right to do so, since Stuck took his pet malamute, Muk, on the *Pelican* and on the winter trail. But the fox had other ideas. The first night onboard she repeatedly tried to jump ship, disturbing the sleep of her would-be companions. The next day she again jumped overboard. Time and again they pulled her back as she dangled over the bow. Eventually the fox broke her chain and plunged into the river. Turning the *Pelican* around, Stuck and Harper mounted a search. They captured her as she swam with the chain hanging from her neck. The next evening, when they were moored, she jumped again, and Muk attacked her as she tried to break loose from her chain. Her shrieks awakened Walter, who rushed to her rescue. This time he made a bed for her in the stern of the boat and barred her escape. Finally she rested quietly.[90] Stuck, who related the drama in his diary day by day, never mentioned the fox kit again. Whether the wounds proved mortal or Walter set her free, the episode offered a learning experience.

Late in August, as Stuck and Harper traveled up the Yukon River toward their home base at Fort Yukon, disaster struck. As Walter oiled the engine, a cotton wad slipped from his hand and lodged between the shaft and the cylinder, stripping the gears and freezing the engine. The *Pelican* lay stranded midstream in the Yukon River. A two-week roller coaster of hope and despair ensued, as successive breakdowns followed repairs.[91] Stuck grew frantic with the rising certainty that the *Pelican* was disabled for the season. The breakdown jeopardized the much anticipated Denali ascent of spring 1913. He and Walter had planned to use

10. Walter Harper with fox kit. Yvonne Mozée Collection, #2002-98-11, Mozée Family Papers, APRCA, University of Alaska Fairbanks.

the launch that fall to cache their climbing outfit at the mouth of the Kantishna River, close to the base of the mountain. Doing so would expedite the ascent in spring. When the gravity of the *Pelican*'s breakdown had sunk in, Stuck wired Karstens, asking him to assume responsibility for transporting and caching the gear.[92] Karstens's willingness to take on that burden put the expedition back on track.

In mid-September, as the *Pelican* lay broken down at Tanana, Jessie and Margaret Harper returned home. Walter's sisters had accepted positions as schoolteachers at Tanana after earning their teaching credentials in San Francisco. They were now sophisticated young women, twenty-two and twenty-one years old.[93] Nearly fifteen years had passed since the girls had gone Outside to school. During the week that Walter remained in Tanana following their return, he and his sisters became reacquainted, and their attachment deepened. They kept in close contact in the years that followed, even when great distances separated them.

The disabled *Pelican* remained at Tanana that fall. In its fourth season it had logged about three thousand miles.[94] Stuck and Harper returned to Fort Yukon aboard the *Schwatka*, a miserable four-day journey.[95] Thanks to their late booking on the steamer, Harper slept on a cot in the "ladies parlour" and Stuck in a room with "two of the lowest blackguards" he had ever met. In the midst of these discomforts Stuck held Sunday church services in the steamer's saloon, with most of the passengers in attendance.[96] Such incongruities typified life on the Alaska frontier throughout the gold rush era. Mainstream American norms clashed with Alaska Native traditions. The highly masculine, liberal alcohol culture competed with conservative, mainstream Christian mores. Insufficient law enforcement, coupled with antiauthoritarian attitudes among non-Natives, contributed to an "anything goes" atmosphere in which migrants exploited Alaska Natives. In the midst of this free-for-all, missionaries took opportunities where they arose, often in unconventional venues, to rein in lawlessness and promote Christian teachings.

Back at Fort Yukon, Stuck and Harper pursued their fall activities through the New Year. Stuck planned steadily for the Denali ascent, ordering most of their equipment from East Coast suppliers. A cold spell in January delayed their departure on their winter circuit. When the temperature rose from 56 below zero on January 21 to 24 below on January 22, they departed. The next day another cold air mass moved in, and the mercury dropped below minus 50 again, where it remained for more than a week. Fighting the bitter cold, the pair made their way westward to Beaver and Stevens Village. Despite its location on the Yukon River, Stevens Village was one of the most remote villages in the Interior. It lay in the Yukon Flats, inaccessible to steamers because of the sandbars between the main channel and the village. It had no mail service in winter.[97]

During Stuck and Harper's visit, residents clamored for a mission. Stuck promised that if they built the structure, the Episcopal diocese would plant a mission there.[98] Residents did so, and the missionary Effie Jackson arrived in 1915 to teach school and hold worship services. This sequence of events followed the pattern at other locations, where the Native people had requested missions. They cut the logs, built the buildings, carved the furnishings, and beaded adornments for the altars.[99] As the social gospel era came to a close in the 1910s, the Episcopal Church's mission society struggled to meet its expanding obligations in Alaska's Interior. Appeals for support for the Alaska mission work increasingly fell on deaf ears.

Two days on the trail from Stevens Village, Stuck and Walter met Sam and Louise Harper, who were staying in a cabin at Coalmine while Sam cut wood for the riverboats. Stuck baptized the couple's one-year-old daughter, Elsie, their second surviving child. Seeing Sam and Louise struggling to feed their family disturbed both Walter and Stuck.[100] Surviving in Alaska's Interior with relatively little wild game had always been difficult, especially in harsh winter weather. Wage labor helped, but such opportunities varied from year to year.[101]

In mid-February 1913 Harper and Stuck arrived in Fairbanks, where they met with Karstens to finalize plans for the Denali climb.[102] They carefully reviewed the minutest details to ensure they had overlooked nothing. Before they could launch the expedition Stuck and Harper had to deliver materials to the remote mission at Tanana Crossing. The two missionaries there had had no contact with the outside world since fall. The eighteen-day excursion, much of it over rough terrain, posed all the usual late-winter hazards, including rotten ice and overflow. But the missionaries' joy at their arrival, and the satisfaction Stuck and Harper derived from the finishing work they did at the mission, repaid their effort.[103]

Back in Fairbanks on March 9, Harper and Stuck spent the next days resting and organizing their outfit together with Karstens. They worked hastily, as the trek to Tanana Crossing had delayed their departure. The trio eagerly anticipated joining the rest of the team in Nenana to launch the Denali expedition.

3

Ascent of Denali

DENALI—THE GREAT ONE—WAS the highest mountain peak in the Athabascan people's homeland. They called its companion peak Sultana—His Wife.[1] The British explorer George Vancouver mentioned seeing Denali in 1794 from the Gulf of Alaska; he was the first European to note the landmark.[2] In 1878 Arthur Harper and his trading partner Al Mayo traveled up the Tanana River and saw a "great ice mountain to the south," Harper later reported.[3]

Denali and Sultana inspired awe in the Native people, but it was the "hunter's paradise" of their foothills, not their eternally snow- and ice-covered peaks, that enticed them.[4] When James Wickersham led the first attempt to climb Denali in 1903, Athabascans near the mountain's base expressed bewilderment at Wickersham's plan.[5]

Henry David Thoreau and later John Muir had inspired Euro-Americans to appreciate mountains' natural beauty and spirituality. By 1885, when Hudson Stuck arrived in the United States, mountaineering was becoming increasingly popular, although intense competition and negative publicity detracted from the activity. Bitter controversies surrounded the ascents of Mount Rainier and the Grand Tetons and would later surround several attempts on Denali.[6]

As a young man Stuck had climbed in Wales and England. After immigrating to the United States, he mountaineered in the Colorado and Canadian Rockies. Mount Rainier was the tallest peak he had scaled. Although he was an amateur, Stuck read mountaineering literature avidly. Denali was one of the features that had drawn him to Alaska.[7]

The 1913 ascent of Denali, the first successful summit, presented a complex set of hardships and hazards. At 63° north latitude, Denali is the farthest north of any mountain of great stature. It stands 18,000 feet from base to summit and rises 20,237 above sea level. Its far northern latitude and high altitude required the ascent team to bring one and a half tons of supplies to the base of the mountain. Above 11,000 feet, dogs could not freight the cargo. The men had to pack their outfit on their backs. They relayed the items in forty-pound backpacks from camp to camp. In ascending the 20,000-foot peak the men likely climbed 60,000 feet altogether.[8]

The unique climate system that surrounds Denali posed further difficulties. The mildest temperatures occur in summer. But from June 1 forward, thick clouds shroud the summit almost continuously, reducing visibility nearly to zero. Therefore late spring offered the best ascent conditions. In 1913 a completely unexpected obstacle—giant ice and snow boulders covering the Northeast Ridge—confronted the ascent team. An earthquake the year before had triggered an avalanche that buried the ridge. This ridge was their pathway to Denali's upper basin and the summit.

Eleven attempts on Denali preceded the successful 1913 Stuck-Karstens-led expedition. In 1903 James Wickersham, a judge and later congressional delegate, along with a party of four others attempted to climb Denali with two mules. In his memoir *Old Yukon: Tales, Trails, and Trials* Wickersham described meeting a band of Athabascans on the mountain's north side. Speaking through two youths who knew some English, the Natives asked the men what brought them to the region. After translating their goal, one of the interpreters commented that "mountain sheep fall off that mountain." He then expressed doubt that the climbers would be able to "stick" to the mountain better than the native sheep. Without metal-spiked crampons, scaling the higher, steeper reaches of the mountain would certainly be impossible. Apart from the problem of the icy slopes, avalanches regularly crashed down Denali's sides, taking everything in their paths. The Native group then asked the climbers if they were seeking gold at the summit. Upon hearing that the men simply wanted to be the first to climb to the summit, the Natives guffawed. Olyman Cheah, their leader, called Wickersham a fool.[9] The Wickersham team tried to ascend the mountain by the Peters Glacier, but upon reaching its upper limit they came to an impasse. At ten thousand feet they retreated.[10]

In the years that followed, several teams undertook the quest. The renowned physician and explorer Dr. Frederick Cook made two summit attempts. The second time, in 1906, he claimed success, but his tale was so implausible that many doubted him.

In December 1909 a group of "sourdoughs" from the Kantishna region on Denali's north side tackled the mountain.[11] That team included the miners Thomas Lloyd, Charles McGonagall, Bob Horne, William Taylor, and Peter Anderson and the surveyor E. C. Davidson. Lloyd, Horne, and Davidson backed out early in the expedition. McGonagall, Taylor, and Anderson, in an astonishing show of strength, carried a fourteen-foot pole in one stretch from eleven thousand feet to the Grand Basin at eighteen thousand feet. At this point McGonagall turned back, while Anderson and Taylor continued. Upon reaching the north (lower) peak, they planted their flagpole.[12] The team never received the credit they deserved for their feat, however, because Lloyd later boasted that he, McGonagall, Taylor, and Anderson had climbed both peaks, a tale that invited derision. Regardless of the uncertainty surrounding their summit, the sourdough team's discovery of the prized access route to the mountain was a boon to the Stuck-Karstens-led team a few years later. Knowing the elusive pass's location spared the 1913 ascent team a potentially lengthy reconnaissance.[13]

In 1912 a team led by professor Herschel Parker and the artist Belmore Browne nearly reached Denali's south peak. The seasoned climbers had been members of Dr. Cook's first Denali attempt. Just a few hundred feet below the summit, blizzard conditions forced them back. With their food supply exhausted, they could not wait out the storm and had no choice but to retreat.[14]

In 1913, as the Stuck-Karstens team prepared for their historic expedition, controversy and intrigue surrounded Denali. Various claims about conquering the peak mystified the public. A Phila-delphia attorney declared it should be called Mount Denial rather than Mount Denali.[15]

Hudson Stuck's dream of climbing Denali had crystallized in 1907, when he viewed the peak from Pedro Dome, near Fair-banks. He declared in his diary that day, "I would rather climb that mountain than discover the richest gold-mine in Alaska."[16] As he traveled by dogsled among the Episcopal missions in his dis-trict, Stuck often dreamed of the mountain. Many times he tried but failed to capture the perfect photograph of Denali.

Finally in spring 1913 the plan materialized. Bishop Rowe had approved a leave of absence for the archdeacon, and Stuck had gath-ered a team of four men, including himself, to make the ascent. He found two youths to assist them and secured private funding and the gear and supplies the climbers would need.

As for the men who would accompany Stuck, Walter Harp-er's participation was implicit. By now Stuck relied heavily on his assistance and companionship. Harper's subsistence skills and cool competence in crises ensured his selection.

Several years earlier Stuck had identified Harry Karstens as the ideal climbing partner to co-lead the expedition. He consid-ered Karstens one of his closest friends in Alaska.[17] Karstens had gone to the Klondike as a sixteen-year-old. Mining in the Seventy-mile area near the Alaska-Yukon border had earned him the nick-name the "Seventymile Kid." In 1907 he and Charles McGonagall had broken the trail from Fairbanks to Valdez. Later they had car-ried mail over the wilderness route. Karstens piloted riverboats as well, on the Yukon and Tanana Rivers.[18]

For more than a year, first in the summer of 1906 and again from 1907 to 1908, Karstens had guided the naturalist and hunter Charles Sheldon in the foothills of Denali. The wealthy, well-known conservationist had come to Alaska to study Dall sheep.[19] He and Karstens got along fabulously and developed a deep mutual respect. They had talked of climbing Denali together.[20]

When Sheldon married and settled Outside, Karstens aban-doned his dream of climbing the peak with his friend and accepted Stuck's appeal. The two agreed to be full partners in the effort.

Stuck would finance the climb and conduct scientific observations. He would publicize the feat afterward, through articles, a book, and speaking tours. The two would split any profits. They expected substantial earnings, given that Dr. Cook had made tens of thousands of dollars on his Denali ascent claim.[21] Stuck, however, was more interested in the attention the expedition would bring to the mission work than in earning income for himself. Karstens would provide his experience and expertise in alpine conditions. The men sealed their agreement with a handshake.[22] Having met Walter Harper and knowing of his wilderness skills, Karstens supported his participation.[23]

Stuck chose Robert Tatum as the fourth team member. The twenty-one-year-old theology student from Knoxville, Tennessee, worked at the Tanana mission. He had developed winter travel skills while delivering supplies by dog team to Episcopal missions. Tatum's primary responsibility on the Denali project was cooking for the team. His efforts to prepare pleasing meals earned the others' gratitude.[24] As the least seasoned member of the ascent team, however, he struggled with the mental and physical demands of the expedition.

Stuck planned to choose two youths from St. Mark's Mission to assist the ascent team with freighting their outfit. All of the older boys at the mission dreamed of being chosen. Because several had sufficient hunting and dog handling skills, Stuck planned to choose top students. The boys threw themselves into their studies as they vied for the honor of joining the much discussed expedition and accompanying the archdeacon and Walter.[25]

Seventeen-year-olds Johnny Fred, who was raised at the mission at Fort Yukon, and Esaias George, whom Stuck had brought to St. Mark's in 1911, won the positions.[26] Their delight waned when they learned the limited scope of their duties. They would accompany the team to the base camp, hauling supplies and hunting for food along the way. Then Esaias would return to Nenana with one dog team and an empty sled. Johnny would maintain the base camp while the men scaled the mountain.[27] Stuck gave each of the boys a brand-new Winchester rifle, one of the best sporting models on the market at the time.[28]

Stuck spearheaded the expedition and collected $1,000 to fund it. He wrote in *Ascent of Denali* that he could not have assembled a "more desirable party."[29] Determined to avoid the negative impressions people had about previous attempts on Denali, Stuck's book glossed over the tensions that arose among team members and the weaknesses those conflicts revealed.[30] His depiction of Walter's performance, however, reflected the unvarnished truth: "Twenty-one years old and six feet tall, he took gleefully to high mountaineering, while his kindliness and invincible amiability endeared him to every member of the party."[31] In fact Walter's energy and charisma often lifted the others' spirits.[32] Karstens, too, later expressed unqualified praise for Harper: "The deacon[']s boy Walter was a good one 21 years old strong fearless and as fine & lovable disposition as I ever saw in a man he was my main standby."[33]

Following their emergency run to the Tanana Crossing in late winter 1913, Stuck and Harper met Karstens in Fairbanks to launch the expedition. On March 13 the three left St. Matthew's Church in Fairbanks for Nenana, seventy-five miles away. There they would join Robert Tatum, Johnny Fred, Esaias George, and the second dog team and then proceed.[34] The day of their departure the *Fairbanks Daily Times* broke the story, proclaiming Stuck "head" of the expedition. Six paragraphs down, the article identified Karstens as Stuck's "guide."[35] This portrayal of Stuck as expedition leader and Karstens in a subordinate role irked Karstens, fueling a rift that grew between the two on the climb.

After two days spent reorganizing their supplies at St. Mark's in Nenana, the team struck out toward the Kantishna River on March 16. Fourteen dogs and two sleds supported the six team members. Excited children at St. Mark's ran with the team across the ice-covered river and waved goodbye as they set off. The party arrived at Diamond City a week and ninety miles later.[36]

When the *Pelican* had broken down the previous fall, stranding Harper and Stuck in Tanana, Karstens had taken over responsibility for assembling the team's outfit in Fairbanks. He loaded more than two tons of materials into a poling boat and a riverboat. Next he pushed the poling boat ahead of the riverboat from Fairbanks, on the Chena River, to Diamond City, at the headwa-

11. Striking across from the Tanana River to the Kantishna River, March 1913. From Stuck, *Ascent of Denali.*

ters of the Kantishna River. This was as close to the base of the mountain as he could travel by water.[37] The effort, which occupied Karstens for nearly a week, saved the team from packing their outfit over the lower foothills of the Alaska Range, as other climbers had done.[38] When the team arrived at Diamond City in late March, they found the food in good condition, except for the loss of thirty pounds of cornmeal and fifty pounds of oatmeal to hungry mice.[39]

In 1913 Diamond City was a shadow of its former self. At the height of the Kantishna gold rush in 1906, thousands of prospectors had worked in the area. Several mining camps had sprouted, including Diamond City. A year later the vast majority of the prospectors had left, after recognizing the area's limited gold deposits.[40] The thirty or so men who remained in 1913 were experienced miners who earned a modest living.[41]

The party spent several days in the Kantishna, relaying supplies and talking with miners, including Pete Anderson and Charley McGonagall. They discussed details of the 1909–10 ascent, including the premier route they had discovered. The miners also solved the climbers' footwear dilemma. The boots that Stuck had ordered were too small for the multiple layers of socks they

12. Co-leaders of the 1913 Denali expedition: Hudson Stuck and Harry Karstens. From Stuck, *Ascent of Denali*.

needed for insulation. McGonagall recommended that the team buy large-sized moccasins from area miners. They did, and the moccasins, with layers of warm socks, proved superb.[42]

Now the team had to haul their outfit fifty miles to the base of the mountain. They erected their first camp at two thousand feet, at the tree line, where Denali rose majestically above them. For five days, as some of the crew relayed supplies from their cache site and advanced them forward, others cut several cords of wood and hauled it to the next camp.[43]

During these first weeks of the expedition, spirits were high. Moments of hilarity punctuated the days of heavy physical labor. Walter divided his time between hunting and hauling freight with Johnny and Esaias. The trio thrived in subsistence activities. From March 31 to April 1 they moved a load forward and cached it at the base of the mountain. Back at the lower camp, Walter, in a serious voice, told Stuck that he had a "patient" for him. The other dogs had torn Stuck's pet malamute Muk "to pieces," he reported. Stuck dashed to the sled, demanding who was to blame. As Stuck pulled a blanket off Muk, Walter shouted, "April fool!"

ASCENT OF DENALI

13. Members of the 1913 Denali climbing team: Robert Tatum, Esaias George, Harry Karstens, Johnny Fred, and Walter Harper. From Stuck, *Ascent of Denali.*

and the pranksters howled with laughter.[44] About a week later, as Walter and the boys repaired snowshoes and Karstens slept, Tatum mixed sourdough pancake batter for breakfast the next morning. As he tried to hang the pot, he dropped it, spilling the batter. In a takeoff on Karstens's nickname, the others dubbed him the "Sourdough Kid."[45]

From the two-thousand-foot-elevation camp the team proceeded up Cache Creek to four thousand feet, where they set up their base camp. Here, where the last of the willows grew, they gathered a supply of branches to mark their trail across the Muldrow Glacier.[46] The willows would guide their descent over the crevasse-ridden ice sheet. At the base camp Karstens, Walter, and Esaias felled enough game to supply fresh meat for the ascent. The men boiled the meat, seasoned it, and made about two hundred baseball-sized meatballs.[47] Meanwhile Johnny and Esaias relayed the remaining equipment and supplies to the base camp. From there they advanced the freight to a cache at the pass to the Muldrow Glacier, a feature later named McGonagall Pass in honor of the sourdough climber who had discovered it. From this pass rose the two walls to the north and south peaks of Denali.[48]

During these frenzied days of preparation for the actual ascent, Stuck spent many hours relaxing, reading, and writing, as was his usual pattern.[49] He read and wrote daily, whether at home in Fort Yukon or on the trail or river. The archdeacon had long relied on assistants to perform various tasks for him.[50] Walter was accustomed to Stuck's habits and likely took them in stride. Karstens, on the other hand, had expected quite a different partnership with Stuck, perhaps resembling his relationship with Charles Sheldon. The wealthy, Yale-educated Sheldon associated with the likes of Theodore Roosevelt, Gifford Pinchot, and Alexander Graham Bell, yet he shared daily tasks with Karstens when they camped.[51] Karstens assumed that Stuck would also help with such chores.[52] He certainly had not planned to serve as one of the archdeacon's trail boys.

Karstens also resented Stuck's demands on the "boys" after they had worked hard all day. The respect that the four younger team members showed the archdeacon likely annoyed Karstens as well, especially when he felt that Stuck was shirking his duties. Moreover Stuck could be quite critical of the others' work. For instance, he complained about Tatum's cooking despite his efforts to please Stuck.[53] Tension thus mounted between the project's co-leaders.

According to Karstens's biographer, Tom Walker, Karstens was "combative and possessed of a volcanic temper. . . . He was a proud man, a self-made man. . . . Notoriously thin-skinned, he took criticism personally."[54] Given Stuck's domineering personality and Karstens's feistiness, the two were bound to clash. Harper, on the other hand, was both personally and culturally disinclined toward confrontation. The traditional Athabascan values of nonconfrontation and nonintervention had fostered harmony and promoted survival within Athabascan bands for millennia.[55] Harper's personal charisma, congeniality, and stoicism deescalated tension, while his strength and stamina moved the project forward.

On April 11, with the preparatory work for the ascent completed, Stuck and Karstens scouted ahead from the base camp. Advancing through McGonagall Pass, their eyes surveyed for the first time the dazzling Muldrow Glacier, the "highway of desire," as Stuck called it.[56] The glacier's huge expanse held many barriers to the team's ascent, including gaping crevasses, avalanche rubble, and icefalls thousands of feet high.[57] But it provided the golden pathway to the upper reaches of Denali.

Three days later Walter took advantage of the opportunity to write to his sister Margaret. Esaias would return to Nenana the following day, carrying letters with him. "It is almost a month since we left Nenana and not a single day is wasted," he wrote. "We brought a ton and a half of provisions and were kept pretty busy hauling and relaying it. We just made a trip up to Muldrow Glacier today with a load and coming back we tobogganed most of the way. . . . There is the wood to be hauled up which we already hauled eight or nine miles up the Clearwater creek. The wood up in this region is worth its weight in gold. . . . Please excuse a hasty note. Yours lovingly," he signed off, "Walter Harper," as if the surname were necessary.[58]

The next day the men sent Esaias, with a dog team and sled, on the one-hundred-mile journey back to Nenana. The team of five now finished preparing their camp on Muldrow Glacier. They moved the climbing outfit a mile upward from the base camp, through McGonagall Pass to the West Fork of the glacier at 11,500 feet.[59] Giant crevasses posed the greatest risk on Muldrow Glacier. Drifted snow completely covered some of them. With one step on the soft surface, the snow would give way and the climber could plummet into an abyss. Karstens devised their plan for crossing the glacier using a sounding pole to test the surface. He invented various means of bridging the crevasses, including arched ice bridges that held like stone.[60]

Thrusting the pole into the snow required muscle and force. Once, when the snow covering a crevasse broke away, Stuck lost his grip on the shaft, and it hurtled out of sight.[61] Karstens carved a new sounding device from their tent pole, and Walter took over Stuck's turns with the rod.[62] Already the older man was beginning to recognize his physical limitations.

As a second precaution against falling to their deaths in a crevasse, the men roped themselves together. At least twice Karstens

14. Bridging a crevasse on the Muldrow Glacier. From Stuck, *Ascent of Denali*.

fell through snow bridges and had to be pulled back.[63] When Snowball, Walter's favorite dog, fell into a crevasse, he rescued the animal. In his typical matter-of-fact tone, he related the incident in his diary: "We had [a] little trouble in crossing some of the crevasses with the dogs, and one place poor old Snow Ball fell through . . . so they let me down with a rope and I tied a rope around his body and we were both hoisted up by the others."[64]

Occasional comments in Karstens's diary reveal his growing frustration with Stuck. On April 25 he wrote, "The deacon is taking his siwashy pictures in important positions which means? I plan everything & will get the bunk."[65] The comment referenced two sore points. First, Stuck needed photos and measurements for the book and articles he planned to write on the expedition— publications Karstens suspected would downplay his role. Second, as Stuck performed these tasks, Karstens prospected and planned, which was work critical to the climbers' safety and success. Leadership responsibilities increasingly fell to him.[66]

Periodically Karstens's resentment boiled over. Once he berated Walter for leaving his things lying about.[67] Two days later he shouted at Stuck for reading in the tent while the others worked, after he himself had said that only four people were needed for the day's tasks. Stuck blamed Karstens's foul mood on an upset

15. Hudson Stuck, May 1, 1913. From Stuck, *Ascent of Denali.*

stomach. Only later did he realize that he had caused Karstens's distress. He decided to ignore Karstens's ill humor, because he relied on him and he truly admired him. "I like him; have always liked him & he must be taken with his limitations," Stuck wrote at the time.[68] By late April various ailments and discomforts troubled both Tatum and Karstens, heightening sensitivities.[69]

Amid these tensions Harper focused on the task at hand, whether it was scouting the route ahead, packing supplies up the mountain, or studying. His brief diary entries reveal no hint of discord among the men. He related their work each day, rarely mentioning the risks the men faced. Sometimes he expressed delight at simple pleasures: "Johnnie [sic] and I went down to base-camp this morning," he wrote on April 20. "We stayed there feasting on the choicest parts of the caribou." On April 27 he noted, "The sun has been shining all day and Mt. Denali stood out in the clear blue sky splendidly." His May 7 entry captured a breathtaking scene: "We saw the finest avalanches this morning coming down from the north ridge of Mt. Denali one after another shaking the whole Muldrow Glacier as it struck it. I rushed out with the Archdeacon's camera and mine and took snapshots of them as they were falling."[70]

On May 2 disaster struck at their cache site midway up Muldrow Glacier.[71] The team had covered their gear with their silk tents. After lunch Karstens and Stuck had smoked their pipes, as usual. When they returned to the site with another load of supplies, they discovered the cache in flames. After a few moments of stunned disbelief, the source of the fire dawned on them. A match that one of the smokers had tossed had smoldered in the silk fabric and burst into flames. The fire destroyed their sugar, powdered milk, baking powder, dried fruit, and pilot bread, along with a sack of woolen gloves and socks, a bag of film, and most of their tobacco. Luckily they saved the wood, and plenty of kerosene remained.[72] And their most calorie-rich food lay at the lower site. Even so, shock and dismay overwhelmed the men, especially Stuck.[73] The whole enterprise might have been ruined.

Walter had been relaying supplies and returned to the camp after the fire was smothered. He took the loss in stride, noting on May 2, 1913, in his diary the team's "great disappointment," without dwelling on the point. He had relied on his resourcefulness to overcome countless predicaments. This was but another.

Karstens took charge of the crisis, calculating their losses and determining what could be salvaged.[74] He, Stuck, and Tatum began the repair work, while Walter and Johnny returned to the base camp to gather replacement supplies for the ascent. Walter insisted that Johnny keep a small supply of the reserve milk and sugar for himself. Johnny immediately decided to save those cherished items for the ascent team's return.[75]

The group spent several days in camp re-creating materials they had lost in the fire. They cut, sewed, and darned tents, mitts, and socks for the next stage of the expedition.[76] Meanwhile precious clear days of perfect climbing weather passed. But remaining in camp offered one advantage: temporary relief from sunburn. Karstens's face and neck were now severely burned. Walter too was sunburned and had blistered lips. Amber sunglasses saved all the men from painful snow blindness. The recently developed glasses provided excellent protection from the sun's glare reflecting off the snow.[77]

As they repaired the damage, the climbers discovered a second catastrophe, even greater than the fire: the shattered Northeast Ridge. On May 5, as Karstens remained in camp repairing their ice creepers, Stuck and Tatum scouted for a route from the head of the glacier to the summit. They searched for the Northeast Ridge that Parker and Browne had climbed the year before. The jumble of ice and snow boulders they saw looked nothing like the ridge Parker and Browne had described.

Above the ice boulders lay a great cleavage. Apparently the snow and ice had broken away from the slope and fallen on the ridge. The significance of the ridge's stunning transformation dawned on the ascent team slowly. On May 8 Karstens, Johnny, and Walter struck out for the ridge. Karstens now realized that the previous summer's earthquake explained the scene. By May 9 the full weight of this disaster had sunk in. After a second grueling day cutting steps through the ice boulders, Karstens wrote in his diary, "Last years shake up has certainly ruined this ridge for good climbing."[78]

16. The shattered Northeast Ridge. From Stuck, *Ascent of Denali*.

The July 1912 earthquake had triggered an avalanche that buried the pathway along the Northeast Ridge, the route to the summit. As it turned out, Parker and Browne were fortunate to have retreated when they did. Two days after they reached their base camp, the earthquake struck, shaking the region violently.[79]

On May 9 the men finished their repairs from the fire, and the camp at the head of Muldrow Glacier was ready. The site lay at 11,500 feet, at the actual base of the mountain. The rise from there was too steep for the dogs, so Stuck and Tatum escorted Johnny and the dogs down over the crevassed area of the Muldrow toward the base camp.[80] Johnny expected the ascent team to return in two weeks, but his vigil extended much longer.

For three weeks the men labored to carve a pathway along the Northeast Ridge to the Grand Basin, with some days off due to bad weather and poor visibility. Karstens and Harper cut each step through the ice boulders in the three-mile route.[81] Almost sheer drops on either side of the ridge heightened the risk. Karstens later described the work: "again & again Walter & I tackled the ridge fogs & storms would drive us back . . . you can hardly imagine what a proposition that ridge was . . . a jumbled up mass of ice . . . some [blocks] balancing on the ridge 2 blows of my axe sent one as big as a two story house crashing and [roaring] into the basin thousands of feet below."[82]

As usual Walter reported the backbreaking work in his diary in understated terms. He described the work most graphically on May 11: "We had heavy packs on our backs and we toiled up the ridge gasping for breath."[83]

According to Stuck, aside from this unexpected barrier, Denali did not present exceptional technical challenges. The greatest hurdles were its remoteness, size, and the expanses of ice and snow that had to be crossed while carrying heavy gear.[84] But the Northeast Ridge of 1913, with its "miles and miles of ice-blocks" rising three thousand feet, presented "all the spice of sensation and danger that any man could desire."[85]

The camp itself was reasonably comfortable. A floor of wooden food crates shielded them against the cold and moisture of the glacier. Upon the wood the men spread caribou and Dall sheep pelts from the game they had shot.[86] Snug in their sleeping bags atop the platform, they slept more than usual during these weeks, to conserve precious fuel and relieve boredom.[87]

Although they kept warm in their cozy quarters, team members suffered from digestive ailments, headaches, anxiety, and depression during this phase of the ascent. Their meals consisted of hearty meatball stews that some had trouble digesting.[88] The men longed for the treats that had perished in the fire, especially sugar to sweeten their tea and hot chocolate. The constant rumbling and roaring of avalanches set their nerves on edge.[89] Tremendous icefalls tumbled from between the two peaks, jarring the glacier and sending plumes of ice particles thousands of feet high.[90] Tatum suffered severe headaches and other ailments.[91] The team considered replacing him with Johnny, but he recovered, thus resolving the dilemma.[92] Walter found the waiting for clear weather "tedious," but showed no signs of distress. He and Stuck passed the time studying, which both enjoyed.[93]

Finally on May 24 the men packed the most essential gear and proceeded up the ridge. They carried the tent Karstens had fashioned, which was so small they had to change sleeping positions in unison. Fifteen hundred feet above the glacier camp, at thirteen thousand feet, they cleared a small space and made a camp on the ridge. The following day they descended and returned with the remaining gear. Walter wrote that evening of his relief that they would not have to descend that part of the ridge again. He knew every step of the way by heart now.[94]

The climb that day had pushed Stuck to his physical limit. Repeatedly he had stopped to catch his breath. Anxiety about "the deacon's" rapidly declining capacity caused Karstens to lie awake fretting that night. The following day, feeling out of sorts, he stayed in camp while Harper and Tatum cleared steps toward the top of the ridge.[95] The day's work and the prospect of climbing the ridge deepened Tatum's fear and depression. He dreamed of his father's death and cried in his sleep that night.[96] Only Walter slept well by this time. "I envy that boy his splendid rugged strength & adaptability," Stuck mused.[97]

Feeling better the next day, Karstens, along with Walter, proceeded up the ridge. Karstens plotted their moves carefully as they advanced from the top of the ridge to the smooth snow slope above the cleavage. They carved a pathway along drifted snow, cutting a secure foothold into the ice every few feet, in case the snow broke away. They took turns in the lead, with one of the two always remaining on solid footing. Walter strictly followed Karstens's directions, even on this perilous stretch.[98]

At four o'clock that afternoon Stuck scanned the ridge and held his breath as Karstens and then Harper stepped onto the unbroken snow above the cleavage. Overcome with joy and relief, he wrote, "This is the best thing I have been able to record for three weeks." Their hope of reaching the summit was revived. At last the team could advance to the Grand Basin between the two peaks. Yet they still had to climb, descend, and reclimb that treacherous passage multiple times to bring up their outfit. The packs on their backs increased the odds of losing their balance.[99]

On May 29 Harper and Karstens reached the Grand Basin, a breakthrough that transformed the mood in camp. Walter wrote

May 25th 1913
Sunday

We took all our belongings and started up to the camp on the ridge this morning with a great deal of pleasure and satisfaction that we won't have to come down the old ridge which we were all tired of, and I specially for I am at the head always cleaning out the steps I think I know every step of the way nearly. After we had lunch Mr. Karstens and I went up the ridge toward the col, and after a hard work of seven hours we returned failing to reach the col.

17. Walter Harper's diary. Yvonne Mozée Collection, #2002-98-diary-Harper, Mozée Family Papers, APRCA, University of Alaska Fairbanks.

that night that they were "all happier tonight than we have been for three weeks." Two days later Tatum and Harper descended the "dreadful ridge" to bring up the last gear.[100] After gathering supplies at various caches below, Walter bore so much weight on his back that he had to fashion a head band to shift some of the burden to his head. At several places on the ridge the wind blew so fiercely he nearly lost his balance.[101]

In the Grand Basin, at fifteen thousand feet and higher, the altitude affected all the men. With each additional foot they ascended, the air's density diminished. The forty pounds they packed on their backs felt like eighty. None of the men suffered from the motion sickness mountaineers often experience at high altitudes, but Stuck in particular had trouble breathing.[102] Walter and Tatum divided the contents of his backpack between them.[103] Only at the highest reaches of the mountain did Harper, Karstens, and Tatum have serious difficulty breathing.[104]

The team's spirits soared as they neared the summit. Karstens's annoyance with Stuck waned as the older man stopped every few steps, gasping for air, and a sense of camaraderie grew among the men. By June 3 Stuck was carrying nothing but the mercurial barometer, a rather cumbersome thermometer. On these final ascent days he waited with the gear while the others relayed supplies forward. He ascended with the team on the final relays.[105]

On June 3 as the team rested at about 16,500 feet in the Grand Basin they discussed the Kantishna sourdoughs' ascent of the north peak three years before. The sky was completely clear for the first time in weeks. Scanning the north peak, Walter suddenly shouted, "I see the flagstaff!"[106] Excitedly the men took turns viewing the flag through their binoculars, relishing in this proof of their friends' achievement. That day for the first time Walter's feet nearly froze.[107]

On June 4 altitude sickness overpowered Harper after he and Karstens had climbed to eighteen thousand feet in the blazing sun.[108] That night as Walter lay in the tent feeling ill, Stuck wrote, "He has done one yeoman's service." Stuck now doubted whether he could reach the summit, given his shortness of breath, but "K. says I shall get to the top if he has to pack me," he wrote.[109]

By the evening of June 6, just before their final trudge to the summit, Walter had recovered. Determined to make use of the flour they had been packing but unable to use without leavening, he tried to make noodles for dinner but failed miserably. The pitiful results caused all but Walter stomach upset. Stuck marveled at Walter's digestive and sleeping capacities.[110] After resting for three hours, the men arose at 10:00 p.m. in bright sunlight, lit the Primus stove, and gathered around it. Walter described the atmosphere in the tent: "Mr. K. had a headache and Tatum had another and the Archdeacon could not move without losing his breath." Their spirits were low. A daunting task lay ahead: reaching the summit and returning in one day.[111]

But the glorious weather offered a chance at the summit, so at 4:00 a.m. the men set forth, despite their maladies. Only Harper felt "entirely himself."[112] Karstens wrote, "I put Walter in lead [and] kept him there all day." He took second position on the rope so he could instruct Walter. And Walter "worked all day without a murmur."[113] They chopped steps as they zigzagged their way up the steep slope.[114]

By 11:00 a.m. the team was advancing toward the horseshoe ridge that had Denali's south peak at its center. Even this close to their goal, the bitterly cold north wind caused the climbers "grave doubts" that they would summit. Painfully cold feet plagued them, despite multiple layers of footwear. Stuck wore six pairs of thick woolen and felt socks along with felt inner soles in his size 16 moccasins.[115] The men agreed that if anyone's feet were actually freezing, they would turn back.

Seeing Stuck struggling with each step, Walter took the mercurial barometer from him and put it on his own back. After they rounded the ridge and the peak they stopped for lunch. Sheltered from the north wind, they absorbed the warmth of the sun. Scalding tea revived the team's confidence, and they continued.[116]

Upon reaching the top of the ridge the men thought was the summit, Walter shouted back to the others, "There's another ridge!" After trudging up the final stretch, he still had the lung capacity for a victory shout at the peak.[117] In typical fashion Walter downplayed the final day's ordeal in his diary: "After a long and tedious grind we reached the first level about half way to the top . . . and from there we [plodded] slowly but steadily. . . . I was ahead all day and was the first ever to set foot on Mt. Denali."[118]

Karstens arrived next, then Tatum, and finally Stuck, who almost had "to be hauled up the last few feet, and fell unconscious for a moment," as he described it. It was 1:30 p.m. on June 7. Stuck concluded that Harper and Karstens could have climbed another ten thousand feet, based on their condition at the summit.[119]

Once Stuck had caught his breath, the men shook hands and said a brief prayer of thanks "to Almighty God" for bringing them safely to the summit.[120] The men quickly set up their instrument tent. Stuck took the reading on the mercurial barometer, and Harper boiled water for the boiling point thermometer.[121] They had rehearsed their moves multiple times. Nevertheless, as Stuck put it, they suffered from "high altitude stupidity." He later discovered mistakes in their data, including recording 7 degrees Fahrenheit on one thermometer and 20 degrees on the other.[122] Considering the intense effects of altitude at twenty thousand feet, it is a wonder that the men functioned as well as they did. The air contains less than 50 percent of the oxygen it holds at sea level.[123] Disorientation at high altitude has led to numerous tragic accidents in the early stages of descents.[124]

After completing their tasks, the team members surveyed the breathtaking view in all directions.[125] Tatum tied onto the tent pole a small U.S. flag he had made of two silk handkerchiefs. Walter drove the pole into the snow. Tatum then removed the flag, and Walter lashed to the pole a slender birch crosspiece that Stuck had fashioned. Walter thrust the cross into the snow permanently, and the men gathered around it and recited the Te Deum, a hymn of praise.[126] Then they prepared to descend, having spent a mere one and one-half hours at the summit.[127] They took a last view of Denali's north and south peaks, donned their creepers, and descended to the camp above the Grand Basin in just two hours.[128]

The stunning panorama at the summit had induced such euphoria in the men that they felt no exhaustion on the descent. Gratitude for the privilege of the experience overwhelmed them.[129]

Nearly two decades later Tatum told a newspaper reporter, "It was like looking out of a window of Heaven."[130] Harper's diary entries suggest that he took the risk, labor, and discomfort of the expedition in stride. But that spectacular view of his homeland surely remained with him for the rest of his days.

The men slept soundly at their eighteen-thousand-foot camp that night. In the morning they stashed the supplies they no longer needed. Then they wound their way downward in the Grand Basin, until they came to the Northeast Ridge.[131]

Now Karstens and Harper put their skills and experience to work as never before. Guided by their experience and aided by ice creepers and blessedly clear weather, they traversed the "sensationally steep" ridge above the earthquake cleavage. They had to shovel their steps on the descent, because two feet of snow had fallen since their ascent. The four were tethered with a rope, with Karstens in the lead. In one and one-half hours they reached the cleavage, the most critical point of the descent. Now the men crept like cats across the slope, placing their feet carefully onto their shoveled steps and thrusting their ice axes into the holes in the ice wall. They moved forward in silence, the rope taut between them.[132]

Next they descended the staircase Harper and Karstens had carved over the ice chunks on the ridge. At 9:30 p.m. on June 8 they reached their camp at the head of Muldrow Glacier. Twelve hours had passed since they had left the eighteen-thousand-foot camp. Suddenly Denali's usual cloud cover descended, obscuring the summit. It was as if by design the clouds had been held aloft until the men reached safe ground.

In the morning they placed their backpacks on the Yukon sled they had left at the camp and donned their snowshoes to descend the glacier. Now their thoughts turned to Johnny, who had been waiting for four weeks, knowing nothing of their fate. The willow branches they had planted marked their ascent path, but some of the snow bridges had collapsed. Carefully testing the snow with each step, they crossed the glacier.[133] Beyond the crevassed region of the ice sheet, soft, wet snow and finally pools of water soaked their footwear. At McGonagall Pass the men abandoned their sled and snowshoes. Looking down through the pass, they

18. Harry Karstens wearing climbing irons. From Stuck, *Ascent of Denali*.

19. Johnny Fred at the base camp. From Stuck, *Ascent of Denali.*

gazed in wonder at the carpet of purple moss flowers clinging to the rocks. Spring had arrived while they struggled up the mountain. An unwelcome sign of the season greeted them too: swarms of mosquitoes. To their dismay they had forgotten to bring nets.[134]

Back at the base camp Johnny had passed the days with Stuck's seven dogs, hunting for game as needed. He felled and butchered three Dall sheep and two caribou, dividing the meat between himself and the dogs, while saving plenty for the men. He knew they would be famished when they returned.[135] Finally on the evening of the thirty-first day after he left them Johnny heard a shout and then another. Overjoyed, he ran to greet the men. Upon meeting them, Johnny took Stuck's pack from his shoulders and placed it on his own back.[136]

A jubilant reunion followed. The men devoured the fresh meat and biscuits Johnny had prepared, accompanied by cup after cup of coffee with the milk and sugar he had saved for them. Between bites and gulps they excitedly exchanged adventure stories.[137] The praise the men heaped on Johnny for saving the sugar rang in his ears for the rest of his life. He was forever known as the boy who would not eat the sugar.[138]

The next day at base camp, the men reorganized their gear, bathed in the icy stream nearby, and ate dozens of biscuits Johnny continuously baked, washed down with coffee. They sewed canvas bags so that the dogs could be fitted with them and carry some of the weight on their backs. The following morning, June 11, they left their sled and base camp and walked toward the Clearwater River.[139]

Travel through the foothills was awkward and unpleasant. Their feet sank in the moss, and mosquitoes tormented them. Torrential rain soaked their clothes, and hail pelted them.[140] Crossing the glacial streams required ingenuity. The mile-and-a-half-wide McKinley Fork was a tapestry of rocks and glacial silt. Walter carried Stuck, who was wearing moccasins, on his back through the running water.[141]

From the McKinley Fork the men hiked to Eureka, a mining camp on Moose Creek. The miner Jack Hamilton fed the team and provided them comfortable bunks for the night. The next day, on

Caribou Creek, they visited the miners Charley McGonagall and Joe and Fannie Quigley, who fed them royally.[142] For hours they relived their adventures with McGonagall. From Caribou Creek they retraced their route to the Tanana River and to the village of Tanana. They arrived at the mission on June 20, three months and four days after their journey began.[143]

First thing in the morning Stuck wired the *Seattle Times* and the *Fairbanks Daily Times* of the team's success. Articles in these and other newspapers hailed the achievement. Virtually all accounts identified Stuck as team leader and downplayed others' contributions. Stuck's stature as Episcopal archdeacon and his membership in the prestigious Explorers Club, a New York–based society of explorers and scientists, contributed to the press's emphasis on him. His later articles, and especially his book, reinforced the perception that he singularly led the expedition. Stuck praised others, especially Karstens, for their skill and stamina, but he left the impression that he was the driving force behind the undertaking.[144]

The media's overemphasis on Stuck's leadership aggravated Karstens's residual anger from the ascent, and a deep rift developed between the two. Stuck tried repeatedly to repair the relationship. Following the climb, he had Tiffany's fashion lapel pins for the ascent team members from pieces of granite he had gathered near the summit.[145] He wrote to the *Fairbanks Daily Times* that in overcoming challenges and unexpected conditions on the mountain, "Karstens was always the real leader." He declared that he never would have tried the ascent without partnering with Karstens.[146] He repeatedly praised Karstens in *Ascent of Denali*, and he renamed the Northeast Ridge in honor of Karstens. On the other hand, Stuck did sometimes overstate his own part in the achievement.[147] After the climb the two never spoke again.

The falling out between the co-leaders of this historic expedition illustrates both men's foibles. The explosive combination of Stuck's forcefulness and Karstens's quick temper could have derailed the enterprise. Stuck's frailty heightened the risk of failure. However, individual team members' grit and resolve, spurred by Harper's mild temperament, surmounted these interpersonal tensions. If anyone had reason to resent the overshadowing of his role by the praise lavished on Stuck it was Harper—the peace-maker and superathlete.

The expedition shaped the participants' identities for the rest of their lives. The triumph enhanced Stuck's and Karstens's prominence and advanced their careers. Considered in this light, Walter's critical role in the pioneer summit takes on more profound and enduring implications. His strength, stamina, and steadfastness not only sealed the expedition's success but bolstered team members' reputations.

Already the Episcopal Church's most well-known missionary in Alaska, Stuck capitalized on publicity about the ascent to increase awareness of mission needs. He traveled extensively to raise funds for the mission work and recruit missionaries. Publicity for the triumph aided his efforts in Washington DC to protect Native subsistence interests as well.[148]

Harry Karstens became the first superintendent of Mount McKinley National Park. President Woodrow Wilson signed a bill creating the park in 1917. Efforts by Charles Sheldon, the mountaineer Belmore Browne, and James Wickersham, who was Alaska's delegate to Congress at the time, had influenced the act. Karstens served in the position for seven years. He established rules to protect the wildlife, developed a snowshoe-equipped ranger corps that patrolled the park with dog teams, and had park headquarters facilities constructed.[149] Karstens's storytelling was legendary. In the evenings he would gather park visitors around a campfire and regale them with tales of his exploits.[150]

Johnny Fred and Esaias George returned to St. Mark's Mission. In 1916 they became the mission school's first students to pass exams and graduate eighth grade.[151] Johnny entered Mount Hermon School that fall. After earning a college degree, he returned to Alaska and served the Athabascan people in several roles, including through Episcopal Church work. Esaias remained in Alaska's Interior and worked for a time at the newly opened St. Stephen's Hospital at Fort Yukon.[152]

Robert Tatum considered the experience "one of the greatest privileges" of his life.[153] He later attended Mount Hermon School. In 1921 he earned a bachelor of arts degree in theology at Stuck's alma mater, the University of the South. That year he became superintendent of the Tanana Valley missions. The following year he was ordained an Episcopal priest.[154] In fall 1922 Tatum enrolled his protégé, Moses Cruikshank, at Mount Hermon.[155] Like Johnny, Moses had followed in Walter Harper's footsteps. Tatum oversaw the Tanana missions until 1924, when he returned to Tennessee. He pastored Episcopal churches in several states in later years.[156]

The crucible of the ascent experience deepened Stuck's affection for Walter and his commitment to the young man's future. Walter's concern for Stuck's well-being had helped Stuck achieve the summit. Following the expedition, Stuck devoted more of his time and thought to "the boy." They traveled extensively together Outside, and Stuck sponsored his education at Mount Hermon School in Massachusetts. Visits to national landmarks and cultural institutions, as well as encounters with wealthy and influential figures in Stuck's social circle, continually expanded Walter's understanding of the world.

Stuck bestowed several place names on Denali, in addition to renaming the Northeast Ridge for Karstens. He named the glacier in Denali's Grand Basin the Harper Glacier in honor of Walter and his father, Arthur Harper. None of the place-names meant as much to Stuck as the restoration of the Athabascan name Denali to the mountain itself and the name Denali's Wife to its companion peak.[157]

4

Mount Hermon School

BACK AT TANANA, Walter Harper spent several days preparing the *Pelican* for the summer season, with Robert Tatum's help. Walter tuned the engine while Tatum repainted the rooms on the boat. The Denali expedition had made fast friends of the two, and Tatum regretted that in the fall Walter would be headed Outside, to attend school.[1]

During most of July 1913 Harper and Stuck traveled the Yukon and Tanana Rivers, visiting fish camps and Episcopal missions. Late in the month Harper returned to Tanana to see his sisters before leaving for school.[2] He remained in Tanana a full week before returning to Fort Yukon.[3]

Jessie and Margaret now taught at St. Mark's Mission.[4] The two sisters had developed a glamorous sense of style during their school years in California. Their makeup, modern hairstyles, and fashionable clothing won them many admirers. They had become well acculturated in mainstream American society, and both soon married white men. Margaret married Frank O'Farrell and Jessie married Ben Mozée, who had come to Tanana to take a teaching position.[5] Walter's sisters navigated easily among both Alaska Natives and non-Natives, in contrast to their brothers, who often were subjected to sneers and insults from both full-blood Natives and whites.[6] Discrimination against mixed-race individuals tended to keep them on the fringes of Alaska society.[7] Walter, on the other hand, like his sisters, integrated into both cultures effortlessly.

In fact Walter was so sociable that Stuck feared he might be easy prey for "low down white men" who exploited Natives.[8] The drunkenness in Tanana epitomized missionaries' worst fears of the downfall of Alaska Natives through corruption by whites. Stuck only reluctantly permitted Walter to stay the week in Tanana, owing to his anxiety about "the boy's" vulnerability. What Stuck did not yet fully understand was that beneath Walter's mild demeanor and charisma lay firm convictions. Furthermore, witnessing alcohol abuse as a child and his one experience with drinking it had left Walter wanting no part of it.

About the time Walter arrived back in Fort Yukon, the well-known writer and conservationist Emerson Hough and friends turned up at the mission, hungry and exhausted. They had navigated the Mackenzie River in northern Canada to the Porcupine River and down to Fort Yukon.[9] Their route followed the course Arthur Harper had taken to Alaska in 1873. Happy Burke's wife, Clara Burke, fed the men a hearty meal, and Stuck gave them clean sets of clothing.[10] Hough was an avid outdoorsman and friend and supporter of President Theodore Roosevelt. For hours the men talked on wide-ranging topics, including the Denali expedition and Hough's effort to establish a national park system.

On August 11 Harper, Stuck, and the Hough party boarded the *Schwatka* to travel Outside.[11] The steamer carried them upriver to Whitehorse, where they took the Yukon & White Pass Railway to Skagway on Alaska's "panhandle."[12] From Skagway they traveled on the newly commissioned Canadian Pacific Railway–owned *Princess Sophia*. The ocean liner was designed to serve the northern region of North America's western coast.[13]

As they waited to board the ship, passengers heard the dreadful news that the steamship the *State of California* had foundered ninety miles south of Juneau three days earlier.[14] The ship had struck an uncharted jagged pinnacle that cut a gash the whole length of its hull. It sank within minutes. Thirty-one of the people aboard drowned, despite heroic efforts to save them by the ship's crew and men in rescue boats. Alaska's beautiful Inside Passage was known for its hidden perils—reefs and pinnacles that had caught many a captain unaware.[15]

The *Princess Sophia*'s voyage of August 1913 from Skagway to

Vancouver, British Columbia, proved uneventful. Perfect weather allowed passengers to enjoy the spectacular scenery. By popular demand Stuck held a short talk on the Denali expedition, and Walter stood to be recognized. Members of the audience snapped countless photos of the two. Upon their arrival in Vancouver, they took an automobile tour of the city and the world-famous Stanley Park courtesy of friends. That evening Stuck and Walter went swimming in English Bay, one of many firsts for Walter.[16]

The two spent a few days sightseeing and doing business in the Seattle and Vancouver region, as well as taking an excursion to the charming, British-influenced city of Victoria on Vancouver Island. Next they boarded the *Imperial Limited*, Canada's premier passenger train between Vancouver and Montreal. The train failed to live up to its luxury image, but the ever-changing landscape provided continual diversion.[17] The train coursed through the peaks and canyons of the Cascade and Rocky Mountains, through Alberta's Badlands, across the grain fields on the prairies of Saskatchewan and Manitoba to Winnipeg. There the duo paused their journey to attend church services and see the sights. Back aboard the train the next morning, they traveled through southwestern Ontario's lush rolling hills, past Lake Superior, and on to Montreal. They spent a day touring the francophone city before boarding another train to New York City.

Stuck took great delight in showing Harper New York's attractions. He proudly introduced him to Episcopal officials whom he hoped would support Walter's education. The two lunched with Bishop Arthur Lloyd, president of the Episcopal Board of Missions, and his son at the National Arts Club. Later the two young men took in a ball game while Stuck saw his publishers.

The highlight of the visit to New York was an evening at the Hippodrome Theatre, where they viewed a "spectacle" titled *America*. For eight years extravaganzas designed and produced by Arthur Voegtlin had mesmerized audiences at the Hippodrome. The theater boasted the grandest stage in the world, one where major feats of technical design, lighting, and magical effects played out. A huge water tank on the stage supported dramatic scenes. A two-ring circus featured dancing horses, elephants, and strong-man acts.

Usually the shows took audiences on virtual excursions around the world with as many as fifteen separate scenes. *America* took place completely within the nation's shores except for one scene of a ship sailing through the Panama Canal. In the most thrilling act, three New York City fire engines pulled by galloping horses, sirens shrieking, rushed to put out a fire. More than sixteen hundred electrical lights lit the stage, a spectacle in itself in 1913.[18]

As Stuck and Harper walked back to their hotel at Union Square, a downpour drenched them.[19] The sights and sounds of Vancouver, Victoria, Seattle, Winnipeg, Montreal, and finally New York surely fascinated and disoriented the twenty-year-old Walter. Just five years had passed since Stuck had discovered him at his family's fish camp on the Yukon River.

The following evening he and Stuck arrived at Mount Hermon School in Northfield, Massachusetts. Arthur Wright, who had just completed his third year of studies at Mount Hermon, met the two as they arrived. The next day Stuck spoke in a Saturday service at the chapel. That afternoon he took Walter and Arthur on a drive to nearby Greenfield before leaving.[20]

In his application to Mount Hermon, Walter had written that he was a dog musher, guide, trapper, and wood chopper.[21] On another form he had listed "traveling guide" as his occupation.[22] When he entered the school, he planned to become a vocational-technical teacher at a mission school in Alaska, a career that would earn him respect and dignity.[23] Walter's plans evolved at Mount Hermon. He later aimed to attend medical school and become a medical missionary.

America's most well-known Christian evangelist, Dwight Moody, had founded Mount Hermon Boy's School in 1881. In the mid-1880s Moody dropped the word "Boy's" from the school's name. He had established Northfield Seminary for Young Ladies two years earlier.[24] Mount Hermon offered an education to "young men of sound bodies, good minds, and high aims" with "limited means." Neither "vicious" nor "idle" boys nor boys who had previously failed in school were welcome.[25] Moody's lack of schooling and spiritual direction in his youth, and his work with homeless boys in Chicago, had inspired him to found Mount Hermon. He believed boys and young men needed a rigorous Christian education to mature into responsible adults.[26] Several wealthy men, mostly Moody's friends, had supported the school. They included Hiram Camp, who chose the school's name: Mount Hermon, a mountain in Israel mentioned in the Bible.[27]

Moody chose a pastoral setting for the schools, near his birthplace in northwestern Massachusetts. The Mount Hermon campus lay on rolling hills overlooking the Connecticut River and the hills beyond. Stately buildings, graceful elm, oak, pine, and maple trees, and undulating lawns lent character to the peaceful landscape.[28]

In the late nineteenth century, as Moody established the Northfield schools, the U.S. government began a new era in Native American policy: the allotment and assimilation era. A new set of policies sought to remedy earlier mistreatment of Native Americans by assimilating them into mainstream society. The Carlisle Indian Industrial School exemplified assimilation-based boarding schools. Richard Henry Pratt, a former cavalry officer, established a school in Carlisle, Pennsylvania, in 1881, to prepare Native Americans for citizenship.[29] In an 1892 speech Pratt explained his aim as a revision of a famous general's well-publicized declaration that "the only good Indian is a dead one." Pratt believed instead that the solution to the so-called "Indian problem" was to "kill the Indian in him, and save the man."[30] The U.S. government erected many boarding schools in the Carlisle model. Reservation schools later became the norm.[31]

The same year that Pratt established Carlisle, Dwight Moody learned of a need for Native American teachers on reservations. Tribal members preferred that their children be taught by Native teachers who were acculturated to Western society, and missionaries in Indian Country preferred Christianized Native teachers. Moody sent a recruiter to several eastern reservations to identify promising young women for Northfield Seminary. Sixteen Native American women entered the school in 1880. The students experienced a variety of adjustment difficulties, including frustration with the regimented academic schedule and homesickness. School officials tried to create as homelike an experience as possible for the Native American students, housing them in a small cottage during the summer, for instance. The majority did not graduate, but their graduation rate exceeded Northfield's average rate in the 1880s. Most became teachers.[32]

Unlike federal boarding schools, the Northfield schools prepared Native American students to return to their reservations as professionals, such as teachers, doctors, government employees, and pastors. Moody believed Native students could serve their people more effectively if they remained immersed in their own cultures. Personnel therefore neither denigrated Native students' heritages or cultures nor did they mock or forbid the use of their native languages, as industrial schools typically did. Moody sought to prepare Native American students to bridge mainstream American and Native American cultures in their capacities as professionals in their communities.[33]

By 1900 twenty-three Native American women had attended Northfield Seminary, including five from Sitka, Alaska. Six Native American men had attended Mount Hermon. Frederick Moore, a Tlingit man, became Mount Hermon's first missionary. Following Moody's recruitment efforts among Native Americans, word of the schools' program for Native American students spread through his extensive Christian network.[34]

By the time Walter Harper entered Mount Hermon, it had earned an outstanding reputation for preparing Native American students for leadership roles in their communities.[35] Several other Alaska Native youth who assisted Hudson Stuck also attended the school, including Arthur Wright before Walter and John Fredson, Tony Joule, and Moses Cruikshank after him. As men they filled prominent roles in the Episcopal Church in Alaska.[36] Arthur Wright's early experience at the school enhanced Stuck's view that it was an excellent environment for Alaska Native students. The students' deep personal faith inspired Wright.[37]

In fall 1913, when Walter enrolled, 663 students attended Mount Hermon, including one other from Alaska—Arthur Wright. At midsemester another Alaska Native student would arrive—Tommy Reed, from Anvik on the lower Yukon River. The diverse student body included 165 foreign students. The average student age was

20. Mount Hermon School, 1913, engraving. Courtesy Northfield Mount Hermon Archives, Mount Hermon, Massachusetts.

twenty years, six months—almost precisely Walter's age.[38] Tuition, including room and board, cost $120 a year. Alaska's Bishop Rowe, and later the congregation of St. Peter's Church in Morristown, New Jersey, paid Walter's tuition.[39] Stuck gave him spending money throughout his years at the school, sending $50 to be credited to his account from time to time.[40]

Mount Hermon's rigorous academic program included challenging final exams each term.[41] In addition each student had to work 13.5 hours per week at physical tasks. Such labor included assisting on the school farm or in the carpentry shop, power plant, or kitchen and dining hall. The administration aimed to teach the students useful skills and to instill in them a strong work ethic.[42] Students could work additional hours to offset their tuition.[43]

Upon his arrival at Mount Hermon, Walter had had little prior formal education. One year at St. Mark's Mission followed by three years of tutoring by the archdeacon in their spare time had not brought him to high school standing. He had basic arithmetic skills and some U.S. history, but no training in English grammar or in science.[44] Having learned to speak, read, and write English rather recently, Walter struggled academically at Mount Hermon. Letters from home, as well as Stuck's high expectations of him, spurred him on.

Walter's correspondence while at Mount Hermon reveals homesickness. He longed for family members, for the Alaskan landscape, and for the seasonal subsistence activities he loved. And he missed the companionship and mentorship he had grown to appreciate with Stuck. Yet his letters also capture his fascination with the setting, novel experiences, and opportunities. Native American memoirs of boarding schools often reflect such ambivalence and loneliness, especially because so many children could not return home for holidays and summers.

Three weeks after arriving at the school Walter wrote Jessie, "I have just come in from gathering chestnuts in company with another fellow. The trees around here are just loaded with all kinds of nuts." He enrolled in music classes, planning to take "as much musical instructions as I can afford." He joined the Agricultural Club to improve his ability to express himself.[45] Throughout his years at Mount Hermon the mild-mannered Walter struggled to develop the assertive style and voice expected in formal schools. His communication style reflected his Athabascan upbringing, which emphasizes nonconfrontation and noninterference.

Recreational activities allowed him to draw on his athleticism and experience. He bicycled and took part in several sports, breaking the record in cross-country running.[46] Winter sports included downhill skiing, tobogganing, and ice skating—all familiar pursuits.[47] Students skated on Shadow Lake on the Mount Hermon grounds during winter. In summer they swam and kayaked on the lake.[48]

The school's highly programmed days flew by at a dizzying speed. "You get up in the morning and the first thing you know it is night," Walter wrote Jessie.[49] Each school day included classes, physical chores, work on the school farm, sports activities, and studying. Mount Hermon's Christian grounding permeated daily routines. Formal prayers preceded meals. The principal, Dr. Cutler, enforced a day of rest on Sundays, with three compulsory church gatherings in Memorial Chapel. He allowed no secular work, and he forbid games and bicycling. He even banned studying on Sundays. To encourage compliance with that rule, the school held no classes on Mondays.[50]

Teachers and administrators stressed proper etiquette and moral training. They expected courtesy and refined table manners at

21. Crossley Hall, Mount Hermon School. Courtesy Northfield Mount Hermon Archives, Mount Hermon, Massachusetts.

all times. The students took their meals each day in West Hall, a large brick and stone dining room, where Cutler delivered official announcements and lectures on behavior, including table manners. Cutler's "right hand man," Richard Watson, known as "the King," patrolled the tables during meals. From time to time he seized a misbehaving student and marched him outside.[51] Examples of official rules included: "When a master or adult, man as well as woman, comes into a room, rise. . . . Don't curse. . . . At meals, do ask for things with a 'please' tacked on. Don't yell, 'Bread down!'"[52] Of course these rules were second nature to Walter, having spent nearly a year under Annie Farthing's guidance at St. Mark's Mission and three years with Hudson Stuck.

Shortly before Walter arrived in fall 1913 construction of the campus had been completed. Harper lived in Crossley Hall, which housed three hundred boys, two to a room.[53] In 1910 the James Gymnasium was built, reflecting the school's growing emphasis on physical education and intramural sports. The building housed a twenty-meter-long swimming pool, a running track, and a full-sized basketball court. Open playing fields lay outside the gym.[54]

In 1913 Mount Hermon was the largest independent school in the United States. Principal Cutler increased the school's academic standing by creating disciplinary departments and appointing the strongest teachers to lead them.[55]

Walter enjoyed minor celebrity status at Mount Hermon, having recently climbed Denali. The fall edition of the school's newspaper, the *Hermonite*, announced his arrival, noting that he was "the first person to actually put foot on the summit of Mt. McKinley."[56] During his first semester at the school a stranger sent him William Ogilvie's book *Early Days on the Yukon*, which featured Arthur Harper prominently as the discoverer of the gold potential in the Alaska-Yukon region. His father was somewhat a mystery to Harper, yet he took pride in his accomplishments and reputation. He wrote Jessie, "Glancing through it I found my father's picture in it. I have not yet read the book. I only got it last night. I am sure it will be interesting, more so because my father is in the story." Hudson Stuck had recently told Walter that Arthur Harper and Al Mayo had been the first white men to report seeing Denali. Walter told Jessie, "My father was one of the first white men that ever reported the great mountain of North American Continent & it is appropriate that I should be the first one ever to set foot upon the mountain."[57]

In late October 1913 Charles Sheldon invited Walter for a visit to his home in Woodstock, Vermont. The wealthy naturalist had wanted to meet Walter, having heard so much about him from his friend Harry Karstens and from Stuck. Sheldon wanted to encourage Walter's ambitions to educate himself so he could be of service to his people.[58] He sent a ticket for Walter's travel by train from Northfield to Woodstock. During the visit Sheldon drove him on a tour of the countryside.[59] New England's brilliant fall colors provided the backdrop for their conversation.

Autumn activities at Mount Hermon included apple picking, potato digging, and other harvesting tasks on the school's farm lands.[60] A highlight of the season was Mountain Day, which Moody initiated in 1881. Students never knew just when the prized school holiday would fall. Moody would announce it in the morning, freeing students to spend the day hiking, picnicking, and mountain climbing. According to tradition, Mount Hermon seniors climbed Mount Monadnock, a 3,165-foot peak thirty miles to the north, in Jaffrey, New Hampshire.[61] Underclassmen climbed a lesser range to the east of the school. Climbing such hills was child's play for Walter, but he appreciated the day off from school and enjoyed the outdoor activities.

On a Sunday morning in mid-November, after the first snowfall, the three Alaskan students, Walter, Arthur Wright, and Tommy Reed, went for a long stroll down to the Connecticut River. The beautiful scene at the river reminded the young men of home. Walking back toward the campus they stopped to watch the school's pigs feeding, a noisy and amusing scene to their ears and eyes.[62] Arthur returned to Alaska later that winter and joined the St. Mark's Mission staff at Nenana as an industrial engineer.[63]

Walter was "tickled to death" when a package arrived with a cap and gloves from his mother that first winter at Mount Hermon. He wore the garments to a memorial service at the Northfield School for Girls. "Everybody thought the cap I had on [had] a queer style," he wrote Jessie. "I told them it was a new style I was getting out. They all think it's a [dandy] cap."[64] Such grace and wit typified Walter's knack for easing awkwardness with humor.

In a more serious tone he asked Jessie to thank their mother and tell her he thought of her often. Family members might imagine he was having the time of his life and had forgotten all about them. But struggles with his schoolwork left him feeling "blue nowadays," he wrote. "Your letters are always a great inspiration to me so do write even if I don't write enough to deserve them. To use strong language I am having a deuce of time getting out my lessons this term." Graduation would require four years of coursework. "I will feel proud that I have accomplished something if I ever graduate from here. . . . To this end you all must help me by inspiration," he wrote.[65] Two months later he began a letter to Jessie with the words, "Your last letter was quite a comfort. Keep it up. [Urge] me on. I might succeed yet."[66]

Walter missed not only family but the way of life in Alaska. Springtime brought thoughts of duck hunting. In April 1914 he wrote Jessie, "The ducks and geese must be nigh Alaska by this time. Look at all the hunting I shall miss this year. I shall have to make up for it when I get back."[67] That July he asked Jessie to send him chair cushions with an image of Denali on them. "Any curios that you yourself don't want just send it on," he wrote. "I kick myself for not taking any when I came."[68]

Walter closed each letter with "love" or "abundant love" to his mother, sisters, and "the boys," his brothers.[69] The letters affirm his special bond with Jessie and Margaret. He fretted over Margaret's being "all alone up there at the mission" when Jessie taught nearby in the town of Tanana.[70] After a fire had burned numerous houses in Tanana, he asked Jessie, "What are [you] going to do next year? Are you still going to teach at Tanana? Gee I don't like the idea of you and Margaret separating at all."[71]

Hudson Stuck remained a strong influence on Walter. He wrote his protégé regularly and visited him twice a year at Mount Hermon. In early March 1914 Stuck sent for Walter to join him in Boston, where he was giving a lecture on the Denali expedition.[72] He had sent Walter twenty-five dollars for a new suit for the occasion.[73] The young man cut a striking figure as he entered the room with Stuck and later stood with him on the platform as Stuck delivered his speech. Stuck showed photographs of the expedition, some of which Harper had taken. According to Stuck, Walter appeared completely relaxed as he dined with Boston's "aristocrats," with a waiter in formal attire standing behind his chair.[74]

Walter took interest in Stuck's travels and clearly identified with him. In April he wrote Jessie, "The Archdeacon is now in England visiting his old home and sisters." Touchingly he added, "You see he has sisters, too, like me." Fear of letting his father figure down pushed him to persevere in his studies. "You know I wouldn't disappoint the Archdeacon for the world if it lies in my power to do so," he wrote. "You yourself know how much schooling I had before I came out here. Give me more chance and I will with God's help succeed."[75] In spring, summer, and fall of 1914 Walter did well in his English, French, and Bible studies, as well as in agriculture. But he fell behind in algebra, which would hinder his later math work.[76]

In early summer 1914 Stuck sent for Harper to meet him in

22. Walter Harper, school portrait, Mount Hermon School.
Yvonne Mozée Collection, #2002-98-13, Mozée Family Papers,
APRCA, University of Alaska Fairbanks.

New York City.[77] They attended a baseball game, visited museums, went to a circus, and spent a day on Coney Island. At the theme park, according to the *New York Times*, Walter created a sensation by breaking the strength-testing machine, firing three perfect shots in the shooting gallery, and hitting the target at a dunking tank on all three tries.[78] What actually occurred is anyone's guess. Stuck sent the article to the *Fairbanks Daily Times* with a note saying that it was "largely out of whole cloth," but the newspaper still reprinted it.[79] Whatever feats Walter performed at the park, they had such fun that Stuck kept him from school an extra day.[80] Exposing Walter to art treasures, great musical performances, and grand architecture furthered Stuck's vision for "the boy." He wanted him to appreciate the accomplishments of Western culture as well as his Athabascan culture.[81]

Mount Hermon's Fourth of July celebration that year fell short of Walter's standards. He was used to a full day of festivities in Alaska, with rounds and rounds of gunshots fired at night. Mount Hermon set off some fireworks in the evening, but "during the day it was dead," in Walter's opinion. Actually hundreds of friends and family members of other students visited the campus, which may have left Walter feeling forgotten. He served as "a regular errand boy," running up and down campus locating his schoolmates for their parents, siblings, and girlfriends. In a remarkable coincidence several women who visited Walter's roommate greeted him by name. They had seen him at the luncheon in Boston, on the platform with Archdeacon Stuck.[82]

In the fall of 1915 Robert Tatum enrolled at Mount Hermon and roomed with Walter, a happy arrangement for both of them.[83] Walter's academic work was faltering, however. His limited previous schooling was catching up with him, and his lack of independent study skills had become a serious handicap. During his three years of traveling with Stuck, the archdeacon had tutored him intensely. The two had almost always studied together; Walter had never learned to study on his own.

Walter spent the Christmas season with Stuck in New York that year, while Tatum visited family in Pennsylvania.[84] It may have been during Christmas break that Walter settled on becom-

MOUNT HERMON SCHOOL

23. Walter Harper, circa 1916. Courtesy of the Archives of the Episcopal Church, Austin, Texas.

ing a medical missionary. Dr. Happy Burke and Clara Burke had been a godsend to Fort Yukon and Alaska's entire northern Interior. The new hospital at Tanana would need a doctor, too. Medical personnel were few and far between in Alaska.

When Stuck later received Walter's fall report card in New York, it caused a minor brouhaha and set off a flurry of correspondence among Stuck, Walter, and Dr. Cutler. The unsatisfactory grade in "conduct" caused Stuck the greatest alarm. He wrote Dr. Cutler asking for clarification of the "degeneration" in Walter's studies and behavior. Should he drop everything in New York and travel to Mount Hermon immediately?[85] Two days later Stuck received Walter's letter of explanation; he had received the poor conduct grade for not completing his farm chores on time.[86] Incensed, Stuck fired off a letter of protest to Dr. Cutler. Conduct and work were not the same thing, he declared. No one had ever complained of Walter's behavior before, and he had "never known Walter rude or impudent." Stuck emphasized that he was far more concerned about Walter's character than his academic marks.[87]

Walter's low grades in English and geometry reflected genuine academic struggles. The rules of grammar baffled him. Again Stuck defended Walter. Annoyed with the teacher's emphasis on grammar *rules,* Stuck demanded to know whether Harper's *speech* was not "entirely grammatical." He had taught Walter to *speak* correctly. Was that not more important than understanding the rules? Stuck recalled later with amusement that while Mount Hermon teachers had faulted Walter's grasp of grammar rules, he had come home adept in the use of current slang.[88]

The emphasis on debate in his English class required Harper to violate Athabascan values and his character. "I am not a good debater," he wrote Stuck. "I dislike debating and arguing, and that is what our English course consists of this term."[89] Walter had endeared himself to nearly everyone he had ever met with his soft-spoken graciousness. His friendliness had opened doors wherever he traveled. On Denali his congeniality had eased tension and promoted team spirit. Now his deeply ingrained tendency toward nonconfrontation was holding him back. It simply was not in Walter's nature to express himself forcefully in the manner of an effective debater.

Geometry befuddled Walter as well. Just one year of formal schooling at St. Mark's and three years of tutoring with the archdeacon had not prepared him for high school math. He therefore never mastered the algebra that formed the foundation for geometry. Had he done so, he would have recognized the connections between the algebra formulas and geometry proofs that expressed the features of the landscape he knew so well, for instance, the slopes of trails and mountains. He persevered, however, and earned 85 percent on his final geometry exam that fall.[90]

Academic struggles caused Walter internal doubt and anxiety that he would disappoint Stuck. He wrote his mentor, "I am well physically, but *slightly* stupid . . . you must remember that *my* mind is not like *yours*." Asking for advice on how to study effectively, he wrote, "I think the chief trouble with me is that I do not know how to apply my mind properly." He signed the letter "With much love, Walter."[91]

In spring 1916 his grades continued to decline. He seems to have lost faith in his ability to succeed at Mount Hermon. In April 1916 Stuck wrote Dr. Cutler asking him whether he should encourage Walter to go into medicine. Should Stuck bring him home to Alaska to travel and study with him to prepare for college and medical school, or was this dream unrealistic?[92] Whatever Cutler responded, Stuck decided to take Walter home and tutor him for medical school himself.[93] "The boy" would make better academic progress under Stuck's guidance.

Walter therefore left Mount Hermon after nearly three years of study. School records show that his academic work was "satisfactory" and that he was "a man of excellent citizenship and fine character throughout his stay."[94] Dr. Cutler wrote of him, "Walter is a splendid young man, and we have enjoyed very much his being with us at Mount Hermon."[95]

The years at Mount Hermon had shaken Walter's self-confidence. Inadequate academic preparation and homesickness had subverted his best efforts. Nevertheless he advanced in his schoolwork and left with a clear vision of a career path. The Mount Hermon experience would ease his adjustment to college and medical school. Intense study lay ahead in the meantime.

Tommy Reed remained at Mount Hermon for two or three years. Like Walter, he struggled with homesickness. He subsequently transferred to Hampton Normal and Agricultural Institute in

Virginia, where he continued to study industrial arts. Tommy returned to Anvik and became a valued employee of the Episcopal mission there, putting his carpentry skills to use in building a new mission house.[96]

In the summer of 1916 Johnny Fredson arrived at Mount Hermon. He had replaced Walter as Stuck's assistant when Walter left for Mount Hermon. Johnny also suffered from severe bouts of homesickness at Mount Hermon, but his several prior years of formal schooling prepared him academically. Johnny graduated and went on to college at Stuck's alma mater, the University of the South.[97] In 1930 at the age of thirty-five he earned a bachelor's degree, his studies having been interrupted by service in the Great War and illnesses.[98] Fredson returned to Alaska, where he worked in various fields that served the interests of the Athabascan people. In 1982 the new high school in Venetie was named the John Fredson High School.[99]

In 1922 Moses Cruikshank entered Mount Hermon, continuing the tradition among Stuck's assistants.[100] Robert Tatum took responsibility for Moses's expenses, as Stuck had done for Walter and Johnny.[101] Moses supported Episcopal mission work in Interior Alaska throughout his long life. He became a respected Elder and community leader known for his storytelling. His life story is captured in his book *The Life I've Been Living*, published in 1986.

5

Return to Alaska

LIGHTHEARTED AND THRILLED to be heading home, Harper made the most of the journey. He mingled with fellow travelers, relished the wide-open landscapes, and reveled in the delights of city life. Their route to Alaska in July and August 1916 took Harper and Stuck by train across the continent and by boat to Skagway. The highlight of the homeward journey was a trek through Yellowstone National Park.

Episcopal pastor William Thomas joined the two in Chicago. The twenty-seven-year-old was heading to Alaska to work as a missionary and teacher. Stuck had lectured the year before at Christ Church in Xenia, Ohio, where Thomas pastored. The archdeacon had shown lantern slides of Alaska's landscape and told of the need for missionaries to the Native peoples. Thomas enlisted, eager for adventure and inspired to serve.[1]

Thomas and Harper hit it off immediately. At the train depot he charmed Thomas's mother, sister, and Thomas himself with his friendliness and pleasant banter. Thomas, Harper, and Stuck enjoyed a "delightful" dinner the first evening on the train. They visited well into the evening.[2] The following day dawned bright and sunny. The travelers spent the day sightseeing from the train and socializing with others.[3] Harper and Thomas, both good looking and outgoing, easily befriended people throughout the journey.

The trio arrived at Yellowstone on July 10. President Ulysses S. Grant had created the world's first national park in the northwest portion of Wyoming Territory in 1872. The United States was expanding westward rapidly in the late nineteenth century.

National romanticism offered a counterpoint to the country's emphasis on natural resource development. Writers such as George Catlin, Ralph Waldo Emerson, and Henry David Thoreau celebrated nature as a source of inspiration. They called for preserving the country's most exquisite landscapes as national treasures.

Engineers designed the park's roads, paths, and campgrounds to minimize disturbance of the natural landscape. The Grand Loop, a beltline of roads, allowed visitors to tour the park without having to backtrack.[4] The National Park Service took responsibility for Yellowstone National Park in 1918.[5]

Stuck, Harper, and Thomas fell into a comfortable companionship as they hiked, climbed, swam, and visited with others. The day after their arrival, the three walked ten miles from their hotel to their first campsite, taking in the landscape and enjoying the animal life. Some of the wildlife was tame enough that they teased and played with the critters. After dinner Thomas and Stuck took a long walk while discussing pastoring. The elder cleric's wisdom and faith inspired Thomas.[6]

Each day brought new wonders, including geysers, jagged peaks, waterfalls, and boiling pools, as the men hiked long distances. Moonlight permitted early starts to their days. One morning they set out at 4:00, marveled as the sunrise turned the pines a brilliant orange at 5:00, crossed the Continental Divide at 5:30, and reached Old Faithful camp by noon. They had walked twenty miles. That evening they swam in a hot water pool formed by a geyser.[7]

Crystal clear night skies and bright moonlight created enchanted evenings. Nights while camping typically included music by campfire and sometimes dancing. Harper and Thomas often strolled and talked with young women. They spent a few nights in luxury hotels, with Stuck paying the tab.

The men sometimes walked at a leisurely pace, following the trail. On other occasions they scrambled over rocky cliffs. Harper encouraged Thomas to tackle much more rugged terrain than he would have dared attempt on his own. At some points they were above the snow line. Once they slid down drifts of snow, coming to a halt in a bed of wildflowers.

The Grand Canyon of Yellowstone was widely viewed as the

most remarkable site within the park, partly because of the stone's pink and yellow coloring. Thomas described the canyon as "a veritable wonderland" when it was bathed in moonlight. Leaving their hotel at the canyon in the morning, they ascended the pass, and a glorious panorama of the whole park opened beneath them.[8]

The men constantly engaged in conversation, sometimes lighthearted and sometimes serious. At least once the topic of mountaineering arose. Stuck spoke of climbing Denali's Wife one day. "How I hope that I may be included in that expedition," Thomas wrote in his diary. "I think I could stand it. . . . Of course Walter would go."[9]

On July 18, with their tour of Yellowstone concluded, the men boarded a train traveling west to Seattle. The landscape, beautiful by day, took on a magical quality under the moonlight.[10] Four days in Seattle flew by as they saw the sights, shopped for gear for Alaska, visited friends, and attended a live performance of *The Messiah*, a movie, and a vaudeville show. One day Stuck rented a motorboat so they could test it on Lake Washington. He considered buying the boat for Dr. Burke's use at Fort Yukon. Another day he and Walter drove to a community south of Seattle where a Native American boy was confirmed in the church. Stuck wanted the youth to see in Walter a Native American Christian with a strong sense of identity and purpose.

On Sunday, July 23, Stuck delivered a "splendid" sermon, in Thomas's view, at Trinity Parish, the Episcopal church in downtown Seattle. That evening Thomas and Harper dined with some of Thomas's friends. Walter joined the group late, slipped into the conversation, and before long had charmed one and all with lessons in Athabascan.[11]

One afternoon the three toured the U.S. Revenue Cutter *Bear*, which was soon to depart for the Arctic.[12] The *Bear* had a long and storied history of service to Alaska. Since 1885 it had patrolled Alaska's waters. The cutter delivered mail and transported government officials and prisoners to and from Alaska. It provided the only law enforcement along much of the coast. Officials conducted criminal investigations from the *Bear*, and trials sometimes took place on its deck. The Marine Service provided medical care to Alaska Natives and non-Natives when few doctors or nurses served the vast territory.[13]

Harper, Stuck, and Thomas traveled to Vancouver aboard the *Princess Adelaide* and continued on the *Princess Alice* to Skagway.[14] The young men socialized so much along the way that during their stop in Juneau the archdeacon scolded them for not helping him prepare for Sunday services. Thomas accepted the reprimand as a sign of affection. "He has just taken me under his wing along with Walter," he wrote in his diary.[15]

At Skagway the men boarded a train operated by the White Pass & Yukon Railway, and it took them over the Coast Mountains to Whitehorse. They continued down the mighty Yukon River to Dawson aboard the *Casca*. Meals punctuated their days. In the late afternoons they enjoyed "afternoon tea" in the British tradition, which meant another full meal. In the evenings the passengers gathered around the piano to sing ragtime tunes.

The town of Dawson had been a booming gold rush city of about fifty thousand residents in 1899. Now Thomas described it as a "wreck and ruin of [a] city," although he found the small, run-down cabins along the Klondike River charming. He and Walter walked six miles to view a gold-dredging operation. The two gaped at the size of the giant machines. One was said to be among the largest in the world.[16] By 1916 major corporations were dominating the Alaska-Yukon goldfields. Massive dredges combed through tons of earth to extract small nuggets and specks of gold. A small number of hardy individuals still prospected and mined as Arthur Harper had done four decades before.

Rather than waiting for the next steamer, Walter lined up a sixteen-foot boat called the *Lucianne* and fitted it with an Evinrude motor to proceed to Fort Yukon. At Eagle the local Episcopal pastor and his wife hosted the men for a feast of fresh caribou meat and biscuits. Walter surely savored the wild game he had gone without for three years. The following evening they arrived in Fort Yukon, soaking wet from the near constant rain of the previous days.[17] Village residents, especially the Burkes, hailed the weary travelers' arrival.

Two days later Walter continued downriver in the *Lucianne*

RETURN TO ALASKA

24. Walter Harper, William Thomas, and Hudson Stuck in Dawson, August 1916. From Stuck, *Winter Circuit*.

to Tanana. There he joined Johnny Fred on the *Pelican*.[18] The two young men then overhauled the launch in preparation for a late summer travel season. Walter reveled in the familiar sights, sounds, and smells as he reunited with loved ones and put to use the skills that came so naturally to him.

Reimmersion in his birth culture led to at least one comical episode. Walter gave his mother a pair of fashionable "white-

25. William Thomas and Walter Harper aboard the *Pelican*, summer 1916.
Reverend William Thomas Collection, #2010-110-stevet5, APRCA,
University of Alaska Fairbanks.

lady" shoes—red leather high heels with high tops that buttoned. Jenny tried them on, wobbled a few steps, and nearly toppled over. Exasperated with such nonsense, she removed the shoes, marched to the chopping block, picked up an axe, and whacked off the heels—in Walter's presence.[19] The incident became a part of family lore.

While Harper was in Tanana, Thomas and Stuck remained at Fort Yukon, helping the Burkes prepare the new St. Stephen's Hospital for its opening that fall. After a week in the village they headed downriver, and Thomas began his initiation into Episcopal mission work and life along Interior waterways. They joined Walter and Johnny on the *Pelican*, and William Thomas slipped into the summer routine along with them.[20]

Bishop Rowe initially assigned Thomas to St. Mark's Mission in Nenana. He found the landscape, especially the view of the Alaska Range from Nenana, breathtaking.[21] He came to know and appreciate the Athabascan people, but much had changed in Nenana since Walter had arrived there in 1909. Construction of the Alaska Railroad spur from the Gulf of Alaska to Fairbanks had brought increased economic activity to the Interior. The wharf at Nenana bustled with construction workers erecting the depot. The speed of change caught the village unprepared. The laborers were housed in tents.[22]

Nenana's expansion weighed heavily on the St. Mark's personnel. They feared that wage-labor opportunities and Western products, especially alcohol, would lure Natives away from their subsistence lifestyle and from Christian values. The railroad's completion would ease access to the Interior, which in turn would accelerate the pace of socioeconomic and cultural change. Mission personnel considered moving St. Mark's to a more remote area, to shelter it from negative influences. But if they did, what would become of the village residents who remained in Nenana, with no support from the mission?[23]

Thomas threw himself into the mission work. He rejoiced when Native residents, including Chief Thomas, filled his cabin the Sunday evening after his arrival. Before long he had visited all the various fish camps in the region. A September journal entry captures his delight in his new environment and work: "This week has been perfectly wonderful. Over a hundred miles in the Peterboro canoe. Three nights [out] under the stars, two in Indian Camps one in the Tolovana Road House. . . . The indians were very cordial. . . . I feel that I now know many of them quite well. Especially memorable was the noonday luncheon at the household of old Chief Abrcandar."[24]

After completing a shortened summer circuit on the *Pelican*, Harper and Stuck spent the fall and early winter of 1916 at their home base in Fort Yukon. Walter assisted the archdeacon and mission personnel with all sorts of tasks, including responding to crises and hunting food for the mission and the new hospital. He relished his daily chore of running the archdeacon's dog team to keep the animals in shape.[25] The training kept them happy and healthy and ready to respond to emergencies.

In early October the Yukon River suddenly washed away an enormous mass of the riverbank from directly in front of the mission house at Fort Yukon. Residents rushed to protect the bank with brush and sandbags. Soon the river level dropped, and the mission building was spared for the winter. But the threat of further damage, from the spring breakup, remained. The house would have to be taken apart before then and rebuilt in a safer location.[26]

Numerous children, including orphans and others whose parents could not support them, lived at the mission. Several of the children were of mixed heritage. These youngsters frequently suffered from discrimination, partly because their fathers often abandoned them or took little notice of them. Missionaries strove to reduce the stigma they faced.[27]

Walter helped Stuck arrange activities for the boys, including boxing, wrestling, and skating. Dr. Happy Burke organized the older boys at the mission into St. Stephen's Club. The members elected their own officers, took on responsibilities in the community, and planned sporting contests. These important roles boosted the boys' self-confidence.[28]

Happy and Clara Burke had provided health care in Fort Yukon since their marriage in the summer of 1910. But without hospital facilities they could offer only limited care. Now, following years of efforts by Stuck and Bishop Rowe and with government and Mission Board support, St. Stephen's Hospital was preparing to open.[29] In the years that followed, Stuck made repeated appeals to the mission society and individual mission friends for continued support.[30]

St. Stephen's was the first hospital above the Arctic Circle in North America. The nearest facility that served Alaska Natives lay five hundred miles downriver, at Nulato. St. Stephen's treated any Alaska Native seeking care, without charge. It also served white patients needing treatment, but about 90 percent of the patients were Native.[31]

Local residents supported the hospital by volunteering their services. Women helped with laundry, ironing, mending, and cleaning the rooms. Men chopped, hauled, split, and stacked wood to heat the hospital.[32] They also donated fresh meat for the patients and for the mission personnel and children.[33]

Tuberculosis was the most common and serious disease the St. Stephen's personnel treated. The preferred regimen was sunshine and fresh air. Patients slept out of doors in tents well into the fall. The open air improved their health remarkably.[34] Throughout Alaska medical personnel, missionaries, and teachers stressed hygiene, general sanitation, and ventilation in preventing and curing the disease.

Other illnesses and accidents, including pneumonia, broken limbs, and burns, brought people from many miles away to St. Stephen's. In October a woman who had been working with her husband at a sawmill fell against the saw, cutting her neck muscles, exposing her arteries, and severely injuring her arm. She was rushed to the hospital and survived.[35]

Alcohol abuse was not the constant menace at Fort Yukon that it was at Tanana. Burke and Stuck discouraged its use within the community and helped enforce the law against selling or trading alcohol to Alaska Natives. Whiskey still managed to find its way into the village from time to time. When it did, chaos typically ensued. In December 1916 a bootlegger arrived from Circle with a sled full of whiskey, and a drunken brawl erupted at Short's Roadhouse. That evening Stuck and others "laid down the law" to the worst offenders, threatening to banish them from the com-

26. Walter Harper and Hudson Stuck at Allakaket. Drane Family Collection, #1991-46-531, APRCA, University of Alaska Fairbanks.

munity unless they mended their ways.[36] The month before, an overwhelming majority of Alaska Territory residents had voted for complete prohibition of alcohol. Stuck had played an active role in advocating for the policy. The Bone Dry Act would take effect in January 1918. But without major changes in Alaska's lax justice system, Stuck expected little reduction in the liquor trade.[37]

When medical emergencies arose, the injured and disabled could not always travel to the hospital. Sometimes Dr. Burke had to rush to the aid of a patient. In such cases Walter often drove the dogsled or piloted the riverboat. On Thanksgiving evening 1916 Dr. Burke received word of a woman who had been in labor for three days, one hundred miles from Fort Yukon. The next morning, with the temperature at 30 degrees below zero, Hap and Walter set out by dogsled to aid the woman. The two men slept in the open that night. By morning the temperature had dropped to 57 degrees below zero. That day a messenger intercepted them sixty miles from Fort Yukon. The baby was stillborn. Deflated, Hap and Walter turned back. Following another night on the trail, they arrived at Fort Yukon sore, exhausted, and frostbitten.[38]

The bitterly cold winter of 1916–17 tested Harper's and Stuck's survival skills. On January 31 the mercury dipped to 75 degrees below zero. The two huddled in a dark, tiny cabin near the Alaska-Canada border for days as they waited for the weather to break. Traveling in such temperatures was too dangerous and miserable. They fed the fire in the cabin's little stove, feeling grateful for the shelter.[39]

In spring 1917, before they could dismantle the mission house and move it, flooding carried it way. Luckily no one was hurt. Anticipating the move, the Burkes had farmed out the twenty mission children to local families. They themselves had moved into quarters upstairs at the hospital. Harper and Stuck had remained upstairs in the mission house, where Stuck could write in quiet. Now the two also moved into upstairs rooms in the hospital.[40]

That summer two missionary nurses, Frances Wells and Beatrice Nuneviller, arrived from Philadelphia, full of energy and commitment. Like many other devout Christians of the time, the young women embraced the social gospel. They came to St. Stephen's Hospital prepared to serve five years, the normal tour of duty in Alaska.[41] They would earn $33.33 per month, plus room and board.[42]

Frances was born in 1889 in Philadelphia, the first of Guilliam and Margaretta Wells's nine children. Margaretta descended from Episcopal pastors. Guilliam was a successful real estate broker whose fortunes had turned by the early 1900s. In 1905, when Frances was sixteen, her mother died, leaving her father to care for their family.[43] Friends and family cherished Frances's lovable disposition and admired her many accomplishments.[44]

Frances graduated from the Episcopal Hospital of Philadelphia training school in 1915 or 1916. She then served as head nurse at the hospital for a year. Four months of study at Deaconess Carter's Church Training and Deaconess House in Philadelphia prepared her for missionary work in Alaska.[45] Clara Carter had been an Episcopal missionary in Alaska from 1902 to 1912 before becoming deaconess at the Church Training and Deaconess House. She influenced many women to join the mission work in Alaska.[46]

By February 1917 the deaconess had told Frances so much about Fort Yukon that she could hardly wait to go there. Frances had

27. Frances Wells. Yvonne Mozée Collection, #2002-98-21, Mozée Family Papers, APRCA, University of Alaska Fairbanks.

corresponded with Dr. Burke, whose warm and amusing letters had sealed her positive impression. "'Happy' Burke is my crazy nut of a medical missionary with whom we will live," she wrote her brother John.[47] Frances relished the thought of mission work where God "reigns so supreme" in nature. She loved the idea of the pioneer life and imagined experiencing it fully.[48]

She and Beatrice Nuneviller, a graduate of the same nursing school Frances had attended, traveled by train from Philadelphia to Seattle, where John Wood, foreign secretary of the Episcopal Board of Missions, met them.[49] Stuck had been urging his good friend to visit Alaska for years. He wanted Wood to see with his own eyes the needs of the mission field. Episcopal pastor Benjamin Chambers also joined them in Seattle.[50] The company of four boarded the ss Northwestern and traveled through Alaska's Inside Passage to Skagway.[51] The men made amusing travel companions. Chambers was a "court clown" and Wood a "close rival," Frances reported.[52]

At Skagway, Bishop Rowe joined the group. They took the train to Whitehorse and boarded a steamer to travel down the Yukon River into Alaska.[53] At Eagle, just inside the border, Stuck and Harper met the voyagers in the Pelican and carried them downriver to Fort Yukon.[54] The scenery along the final leg of the journey so dazzled Frances that she wrote to family members that "no words of our language no matter how fantastically put together could possibly make you get more than a glimpse of Alaska's beauty and vastness."[55]

Frances quickly won the hearts of hospital personnel and village residents. She in turn learned to love the people and her work. On July 15, just two weeks after she arrived, she wrote to her brother John, "This work up here is wonderful—The most worthwhile I have ever done." Residents' devotion to the mission impressed her. Almost all of the Native people in the area attended church regularly, filling the church on Sundays. Some traveled from five to ten miles on the river to attend services.[56]

Frances divided her work between hospital patients and home visits to treat illness and injuries. She also taught hygiene and sanitation during home visits. Hospital personnel responded to medical emergencies up and down the river via the Dorothy, "a little peach" of a boat that was equipped to carry eight adults, or fewer if there was a stretcher onboard.[57]

In addition to her nursing duties Frances took on various carpentry tasks, using skills she had developed as a child. Before long her handiwork earned her the nickname "boss carpenter." Despite her many duties she found time for leisure activities. She took riverboat rides and enjoyed picnics by campfire. When mission personnel needed logs to protect the riverbank in front of the building, she joined in the adventure of bringing them downriver. She and the crew rode ten miles upstream, where they boarded the huge raft of logs, two logs deep. As the men worked to control the raft, she simply enjoyed the thrilling ride.[58]

Frances mentioned Walter just once in letters to family early that summer. She reported that she and Beatrice, along with the Burke family, the archdeacon, and Walter Harper lived upstairs at the hospital. The two clearly had contact while he, Stuck, and his guests remained in Fort Yukon.[59]

After celebrating the Fourth of July there, Harper, Stuck, Wood, Chambers, and Rowe began the summer circuit on the *Pelican*. With Walter at the wheel, they visited almost every city, village, and fish camp in Alaska's Interior. The several touring Episcopal dignitaries caused considerable excitement wherever the *Pelican* stopped that summer. Visits lasted longer than usual. At some fish camps they stayed two days, because so many Athabascans assembled for the momentous occasion. The clergy officiated at worship services, marriages, baptisms, and burials.

At Nenana the young Moses Cruikshank came aboard to help with manual labor on the *Pelican*. He was thrilled to have the prestigious position with the archdeacon. Walter took Moses under his wing, but that did not keep the lad from falling into the river at Tanana. Stuck fished him out with a pike pole.[60]

At Holy Cross, on the lower Yukon, the men visited at length with Father Jules Jetté.[61] The Jesuit missionary's many years of experience in the region allowed him to speak with authority on conditions and needs. His perspectives lent weight to Stuck's persistent appeals to Episcopal Church headquarters for support for the mission work in Alaska.

The extended visit at Holy Cross delayed the clerics' arrival at St. Michael on Norton Sound. When Walter piloted the *Pelican* into the sound, a steamer awaited the dignitaries. The captain called over the megaphone, "Is that Archdeacon Stuck?" Upon hearing a yes from the *Pelican* he responded, "We've been waiting for you here." Next he bellowed, "And you got Bishop Rowe with you?" Again came a positive response. "Yeah, well, we're waiting for him, too." With that, Stuck, Rowe, and their visitors transferred to the steamship. They would continue their tour of Episcopal missions in south-central Alaska.[62]

After a hearty meal and a good night's sleep at St. Michael, Walter and Moses piloted the *Pelican* back up the Yukon River. Walter stood at the wheel for most of the twelve-hundred-mile run to Fort Yukon. When he needed sleep, he chose a safe section of the river and allowed Moses to take a shift at the wheel. At one point the boy fell asleep while on duty, and the launch ran into the mossy groundcover overhanging the riverbank. Startled from his sleep, Walter raced to the engine room. The evidence spoke for itself. Luckily no harm was done.[63]

Walter dropped Moses at Tanana, where he boarded the *Yukon* to travel up the Tanana River to Nenana. There he began another school year at St. Mark's Mission. Walter then continued his marathon run to Fort Yukon.[64] During the six-week tour the *Pelican* had traveled five thousand miles.[65] That year Stuck published *Voyages on the Yukon and Its Tributaries*, recounting his summer travels on the *Pelican* and doing mission work. He dedicated the book to the three Alaska Native youths who had served him so faithfully: Walter Harper, Arthur Wright, and John Fredson.

Walter had left a strong impression on John Wood that summer. The next year Wood encouraged Clara Burke to enlist Walter to build a frame for a couch in her new home. Wood suggested that Clara simply leave a few nails, a hammer, and some boards about and gently let Walter know that the archdeacon "would like him to produce a masterpiece." He added, "After seeing the things he did last summer on the *Pelican* I have unlimited confidence in his ability to do anything."[66]

In September Walter and Esaias George, who was now working

at the Fort Yukon mission, went hunting for two weeks. They took a steamboat about 150 miles, to the Charley River. After felling seven moose and two caribou they built a raft, piled it high with the game, and floated "triumphantly" to Fort Yukon. The twenty-five hundred pounds of meat would feed the mission and hospital family, personnel, and patients well in the coming months while Walter and Stuck would be away.[67]

Stuck had long planned a winter circuit of Alaska's Arctic Coast. He had promised church authorities that he would write a book on the Episcopal missions in the Alaska Territory. But he refused to write about places and topics he did not know firsthand. He had never visited the Point Hope mission on the northwest coast.[68] Finally in the fall of 1917 the expedition was possible. Of course Stuck planned to take Walter as his assistant and companion. He relied on Walter's expertise on the trail, and there was no other person whose company he enjoyed as much. Stuck planned to tutor Walter during the trip, in preparation for college. They aimed to leave on November 5, but a health crisis nearly derailed their plans.

Not long after Walter returned from his hunting trip he fell ill. In mid-October Frances admitted him to St. Stephen's Hospital, suspecting typhoid fever.[69] Happy Burke soon confirmed her hunch. He told Stuck that Walter would not be strong enough to travel until late November at the earliest. Stuck was crushed. Such a late start would jeopardize the entire trek because they would have to return to Fort Yukon before spring breakup destroyed the trail.[70] Hap and Clara's six-year-old son, Hudson Stuck Burke, also caught the disease. The likely source was peaches that a riverboat steward had brought from Dawson.[71]

Typhoid fever was known to be caused by *Salmonella typhi*, a strain of bacteria that had been isolated in the 1880s. An effective vaccine existed, but it was not yet in wide use. During the Klondike and Nome gold rushes, crowded ship conditions had spawned many diseases, including typhoid fever.[72] By the time Walter became ill, medical experts knew that it was spread by water or food contaminated with the fecal matter of an infected person.[73]

As Walter lay in the hospital, Frances devoted herself entirely to his care, and the two fell in love. Their budding romance attracted little support, however. Hap and Clara Burke dreaded losing an excellent nurse if Frances followed Walter Outside to go to college.[74] It would be nearly impossible to find a replacement for her. Most nurses willing to work "abroad" were serving in the Red Cross during the Great War.[75]

The archdeacon had little patience for romance. He was so intent upon Walter's education that he thought the attraction was one-sided. He told Frances that she should think of Walter as a brother, because she would be forty years old by the time he was ready for marriage.[76] Walter was twenty-four at the time, and she was twenty-eight.

As Harper lay critically ill, his temperature rising to 105 degrees, Stuck sat upstairs in his study agonizing. He now recognized just how much Walter meant to him. He might lose his "high-minded boy with no bad or disagreeable habits." This extraordinary young man now looked forward to an honorable career as a medical missionary. Stuck vowed that if God would heal Walter, he would never speak crossly to him again and he would do his utmost to ensure "the boy" had the career he desired.[77]

With a heavy heart Stuck considered making his winter circuit without Walter. He broached the topic to Esaias, who reluctantly agreed to go, but Stuck's enthusiasm for the venture had vanished. Then, five days after Walter entered the hospital, his fever broke. On October 30 he had strength enough to leave his hospital bed briefly.[78] The overjoyed Stuck dared to resume his preparations.[79] On Wednesday, November 7, Dr. Burke cleared Walter to leave on the winter circuit.[80] Meanwhile little Hudson Burke had also recovered.[81]

After Stuck and Harper departed, Frances wrote Walter's sister Margaret to report the news of Walter's recovery. She told Margaret he was "holding his own" on the trail.[82] Along the winter circuit Harper and Stuck constantly guarded one another's safety. Nightly they collaborated on Walter's studies. Increasingly Walter entrusted his mentor with memories of his childhood and dreams of his future. By the journey's end a close father-son relationship bound the two.

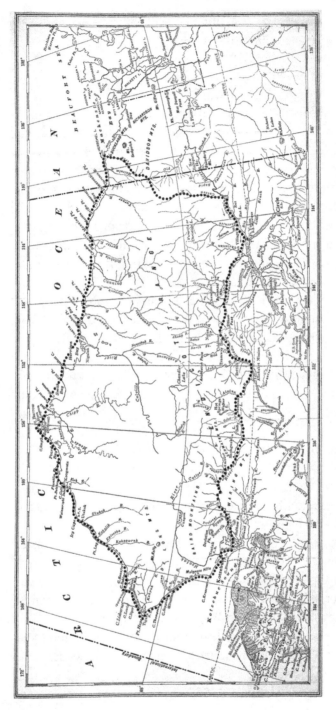

MAP 3. Map of the 1917–18 winter circuit of the Arctic coast. From Stuck, *Winter Circuit.*

6

The Winter Circuit

THE WINTER CIRCUIT of Alaska's Arctic coast would be a unique journey for both Harper and Stuck. The treeless landscape along the coast, the shifting sea ice, and the high winds would be new sensations. The sea and land mammals that inhabited the northern coastal region seemed mysterious. Felling a polar bear stood at the top of Walter's list of aims for the trek.[1]

The circuit would offer the seasoned outdoorsman exotic experiences. Walter had slept out in the open many times in Alaska's Interior, creating shelter with skins or tarps, but he had never built an igloo of ice blocks. And he was not accustomed to creating shelters in the midst of piercing winds—except on Denali. On the other hand, his dog-handling and sled-building skills and his resourcefulness were invaluable anywhere in the north. And his cheerful disposition brightened the most miserable conditions. As Stuck later wrote, "He was past master of the wilderness arts, and I would rather have him at my side in an emergency than any other I ever knew."[2]

On November 8, 1917, Stuck, Walter, and Paul Guinness, a teenage assistant, set out from Fort Yukon westward toward the coast. The long-awaited winter circuit of the Arctic coast had begun, just three days behind schedule. Paul would accompany Stuck and Walter as far as the Koyukuk River; he would do the most strenuous work until Walter was completely recovered from his illness.[3]

On the first leg of the trek Walter took charge of Paul, teaching him subsistence skills and coaching him in English and courtesy. He taught the youth to say "yes, please," and "no, thank you," and to say "yes, Sir," and "no, Sir," to the archdeacon. Paul welcomed the guidance and thrived on the trail.[4] After a few days he begged Stuck to let him "see Husky country too, . . . please, Sir?" Stuck and Harper had grown fond of Paul, but taking him on the full circuit would be too costly.[5]

The smooth trail on the frozen Chandalar River offered easy passage, but crossing from the Chandalar to the Koyukuk River proved exhausting. They struggled over twenty to thirty miles of rough terrain with little snow cover.[6] On the Koyukuk heavy snowfall slowed their pace further. Some days the three put in twelve hours, plodding forward mostly in the dark.[7] Near the abandoned mining camp of Caro, Stuck became separated from Walter and Paul. The mishap ended well, but it could have spelled disaster.

Stuck had struck out early to break trail for the others, who followed with the sleds. Starting before dawn as well, Walter and Paul missed Stuck's trail and continued some distance before noticing their mistake. Walter turned back to find Stuck, but again he misjudged. All day the two searched in vain for Stuck. Finally at 8:30 p.m. they found him, exhausted, chilled, and preparing to spend a cold, miserable night on the trail. Stuck resolved never to lose sight of his dog teams again.[8]

During his thirteen years in Alaska, Stuck had spent many nights on the trail, always in the company of an Athabascan assistant. On November 11 he would turn fifty-four years old. He felt his strength waning and sensed this would be his last long winter journey. The chronic pain in his right shoulder tended to flare up on the trail. Repeated injuries to his muscles and joints over the years had taken a toll.[9]

Miners at Coldfoot greeted the travelers enthusiastically. The first winter mail had not yet arrived, and they were eager to hear news of the Great War. Stuck's report was grim. The Austrians and Germans were overwhelming the Italians, and German submarines were wreaking havoc at sea.[10]

Walter stepped on the scales at the Coldfoot roadhouse and saw that he had regained the twenty pounds he had lost to typhoid fever.[11] His full recovery meant that he and Stuck no longer needed

Paul's help. The boy therefore turned back to Fort Yukon, where loved ones welcomed the good news from the trail.

At a roadhouse two days out of Coldfoot, Walter and Stuck spoke with an old-timer who had known Arthur Harper. Walter listened attentively as the sourdough reminisced about earlier times, speaking highly of the elder Harper. Stuck sat by, pleased for "the boy." He had told Walter earlier that he had never heard anything but praise for the legendary Arthur Harper.[12]

As the days on the trail passed, the two grew closer, and their conversations took on a more affectionate tone. At Bettles, after two and a half weeks on the trail, Stuck told Walter how he had agonized during his illness. He revealed that the crisis had brought home to him just how fond he was of him. At St. John's-in-the-Wilderness, Stuck wrote to his friend John Wood, asking for assistance in finding a suitable university to prepare Walter for medical school. Given that he had not graduated from Mount Hermon, they would have to find a school that would accept Walter as a special student while he overcame his academic deficiencies. There was no time to waste. Six years of medical school followed by a year of internship lay ahead. Walter would be thirty-two years old before he returned to Alaska. Stuck told Wood that he planned to fund Walter's education with royalties from his next book.[13]

This support of Walter's education would repay a debt, Stuck explained. His own accomplishments, he confessed, were due largely to the services others had provided him, in particular Walter. "Have I climbed a mountain?" he asked. "I climbed it largely by his legs. Have I made memorable journeys?—I made them largely by his powers. He has given me his eyes and ears, his hands and feet, his quick intelligence, his coolness and splendid self-reliance in time of stress or danger, his resourcefulness in emergency." Stuck had paid Walter, but "in the account that my conscience keeps with myself I know that the balance is heavily against me," he wrote. Walter and his other assistants had done most of the work, while Stuck stood by.[14] When he sent Walter Outside to school, Stuck would be sending the best in himself, he wrote, the source of his own courage and strength.[15]

Stuck's affection for Walter, other Native assistants, and earlier protégés Happy Burke and Edgar Loomis later raised questions about the nature of the relationships. His life-long bachelorhood, the mental and emotional energy he invested in the boys' development, and the warmth he expressed for them in his diaries fueled such speculation. Church officials suppressed Stuck's diaries for some time after his death, seemingly because of apprehension about these passages.[16] Considering widespread revelations of sexual exploitation by priests, it is not surprising that such concerns would arise. However, no evidence points toward sexual abuse. None of the archdeacon's protégés left any record of inappropriate behavior toward them. On the contrary, they remained devoted to Stuck during his life and to his memory following his death.

Stuck's affection for Walter had begun with his admiration for the youth's amiability and resourcefulness. Walter represented the finest of his generation, in Stuck's eyes. Over the nine years they knew one another Stuck came to see the legacy of his own life's work in the youth.

In the evenings on the trail the two focused on Walter's studies. Lessons covered a wide range of subjects. Stuck believed in the value of a broad liberal education, especially for medical and legal professionals. He had no patience for narrow-minded doctors and lawyers who knew nothing beyond their work.[17] That winter the two read the ancient Hebrew text of the Maccabees, along with Shakespeare and various books they found in mission libraries. They also read the adventure books that Walter so enjoyed, such as *The Adventures of Robinson Crusoe*.

Based on Stuck's assumption that universities expected students to be well versed in Shakespeare's works, the two read all the best-known plays thoroughly.[18] As he read aloud, Walter honed his reading and English diction skills, while immersing himself in the dramas. Walter's interest in his studies and his keen intelligence made tutoring him a joy. Stuck usually gave Walter a quick overview of the play and then read an act aloud. Walter then read the act aloud, with Stuck correcting any mispronunciation. Reading the plays multiple times left Walter with a solid grasp of Shakespeare.

He applied the stories to his own life, testing the characters' actions against his own values.[19] The tragedy of Macbeth reminded Walter of Athabascan stories he had heard. Sometimes he raised objections, to bawdy language, for instance, or unchivalrous behavior. He refused to reread *Othello* because of Iago's offensiveness, and he balked at Hamlet's crude behavior. Why would he treat Ophelia disrespectfully if he loved her, Walter asked Stuck.[20]

Stuck equally admired and praised Walter's subsistence skills. The archdeacon declared to the congregation at St. John's-in-the-Wilderness that knowing how to live off the land was more important than schoolwork. He told them he worried much more about Native youth who "could not build a boat or a sled or make a pair of snowshoes or kill a moose or tend a trap-line, than [about those] who could not read or write." The old chief, Moses, thanked Stuck, telling him he often gave his people the same advice.[21] Walter exemplified the competence in both traditions that Stuck encouraged.

As part of their daily routine, both men wrote in their journals. Stuck's well-established habit of keeping a diary aided him in writing three books about his travels in Alaska and a fourth on the ascent of Denali. He instilled the habit in Walter as well. The only journal by Harper to have survived is the one from the Denali expedition, but because the young man shared his journal of their final winter circuit with his mentor, Stuck knew its contents. In his book *A Winter Circuit of Our Arctic Coast* Stuck noted Walter's recorded thoughts from time to time, providing readers glimpses of Walter's own perceptions.[22]

Harper and Stuck looked forward to their visits to Allakaket. Their arrival always stirred excitement among mission personnel and residents. The two provided company, carried news from elsewhere, and often oversaw festivities and ceremonies. Stuck never failed to bring candy for the children. On this visit he performed marriages and baptisms, along with holding regular Sunday worship services.[23] The Sunday services required dual interpreters— Athabascan and Iñupiaq—to accommodate the congregants on either side of the river.

Stuck hired two Iñupiaq boys from the mission as guides and interpreters for the next leg of the journey, because they would now enter Kobuk River Iñupiaq territory. From Allakaket they fol-

lowed the Alatna River and then portaged to the Kobuk, which
flowed into Kotzebue Sound. They passed through several small
villages in the four hundred to five hundred miles they traveled
to the coast.[24]

On their first night out of Allakaket the temperature dropped
to 56 degrees below zero. The intense cold detained them three
days at Black Jack's Place on the Alatna. Several Iñupiaq families
were overwintering at Black Jack's. Each morning and evening
the men, women, and children gathered around the archdeacon for Bible studies. The extended stay offered ample time for
Walter's studies, while the cozy atmosphere invited storytelling
and sharing of memories. Walter confided in Stuck about childhood experiences he had never before revealed.[25] Along the trail
their mutual trust deepened, and Walter increasingly shared his
thoughts with Stuck.[26]

On December 15 the duo arrived at Kotzebue Sound on the Arctic Ocean. Thirty-eight days had passed since they had left Fort
Yukon. They had traveled nearly eight hundred miles, averaging
thirty miles a day on travel days.[27] The village of Kotzebue was a
traditional gathering place for the Iñupiat of northwest Alaska.
Each summer more than a thousand Iñupiat typically gathered
for weeks of trading, feasting, and sporting competitions. Travelers sometimes came from as far as Siberia.

The Friends, or Quakers, had established a mission in Kotzebue in 1897.[28] In the following decade Christianity spread rapidly
among the Iñupiat. Their conversion was mainly due to the work
of one Iñupiaq Christian, Uyaraq, or Rock, and Friends missionaries Robert and Carrie Samms.[29]

Stuck and Harper stayed at the trading post, where they bought
winter gear suitable for the coastal weather. With no roadhouses
in Kotzebue, travelers tended to sleep at one of the three traders'
headquarters. Stuck bought a fur parka, likely marmot, for himself.
Walter insisted on continuing to wear his caribou coat. Wherever
he traveled, the coat's beautifully beaded shoulders drew attention. The men bought heavy fur mitts with gauntlets, as well as
fur boots, for both of them.[30]

Walter generally took responsibility for purchasing supplies,

THE WINTER CIRCUIT

charging everything to Stuck's account.[31] Years before, Stuck had given him complete access to his credit line at stores throughout Alaska's Interior. Stuck claimed Walter was more careful with purchases on his account than he was himself.[32]

Along the trail Walter built new sleds as the terrain changed, and as the need arose he purchased new dogs for carrying extra supplies over the long distances between Arctic villages. The malamute, a hardy, eager breed with great stamina, was the perfect freighting dog in the Arctic. Stuck assumed they would be easy to find along the coast, "the home of the malamute." But Walter was hard pressed to find suitable dogs. According to Stuck, selective breeding for dog racing had led to the decline of the malamute's capacity for freighting.[33]

From Kotzebue the two began their actual circuit of the Arctic coast on December 17. They aimed to celebrate Christmas with their friend William Thomas, now missionary and teacher at Point Hope, about 170 miles to the northwest. Stuck hired a Kotzebue man to guide them across the unfamiliar terrain. The good-humored "Little Pete" knew the landscape well.[34]

Constant, biting winds and cramped sleeping quarters were the chief discomforts of coastal travel between Kotzebue and Point Hope. All but one night the men shared sleeping space with others in small igloos or cabins. At night Walter wrapped himself in a lynx robe fashioned into a sleeping bag. Stuck had bought fifteen lynx skins and had them sewn together for the bag a year or two before. The cost of Walter's sleeping bag, including the individual skins, their tanning, and the labor involved in sewing them, amounted to about one hundred dollars.[35]

At Kivalina, about two-thirds of the distance to Point Hope, Little Pete declared that he no longer knew the landscape and turned back toward Kotzebue. Continuing without a guide was unthinkable. Harper and Stuck could not distinguish the land from the sea ice that drifted and opened leads that could swallow them. Therefore Stuck hired a local youth named Chester to guide them on to Point Hope.[36] At Cape Thompson they encountered rough trail and hurricanelike "woollies" that Stuck claimed had once swept away a "perfectly sober missionary" and his heavily loaded sled, tumbling them over and over.[37] Nothing so dramatic occurred on this journey. On December 22 the travelers reached safety at Point Hope, to Thomas's relief and delight, as well as their own.

Ideal sealing conditions explained Point Hope's location at 68° north latitude. The seal harvest provided ample food and heating oil for residents. The village lay at the tip of a sixteen-mile-long sand spit constantly pummeled by winds from one direction or the other. The flat landscape offered no protection, but the wind brought seals to either side of the spit.[38]

In August 1826 Frederick Beechey, captain of the HMS *Blossom*, had made first contact with the one thousand or so Iñupiat who inhabited the Tikiġaq, or Point Hope, region. Residents had greeted the explorers enthusiastically, expressed interest in trading, offered food, and danced for them. Beechey noted that the people had metal tools, which had made their way to Point Hope through trade with Siberia. By 1865 two hundred whaling ships a year were hunting the waters at Point Hope.[39]

Between 1887 and 1910 at least a dozen shore-based whaling stations operated in the Point Hope area, including Jabbertown and Beacon Hill, as well as Cape Thompson, which was twenty-two miles away.[40] A multiethnic culture developed around the Jabbertown station, which continued operating for two decades. Iñupiat engaged in whaling and extensive trading, one negative effect of which was severe alcohol abuse among the people.[41] The whaling industry crashed about 1907, largely because steel replaced baleen in corsets.

The Episcopal Church and the Bureau of Education built a mission and school at Point Hope in 1890.[42] Nearly two decades later the reindeer herding program that Sheldon Jackson, the Bureau of Education's agent for Alaska, had introduced in the Seward Peninsula region expanded to Point Hope. The program aimed to relieve starvation in Iñupiaq regions where non-Natives had depleted subsistence resources.[43]

During Stuck and Harper's first two weeks in Point Hope the sun never rose above the horizon, although some sunlight brightened the sky. "Polar night" conditions stretched from December 5 until January 5 at Point Hope.[44] On Christmas Day, however, the moon, stars, and aurora lit the clear sky. Harper, Stuck, and Thomas celebrated the day together with the local Iñupiat. The mission bell rang at 10:30 a.m. to welcome people to Christmas services. Archdeacon Stuck delivered the sermon.[45]

More than two hundred people attended the feast that followed the service. For two days residents had been preparing soup, boiled seal meat, fried lynx, reindeer meat, biscuits, and ice cream for the occasion. The Christmas tree was just a few willow branches gathered from twenty-five miles inland. But strings of popcorn, tinsel, and glowing candles gave it a festive appearance. Following the meal Thomas, Stuck, and Harper distributed gifts and candy to everyone, young and old. At 10:00 p.m. the entertainment began: masterful Iñupiaq dancing. Stuck noted that he never could understand the fault that some missionaries found with this "harmless amusement."[46]

With Christmas behind them Harper, Stuck, and Thomas began a routine that occupied them for the rest of the seven-week visit. Stuck, who adored children, took over Thomas's teaching obligations at the school, while Walter taught the boys industrial arts. Enlisting the older boys' aid, he built a new sled to replace the toboggan he and Stuck had been using. To repay Thomas's hospitality, Stuck and Harper assumed his household tasks. Walter also tended the traveling party's dogs, as well as the mission's dogs. He purchased and butchered seals and boiled the meat with rice or meal to make their feed.[47] Meanwhile Thomas tutored Walter one hour a day in math and another hour in Latin. Stuck continued Walter's literature and history lessons.

On January 1, 1918, the three celebrated Walter's twenty-fifth birthday. He prepared an elaborate meal of stuffed roast ptarmigan, one for each of them, along with baked potatoes, peas, asparagus salad, and sparkling grape juice. Strawberry shortcake made with canned strawberries served as dessert. To create a festive atmosphere Thomas set twenty-five candles down the center of the table. Stuck gave Walter a high-quality Kodak camera for his birthday.[48] Thomas gave him a beautiful pair of reindeer skin boots. He seemed to have grown as fond of Walter as Stuck had.[49]

From January 1 to 8 the wind raged from the northeast, carry-

28. The Point Hope school and children. From Stuck, *Winter Circuit*.

ing with it snow and sand. The temperature ranged from 15 to 30 degrees below zero, with the wind creating a much lower chill factor. The weather kept the small children at home that week, but the fifteen older children braved the blizzard each day to walk a mile and a quarter to the schoolhouse. As the wind pierced the building, they sat at their desks in their reindeer parkas, boots, and mittens. By midday the schoolhouse had warmed enough that they could remove their mittens.[50]

At about noon on January 7, as Stuck stood in front of the classroom, the children shouted, "The sun, the sun!" Peering out the window, teacher and students saw the glowing ball on the horizon.[51] And a welcome sight it was. Just a week later the sun remained above the horizon for two hours.[52]

The children spoke their native language in school. They practiced reading English each day, but some of the content mystified the students. A chapter titled "A Day in the Woods" made little sense to children who had never seen a living tree. The driftwood stumps they had seen looked nothing like the green trees in the illustrations. Efforts were being made to replace the reading material with books written for Iñupiat, but those Stuck saw were far from ideal.[53]

Everyone at Point Hope looked forward to the mail carrier's visits. As the day of his scheduled arrival neared, the men busied themselves with writing letters.[54] Walter no doubt wrote several to Frances during his stay at the village. And she surely posted many letters to him at Point Hope, knowing their plans to spend six to seven weeks there.[55]

One of the highlights of the stay at Point Hope was the first seal-skinning project that Walter initiated. His experience in butchering moose, caribou, and bear gave him the confidence to give seals a try. Thomas, who was eager to develop new skills, agreed to help. Stuck described the process: "The two men, and the back kitchen where the deed was done, reeked with blood and oil . . . never was a kitchen in a filthier, viler mess; the stuff froze on the floor before it could be removed and for days I slipped about on it." Walter described the exercise more simply in his diary: "Mr. Thomas and I skinned a seal; the archdeacon stood around and made remarks."[56]

Walter had yet to fulfill his highest ambition—to shoot a polar bear. Several times he and Thomas wandered out in search of the exotic animal, with no luck. One moonlit night, when they heard of a bear sighting, they went out again. Stuck, who lacked the "red blood" required to kill animals, remained at the mission house, fretting through the night. The hunters returned the next morning having spent a miserable sleepless night in a hut, with the wind howling. They had not seen a bear.[57]

On February 9, after seven weeks at Point Hope, Stuck and Harper continued on toward Barrow. They had mixed feelings about leaving the village. They thoroughly enjoyed Thomas's company and also appreciated the hardy, industrious, and cheerful Iñupiat.[58] At the same time they were eager to move on and see more of the coast and then return to Fort Yukon.

They relied on the mail carrier Andy and his two assistants to guide them northeastward along the coast. Andy set the pace along the grueling trail. The barren landscape and the driving, icy wind were in striking contrast to conditions in Alaska's forested Interior. Gales blasted the coast, and when the air was calm, thick fog set in. Wind from the south brought blinding snowstorms. The pack ice continually shifted, obscuring the boundary between sea ice and land. With no landmarks for long stretches, Stuck and Harper easily could have gone astray. As Walter said, "Most of the time you can't see anything, and when it clears up there's nothing to see!"[59]

Walter took charge of the new sled loaded with four hundred pounds of cargo, mostly dog food. Stuck drove the old sled, which carried three hundred pounds. The first day's travel was most difficult. As they climbed toward Cape Lisburne, bitter winds formed deep snowdrifts and froze their noses repeatedly. Finally they placed the smaller sled behind the larger sled and combined the dog teams to pull the weight jointly. This tactic increased their pace somewhat.[60]

The mail carriers, whose loads were lighter, pulled ahead out of sight. The first night out Harper and Stuck built a shelter using their sleds and snow blocks. Exhausted and struggling to see, they could not make the hut windproof, so the Primus stove kept going out. Finally they each ate a chocolate bar and crawled into the sleeping bags, still dressed in their parkas and boots. All night they shivered as the wind whistled through their shelter. Under such conditions Walter's "invincible good humour" buoyed Stuck's spirits. He told Stuck, shouting above the wind, that he was glad they had discovered "the delights of Arctic coast travel" so soon. "Now we know what to expect," he said.[61]

Three or four miles into the next day's trek, they met up with their guides.[62] Some nights they slept in uninhabited ice huts. Other times Iñupiat invited them into their crowded igloos. At Mut-ták-took Harper and Stuck tasted their first seal meat, which the mail carriers offered them. Others had warned them of the foul taste of seal meat and oil, but Stuck found the meat less offensive than he expected. Harper devoured the meat gratefully, his appetite for meat seemingly insatiable.[63]

After eleven long days on the trail the travelers arrived at Wainwright. The whole village turned out to greet them. The teachers, Mr. and Mrs. Forrest, invited Walter and Stuck to stay in their home. They decided to remain at Wainwright for two days of rest and recuperation, though each had work to do. Harper repaired the lashing on the sled. Stuck held worship services in the school-house, with every village resident in attendance.[64]

Wainwright lay at one of the most favorable locations on the Arctic coast. A lagoon behind the village allowed ice fishing all winter. The sea ice provided access to seals and walruses. Residents had harvested 150 walruses the previous summer. They hunted whales, too. Mr. Forrest oversaw three reindeer herds, including about 2,300 deer that 26 Iñupiaq herders and apprentices tended. About 184 people lived in the region in 1918.[65]

Although Stuck and Walter appreciated Andy the mail carrier's knowledge of the terrain, he disappointed them in other ways. Walter disliked Andy's habit of addressing the archdeacon by only his surname, rather than his title, as virtually all others did. But this was Andy's custom with all white men.[66] Walter took greater offense at Andy's neglect of his dogs. At least one night, after a long and exhausting run, Andy left his dogs hitched to the sled and unfed all night while the men slept in an igloo. Dog men just "don't do" that, Walter declared. He and Stuck had fed their dogs and unharnessed them, so they could curl into balls with their backs to the wind. Walter was so disturbed by Andy's maltreatment of his dogs that he reported him to the postmaster at Barrow. It was the only instance Stuck knew of when Walter "made trouble" for anyone.[67]

The most memorable night between Point Hope and Barrow took place at Sing-i-too-rók, where six family members hosted the five travelers. An eccentric old woman seemed to rule the house. She may have been the only person Walter ever met whom he did not charm. Or perhaps she did find him charming and only meant to tease him. He was not amused.

The woman laughed and chattered as she used the chamber pot noisily amid the others. At bedtime everyone lay down with their sleeping bags slightly overlapping one another in the cramped quarters. The woman curtained off an area for herself. She repeatedly scolded Harper when his feet intruded into her space. When his foot collapsed the framework supporting her curtain, she exploded in screeches and shouts followed by laughter. Horrified, Walter jumped up and reset the curtain. When he again inadvertently knocked the partition down, she poked him in the ribs with a stick until he reset the curtain. The next morning as they loaded the sleds, Walter exclaimed to Stuck, "That's the most awful old woman I ever saw in my life." Stuck agreed that she was "flabbergasting."[68]

On February 25, sixteen days after leaving Point Hope, the men pulled in at Barrow. Alaska's most northerly community, at 71° degrees north latitude, was and remains its largest Iñupiaq village. Actually two Native settlements lay in the area. The larger one, Utkiávik, situated at Cape Smythe, had hosted commercial whaling enterprises in earlier years. A mission and a school were built there in 1890. The smaller settlement, Núvuk, lay ten miles away at Point Barrow. These communities experienced polar night for two months, from November 21 to January 21. As the travelers approached the main village, "the whole population" came out to greet them, Stuck reported. They escorted the men through the community to Charles Brower's headquarters at the Cape Smyth Whaling and Trading Company, where Harper and Stuck stayed.[69]

Brower, a renowned trader and former whaler who was married to an Iñupiaq woman, was Barrow's most prominent resident. He had arrived in Alaska in 1883 at the age of twenty-one as part of a coal prospecting team at Corwin Bluff, northeast of Point Hope. Brower soon took up commercial whaling at Point Hope. He later migrated to Barrow, where he immersed himself in Iñupiaq society and learned much about whaling from Iñupiaq whalers. Brower became a highly respected member of the Barrow community. He also maintained his ties with relatives Outside and with members of the elite Explorers Club in New York.

During his long life in Barrow, Brower had met every person who passed through the community, including scientists, explorers, and travelers, and he had hosted most of them.[70] Stuck and Harper's arrival especially pleased him. Brower was eager to hear the latest news of the Great War, even if it was somewhat dated. With his two sons, Bill and Jim, being "over there," he devoured every morsel of news Stuck shared.[71] He appreciated Stuck's analysis of world events. During their stay at Barrow, Stuck often accompanied Brower on his long daily walks.[72] The two men had much in common. They both admired the Iñupiaq people, and they shared broad knowledge of Arctic and international affairs, past and present.[73]

Walter spent much of his time at Barrow building a new sled, to meet their current needs and the challenging terrain of the high Arctic. He purchased Siberian hardwood from Brower for the runners. And he sawed, chiseled, fitted and shaped, steamed and bent the material into a custom-made sled. Brower proclaimed him to be a "natural born mechanic." With all the pride of a father, Stuck replied that Walter was equally a "woodsman, hunter, dog-driver, boatman, mountain climber—natural born to the whole range of outdoor proficiencies." It was impossible to identify at which he excelled most.[74]

In 1918 the Presbyterian church was the most prominent building in Barrow. The parsonage stood next door. Frank Spence, a physician who served as its pastor, several times invited Stuck to speak to his congregation of three hundred Iñupiat. The services were conducted completely in Iñupiaq, except for the sermon and the scripture reading, which an interpreter translated from Stuck's English. Stuck was moved by the people's spontaneous prayers in their native tongue.[75]

Dr. Spence had practiced medicine for many years before being ordained in the Presbyterian Church just prior to his arrival in Barrow. As Stuck shadowed him on his rounds one day, he agonized over the poor health and living conditions of the people. Many had tuberculosis. Every home had a sheet-iron stove, but the people had no fuel other than seal oil. The cold, crowded, poorly ventilated underground homes would have slowed recovery from any disease, but especially tuberculosis.[76]

Stuck found the health of the Iñupiat all along the coast to be "scandalously neglected." He was so impressed with the work of Dr. Spence and his wife and with the need for a hospital at Barrow that he later contacted the Presbyterian Mission Board and pled for a hospital.[77] The following summer a ship arrived carrying materials for building the hospital and a supervisor and nurse to staff it. In his memoir *Fifty Years below Zero* Brower credited

Stuck with the stunning achievement: "I was willing to admit to the world that Archdeacon Stuck had indeed 'put it across.'"[78]

In mid-March, Stuck, Harper, and their guide, George, departed Barrow, journeying eastward toward the Alaska-Canada border and Herschel Island. On this portion of their trek, which lasted three weeks and two days, the men faced the worst travel conditions of the entire circuit. Fierce, bitterly cold winds blasted them and left the terrain bare and rough. The travel so exhausted them that they took a break from Walter's studies during this leg of the journey. At night he would cook the dogs' food and complete the other chores. Then he would lie down, write a few lines in his journal, and fall asleep. Sometimes he asked Stuck to recite some poetry, or they would sing hymns or other songs they knew by heart.[79]

At one stop along the way, as Stuck and Walter reminisced about their ascent of Denali, Walter exclaimed, "I wish we could climb Denali's Wife before I go [O]utside again!" Stuck replied that he would have to save that adventure "for a vacation when you are in charge of the hospital at Tanana."[80]

Three weeks out, the men reached Tom Gordon's trading post, just west of the demarcation point for the international border. Gordon allowed anyone to lay over at the post, Native or non-Native. The building was crowded when Stuck, Walter, and George arrived. In keeping with his usual routine on the trail, Stuck held a short worship service for those gathered that evening.[81]

As they continued on to Herschel Island, a biting wind drove the chill factor far below the daytime thermometer reading of 40 degrees below zero. The men and dogs struggled over windswept gravel patches and chunks of driftwood.[82] The final night on the trail the mercury dipped to 51 degrees below zero, "some cold for the fifth of April," Walter remarked.[83] Concern for the dogs surpassed their own discomfort. Walter had to ration the dogs' food by now, and their rice and blubber diet gave them digestive trouble. He felt sorry for the dogs.[84]

Finally they reached the village and Anglican mission on Herschel Island. Here in the late nineteenth century hundreds of whalers had hunted the animals year round, drawing Iñupiat and Inuit (related Canadian Indigenous people) into the industry. The whalers also bartered with the Natives for meat and furs from their hunting and trapping efforts. Between about 1890 and 1907, when the baleen market collapsed, the Indigenous peoples of the Mackenzie Delta and Herschel Island region became thoroughly acculturated to Western lifeways and commodities. Among the long-lasting negative effects of commercial whaling activities were deadly diseases and alcohol abuse. Of the estimated population of 2,500 in the mid-nineteenth century only 260 remained in 1910.[85] In 1918 the village was a quiet Royal Canadian Mounted Police outpost. An Anglican mission and a Hudson's Bay Company store served the Iñupiat and Inuit scattered throughout the region.[86]

Two days before Stuck and Harper arrived the renowned explorer Vilhjalmur Stefansson had left the village with a support team and headed for St. Stephen's Hospital in Fort Yukon. Stefansson's five-year Canadian Arctic Expedition had been doing research in the area.[87] He had completed the final mapping of the most western region of the Canadian Arctic archipelago when he fell ill with typhoid fever in January 1918. By April his condition was critical—he had begun bleeding from the lungs. Thus he and medical personnel decided to rush him to St. Stephen's.[88] Stefansson later told Stuck that he thought he would have died had he remained at Herschel Island.[89]

After resting four days at Herschel Island, Harper and Stuck began the final leg of their journey with replenished food and supplies. They followed the Herschel Island River (also called the Firth River) and crossed the Buckland Mountains as they traveled southwest toward Fort Yukon. As they moved inland, the sight of the familiar spruce trees and birds of Alaska's northern Interior heartened them. They saw snowbirds, a hawk, ptarmigan tracks, and then the classic signal of spring—pussy willows. The temperature rose rapidly as they left the coast. Soon they cast off their fur coats and fur boots and drove the dogsleds without wearing gloves. As they encountered deep, soft snow, Stuck donned the snowshoes that they had packed for hundreds of miles. Iñupiat along the coast had chuckled at the contraptions.[90]

On their own now for the first time since leaving Barrow, Harper shared with Stuck the diary he had been keeping. The journal revealed his and Frances's marriage plans, as well as his aim to enlist in the military. During the summer of 1917 the national government had sent out a call for the registration of Alaska men of military age, excluding "all persons of whole or mixed native blood, Indian, Eskimo or Aleut." The announcement had stung Walter and other Alaska Natives.[91] Having learned at Barrow that Charles Brower's sons were serving in the military, Walter's thoughts of enlisting had been revived. He had long been interested in aviation and read eagerly on the topic. Now he hoped to enter the aviation corps in the fall.

Walter knew that Stuck would resist both of his aims, because they would delay his career in medicine and mission work. He must have considered carefully how to tell his mentor before settling on sharing the diary with him. Waiting as Stuck read the little book from cover to cover cannot have been easy. One can only imagine how cautiously their conversation began as Stuck closed the journal.

As Walter expected, Stuck balked at the change of plans. Marriage and military service would delay Walter's college and career plans, *if* he came home. Walter pledged that if he survived the war, he would begin college directly. Ultimately Stuck acquiesced to Walter's decisions.[92]

Surely Walter had hoped for warmer support from his father figure. But Stuck could not muster enthusiasm. He recalled later that Walter's strong writing skills had pleased him. And he felt pride in Walter's desire to serve his country. Given Walter's talents, Stuck *knew* the young man would make an ace aviator. He also took some pleasure in Walter's having "won the heart of a cultivated gentlewoman."[93] But these sentiments did not outweigh his dashed hopes for Walter's immediate future.

The episode marked a turning point in their relationship. This was the first time that Harper deviated from the course he and Stuck had charted together. He did not request Stuck's permission; he asked for his blessing. This Stuck could not give at the time. Yet despite their mutual disappointment their trust in one another deepened through the discussion. Stuck wrote in *A Winter Circuit*,

"Walter had long ago become almost a son to me, and regarded me almost as a father—the only father he had ever known—and I think the relation was established as closely as it can exist without the actual cement of blood, upon this stage of our journey."[94]

Stuck wrote nothing of Walter's revelations in his diary that day or in the following days, although he recorded other events on each of those days. He undoubtedly mulled over their discussion, but he did not commit his thoughts to paper. He would need time to adjust to Walter's independence.

The two encountered the most challenging terrain of the entire journey in the next days. They broke trail in deep, wet snow, as fresh snow continued to fall. They followed the Firth River southwestward and then climbed to a saddle in the mountains that led them to the Coleen River. Stuck went ahead on snowshoes to break trail. Each step required lifting two to three pounds of moist snow, which was toilsome work. Then he backtracked to smooth the trail further. Walter followed behind, controlling both the large and the small sled, with all the dogs harnessed as one team. His was the more demanding work. Stuck recalled, "It was under just such circumstances that Walter shone. . . . He was never irritable or impatient, always cheerful though with not much to say. Stress of any kind added to his customary taciturnity." Their studies lapsed again during this exhausting leg of the journey. In the evening Walter would cook the dog feed, eat his own supper, and crawl into his fur sleeping bag.[95]

As they neared Fort Yukon the pair met the Stefansson party and Dr. Burke, who had traveled north from Fort Yukon to treat Stefansson. The patient had rallied by this point, thanks to the fresh air and the hearty food Dr. Burke allowed him.[96]

In the final stretch toward Fort Yukon, Burke and Stefansson pulled ahead of the heavily burdened Harper and Stuck. After the first party pulled in at the village, word spread quickly of Stuck and Harper's imminent arrival. Villagers formed a welcoming gauntlet and cheered wildly as the travelers entered Fort Yukon. The date was April 27, 1918, ten days short of six months since they had begun their odyssey.[97]

Stefansson remained several weeks at Fort Yukon under Happy

29. Vilhjalmur Stefansson's Canadian Arctic Expedition party with
Walter Harper and Dr. Grafton "Happy" Burke. Courtesy of the
Archives of the Episcopal Church, Austin, Texas.

Burke's care. His presence in the village caused a sensation and
made national news. From New York, John Wood wrote Frances Wells, "We have glowed with conscious and justified pride
this last month as we have realized what the Doctor and nurses
in the Hospital were doing for Mr. Stefansson. It was very gratifying to read in the Monday papers in New York and Boston the
despatch [sic] from Ft. Yukon in which Mr. Stefansson said that
he was being well cared for at the Hospital."[98]

During the several weeks Stefansson recuperated at St. Stephen's
Hospital, he and Stuck engaged in far-ranging and sometimes
heated discussions. The notoriously atheist Stefansson reportedly told Stuck that his antimissionary views had been overstated
in the press. His criticism of missionaries in his own book was
harder to explain away, although he tried, according to Stuck.[99] It
is quite possible that during Stefansson's long stays at Herschel
Island and Fort Yukon, and through his discussions with Stuck,
his understanding of missionary work expanded. He must have

recognized Stuck and Burke's devotion to Alaska Natives' well-being and energetic efforts on their behalf.

In Walter's absence Frances's commitment to the mission work intensified. A March 1918 letter to John Wood illustrated her sentiments: "There is certainly a great field for work and I hope and pray that I can do my 'bit.' . . . This Indian work appeals to me more than ever it did before I was actually sharing in it."[100] However, some, including Wood himself, now questioned the wisdom of investing scarce resources in seemingly dying races.[101] The Great War marked the end of the social gospel era in the United States, when Christians felt moved to help the less privileged.[102] Both voluntarism and donations to missionary work were declining.[103] In an article in the *Alaskan Churchman* Frances refuted such "doomsday" perceptions of Alaska Natives' future and defended the Episcopal mission work. She described industrious people who volunteered their labors to repay the mission's generosity. And she wrote of the broad influence of the mission and hospital in improving health and sanitary conditions in the region.[104]

Just days before Stuck and Harper returned to Fort Yukon, Frances rushed with a dog team to Circle City, where the local schoolteacher lay critically burned. No nurse or doctor lived in the village. Leaving Fort Yukon at 10:00 p.m., she traveled through the night in a blinding snowstorm, barely escaping open water and overflow several times. Halfway to Circle a new driver and dog team took over, so she could continue without stopping to rest. After twenty-one hours on the trail they reached her destination.[105]

The schoolteacher had been cleaning with gasoline when the rags spontaneously combusted. Her prognosis had been bleak, but under Frances's skilled care she recovered. While at Circle, Frances also attended to the medical concerns of the fifty or so Natives in the village.[106] Circle had wire service, so she heard the news of Harper and Stuck's homecoming in Fort Yukon.

A week after his return Walter "called on" Frances, having traveled 192 miles over the same rough trail she had taken to Circle. They spent only an afternoon and evening together. But after the equally punishing return journey, he assured Frances that their reunion had been "worth it."[107]

Breakup—the opening of the ice-filled rivers in the spring—began later in May. The thaw of spring 1918 was the most dramatic in anyone's memory. As the ice in the Porcupine and upper Yukon Rivers loosened and the water flowed, pressure built up downriver, causing ice jams and flash flooding.

At Circle City ice blocks eight feet thick and yards across piled into fifty-foot-high stacks. Ice and water overran the river's banks and flooded the town, leaving water standing four feet high in the houses. Frances and Circle residents grabbed what they could and rushed to the hills, where they slept bundled in furs on spruce boughs for three nights until the water receded. To make matters worse, snow fell continuously the first day of the flood. Yet Frances said that no one complained. The campers were relieved to be safe from the ice and water.[108]

When river traffic opened in late May, Frances returned to Fort Yukon by steamer and riverboat. The distance could have been covered in six hours in summer, but in the spring that year it took forty-six hours, because of the ice clogging the Yukon River. Eventually she escaped the steamer to a launch that sped her to Fort Yukon. She arrived at 2:15 a.m. on May 24, in broad daylight. The normally unflappable Walter stood on the riverbank waiting for her, "having about 40 fits" because of her late arrival and the treacherous conditions.[109] The steamer, the *Washburn*, reached Fort Yukon twelve hours later.[110]

7

Summer and Fall 1918

"I AM HERE alive, very well and happier than I have ever been in my life," Frances Wells wrote her father. "I expect you know by now who is responsible for all this happiness." Walter Harper would soon be going to New York to enlist in the aviation corps. Afterward he would make a "bee line for Germantown" to introduce himself. "I know you will think the world and all of him," she assured her father, adding that she hoped Walter would win over others who might have reservations about his "Indian blood." The couple was not sure when they would marry. They had considered waiting until Walter finished medical school, but with his going off to war they might marry earlier. Frances expected to remain in Fort Yukon, or possibly transfer to the mission hospital in Tanana, Walter's home village, unless the Red Cross needed her.[1]

"What does Walter look like?" she asked in a rhetorical prelude to her answer. "He is taller than I. Weighs about 185[,] is built like [her brother] Joe. Has Joe's olive tinted skin with red cheeks dark brown curly hair, brown eyes. . . . He is generally known as a 'Prince among men,'" she wrote. If her father wanted to know more, he could look for references to "Walter" or "Harper" in Archdeacon Stuck's *Ten Thousand Miles with a Dog Sled*, *Ascent of Denali*, or *Voyages on the Yukon and Its Tributaries*. Since Frances thought he was "the top of everything in the world," she could not describe him objectively. The folks at Fort Yukon were teasing the couple nonstop about their romance, but "we are having our fun out of it too," she wrote. Nothing annoyed either of them now.[2]

Changing her tone only slightly, Frances continued: "Now sit down and give us your fatherly blessing etc." No one would know Walter was part Indian, to look at him, she explained, but his heritage from his mother "makes me love him heaps more."[3] She enclosed a photo of a smiling, rugged-looking Walter.

Meanwhile Walter, Stuck, and other mission personnel scrambled to save the Fort Yukon mission house and hospital from the icy, raging river. Giant slabs of the riverbank in front of the hospital had broken off and been carried away. The hospital grounds and tuberculosis patients' tents lay under water. The river undermined the Burkes' residence as well. It would have to be torn down and rebuilt farther back from the river. The Porcupine River, which drained into the Yukon at Fort Yukon, had broken through its banks and sent several streams through the Native village at Fort Yukon. Numerous cabins had to be moved to higher ground.[4]

In June Frances wrote John Wood at the Episcopal Church's mission headquarters in New York, telling him of her engagement and asking him to release her from her commitment at St. Stephen's. She and Walter had not yet set a wedding date, but Walter planned to go to New York to "do his 'bit'" by enlisting, while she aimed to join the Red Cross. She told Wood she regretted leaving her work at St. Stephen's, as it had "a deeper hold on me than ever."[5]

Replacing Frances at St. Stephen's Hospital would be no easy task. During the Great War nurses who were willing to leave home were signing up to serve "over there" with the Red Cross. In 1918 the Episcopal Board of Missions failed to hire nurses for its stations in Alaska, China, and Japan.[6]

By early summer Archdeacon Stuck had come to accept the pending marriage. He asked both Bishop Rowe and John Wood to write Guilliam Wells of their high opinions of Walter. In Wood's letter to Wells he mentioned the issue of Walter's heritage.[7] Wells responded that he was pleased to hear yet another "good opinion of the young man" but that no one in the family was concerned with Walter's "Indian blood." Wells noted that Frances was nearly thirty years old, and "if any woman is well qualified to make a wise choice of a husband, she is or ought to be."[8] He told Wood he looked forward to meeting Walter.

30. Walter Harper in skiff, circa 1918. Yvonne Mozée Collection, #2002-98-16, Mozée Family Papers, APRCA, University of Alaska Fairbanks.

At Fort Yukon the spring flood and its aftermath had created perfect breeding conditions for mosquitoes. By midsummer a heat wave and swarms of mosquitoes were torturing residents. On July 16 the mercury reached 92 degrees, not an all-time high but well above the average summer temperature. Two days later, with the foundation laid for the Burkes' new home and a contractor hired to build the house, Stuck and Walter began their seasonal rounds on the *Pelican*.[9]

Following their usual pattern, the duo headed upriver. After twenty-six hours of traveling through thick smoke from forest fires, they reached their first destination—Circle City. The smoke was so dense they did not always know where they were, despite their intimate knowledge of the landscape.[10]

In 1918 about one thousand miners worked the creeks in the region and made Circle their headquarters. The community reflected its gold-rush past, with multiple businesses, including saloons and brothels, an Episcopal mission, and a hospital. The chapel and hospital stood empty now. No missionary, doctor, or nurse had lived at Circle City for years. Stuck conducted two services for Natives on Sunday, but he could find no one to interpret during the morning service, so he was unsure how much the people understood.[11] Kutchin, or Gwich'in, Athabascan differed enough from Walter's Koyukon language that he could not help.

The *Pelican* continued on to Eagle and across the border a few miles to an island where numerous Athabascans were camped. Here and downriver Stuck offered Holy Communion services and conducted baptisms at Native and non-Native gatherings. He preached to a full chapel of white congregants at St. Paul's in Eagle. The *Pelican* returned to Fort Yukon on July 30, carrying a little girl with tuberculosis from Eagle to St. Stephen's Hospital.[12]

That summer as Stuck and Harper toured the Interior they noticed changes in the social environments of Native villages. The community of Rampart had lost its Native character. The mining influence dominated, and few Alaska Natives lived there now. Many of the young men at Rampart and other villages had gone or were considering going off to join the fight in the Great War.[13] In Stuck's view the best of the young men were leaving, while the "low-down" ones remained, frustrating the missionaries' work and exerting a negative influence on Native communities and individuals.[14]

Fish traps and canneries at the mouth of the Yukon were taking so many salmon that Interior villagers worried about how they would manage through the winter. The fish runs had been strong in 1916.[15] In 1918 they were shockingly low. Stuck wired Alaska governor Thomas Riggs and congressional delegate Charles Sulzer to protest the cannery at the Yukon's mouth.[16]

After a week's stay in Fort Yukon the two headed downriver toward Tanana and Nenana, stopping at camps along the way. They transported several individuals from one camp to another, even taking one man's canoe onboard. They carried an incapacitated man to the hospital at Tanana and two boys to the school at St. Mark's Mission in Nenana.[17]

They remained several days at Nenana while Stuck underwent extensive dental work. He took a room in the dentist's building so he could have "privacy while partially toothless."[18] After four days in the dentist's chair, he left with an "abominable plate" that he had to remove and clean after each meal. The plate left him "humiliated and mortified," feeling much closer to "old age and decrepitude."[19]

Meanwhile Walter tinkered with boat engines all week. He repaired so many other engines that the *Pelican* was still in disrepair when Stuck was ready to leave.[20] The launch had become more Walter's than Stuck's by this time. He usually slept on the boat, even when they stopped at missions. He kept his academic work onboard, easily accessible, and throughout the boat he had rigged up gadgets and devices for his convenience.[21] Once put on notice, Walter tuned the *Pelican*'s engine in no time.

The pair departed Nenana on August 24, traveling southeast on the Tanana River to Tolovana Hot Springs. Just as they stopped at the springs Stuck received word by telegram of a badly burned four-year-old boy camped with his family on Baker Creek. The child had stepped backward into a large pot of boiling fish and cornmeal just removed from the fire. He simply sat down in it. The boy needed transport to the hospital at Tanana.[22]

Upon hearing the news, Stuck turned to Walter, saying, "It looks as if it's up to us." Walter instantly replied, "I'm with you." Stuck sent word ahead with the signal corpsman from the Tolovana telegraph station that they were on their way and directed the boy's father to stand on the bank with a lantern, so they could see him. As the sky darkened and a storm brewed, the *Pelican* sped three hours to the campsite.[23]

Quickly they placed the swathed boy and his father onboard. Through the night Walter stood at the wheel, peering into the darkness, the *Pelican*'s front window open and the rain beating on his face. With his hand on the throttle and his foot on the reverse pedal, ready for signs of shallows, he raced down the Tanana River. When the rudder line separated, Walter rushed to the stern and guided the launch to the riverbank, where he repaired the line. At the wheel again he resumed the marathon. At dawn they reached the Yukon River and turned upstream. Shortly thereafter they pulled into the Tanana mission. Finding no medical help there, Walter continued the three miles to Fort Gibbon.[24]

Stuck recalled Walter's feat: "I could not have done it myself to save my life or even to win the war. I have not the sight, nor the sense, nor the nerve. No one, save a man with eyes like an owl and reading water [like] a book; no one, I think who has not spent his boyhood in a birch-bark canoe and so come to an intuitive feeling of water, could have brought that launch one hundred miles lickety-split down the Tanana River in the pitch dark and the driving rain, and have touched bottom but once—and then only for an instant." At 7:00 a.m. Stuck and Harper left the boy with a doctor and nurse, and Stuck went to bed. Walter bathed and went to visit Jessie and Margaret, who was due to have a baby soon.[25] Jessie and her husband Ben Mozée had a daughter by this time—Bonnie.[26] Stuck and Harper learned later that day that the burned child had died.[27]

The following day Walter attended a showing of *The Birth of a Nation*. The silent film, set during and after the Civil War, met with sharp criticism for its portrayal of African Americans as unintelligent and threatening and for depicting the Ku Klux Klan as a heroic force. Walter had seen plenty of racial prejudice in his life. Under the archdeacon's wing and accustomed to mainstream American culture, he generally avoided direct insults. African Americans had been among his classmates at Mount Hermon. The film must have puzzled him.

On their return run to Fort Yukon the two stopped at Sixteen Mile Island, where Walter visited with his mother. Although he saw his siblings from time to time on the trail or river, he saw Jenny less frequently. She was close to sixty years old now. Walter told her about Frances, news of his wedding, and details of his plans to join the Air Corps. She asked Walter for Frances's foot size, so she could sew her future daughter-in-law a pair of slippers.[28]

On September 4, 1918, Archdeacon Stuck joined Walter and Frances in marriage at the Fort Yukon chapel. Friends had spent the day decorating the sanctuary and creating an arch of autumn foliage. "It was all very happy and everyone worked mighty hard to do all in their power to make it just as happy for us as was possible," Frances wrote to her new sister-in-law Margaret.[29] An informal reception followed at the hospital, where Clara Burke provided some of her "famously good 'eats.'"[30] Afterward the couple took the *Dorothy* to the Porcupine River, where they spent their wedding night in a tent that Happy Burke had pitched for them.[31] They camped there until a steamer going upriver took them to Walter's favorite hunting area.[32] There they hunted game to supply the mission and hospital with meat for the winter.

Letters Frances wrote to Margaret and Jessie upon their return attest to the couple's love for one another. The letters brimmed with happiness. Thanking Jessie for a note she had written her, Frances wrote, "I feel now that I know you and am glad of it." She said the letter felt like "the grasp of an old friend's hand." A playful remark from Walter conveyed his joy in his marriage: "Walter says 'Tell Jessie I still love her just as much even if I have a wife!'" Frances closed the letter by writing, "And here's a great deal of love from both of us to the Mozée both big & small."[33]

Frances reported to Margaret the "one famous time" they had on their honeymoon-hunting trip. They "roughed it . . . tramping and climbing and watching and sleeping where [they] stopped with and without bedding." After the second night they had forgotten they had a stove and tent. Their luck was "fair." Walter had felled two caribou, two moose, three bears, and some small game, including a porcupine and some ducks. They had seen many more moose, but the animals were too far away to pack them. "It was all miles of fun and I venture to say that no two people could have gotten more real pleasure out of it than we did," Frances wrote. For three days Walter had left her at a camp called Woodchopper while he hunted in territory he felt was too dangerous for her. While she waited, she removed the fat from the hides of the three bears Walter had shot, earning herself the name "Greasy Harper" and having a "heap of fun."[34] She reported to Jessie that they now had three "dandy" rugs for their home.[35]

Frances's thoughtfulness and generosity shone in her letter to Margaret. She sent her sister-in-law a small bag that she had knit and offered to knit her anything else she wanted. "I am almost bold enough to tackle anything in the knitting line if you promise not to be too critical," she wrote. She also offered to be Margaret's personal shopper in Philadelphia, where the shopping was "mighty fine." Frances sent to Jenny a petticoat she had knit. "Be sure to tell her that it brings a heap of love from both of us," she wrote. She enclosed a drawing of her foot and said she was "mighty happy" about the slippers Jenny planned to sew for her.[36]

Walter and Frances had had such a marvelous time on their hunting trip that they had extended it. The delay caused them to miss the steamer they had planned to take to Whitehorse to travel Outside.[37] This decision was to have fateful consequences.

The couple left Fort Yukon on the steamer *Alaska* at about noon on October 10. Just before they departed, village residents learned from the daily news bulletin that Germany was seeking peace and requesting an armistice.[38] This long-awaited news meant that Walter could go directly to college. Frances had a $10,000 inheritance from an aunt that she planned to use to pay Walter's tuition.[39]

After their departure Stuck prepared an advertisement to be placed in a Philadelphia newspaper or perhaps in church bulletins. It sought summer employment for Walter as a wilderness arts instructor or summer camp director. Stuck outlined Walter's work experience, noting that "few men in the United States" were more qualified to instruct "outdoor resourcefulness." Based on his "personal character," no one was more trustworthy with young people's care, he wrote.[40]

In Germantown, Pennsylvania, Frances's family eagerly awaited the newlyweds' arrival. They planned to stay at the Wells residence until they could find a home of their own.[41] They had sent packages ahead, and wedding gifts from friends had begun to arrive.

The couple traveled up the Yukon River to Whitehorse, where they took the White Pass & Yukon Railway to its terminus at Skagway. There they joined hundreds of others from Alaska and the Yukon Territory who waited to board the *Princess Sophia*, the last ship leaving the north before winter. Lighthearted, knowing that Walter would not go to war, the twosome looked forward to a memorable voyage. They knew the scenery along the Inside Passage was spectacular.

The *Princess Sophia* was one of nine *Princess*-named ships the Canadian Pacific Railway (CPR) had built between 1907 and 1914. It was licensed to carry 250 passengers and a crew of 70. With

31. The *Princess Sophia*. William Norton Photo Collection, P226–747, Alaska State Library, Juneau.

special permission it could be retrofitted to carry up to 500.[42] Owing to the high demand for passage on the ship's final voyage from Alaska that fall, the CPR made accommodations for 350 passengers. New regulations following the sinking of the *Titanic* required that the CPR add six "buoyancy tanks" to the *Sophia*. The tanks had ropes for people to grasp as they floated in the water following an accident. Soon after the ship's construction, the CPR converted its coal-burning furnace to oil. At full capacity it carried twenty-nine hundred barrels of oil in two double-bottomed tanks.[43]

The Skagway harbor buzzed with activity on October 23 as the crew prepared for departure and passengers gathered. The daily train from Whitehorse arrived at 5:30 with additional travelers. By early evening all passengers were aboard. At 10:10 p.m. the *Sophia* pulled away from the dock, three hours after her scheduled departure. A careful estimate put the number of people onboard at 353, including about 65 crew members.[44] Many well-known Alaskans and Yukon residents were among them.[45]

Soon after the *Sophia* departed Skagway, a blinding snowstorm from the north overtook the ship. Capt. Leonard Locke continued at the normal speed of 11 to 12 knots, rather than slowing to the recommended speed of about 7 knots.[46] He moved southward through the center of Lynn Canal, to the west of the narrow shipping lane. At 2:10 a.m. on October 24 the ship ran straight onto Vanderbilt Reef, the rather flat top of a mountain rising from the floor of Lynn Canal. At the lowest tide the reef rose about twelve feet above the water's surface. At high tide in stormy seas it may not have been visible, even in daylight.[47]

Captain Locke ordered the lifeboats prepared for use. But he soon decided that the passengers were safer aboard the ship, secure atop the reef, than in lifeboats in the stormy sea.[48] For nearly forty hours as the wind howled, rescuers stood by awaiting Captain Locke's signal to approach.[49] Eight small rescue boats were on the scene in the morning and early afternoon of October 24, when the weather was calm enough to allow transfer of the passengers, but Captain Locke declined their aid. By evening, when the much larger *Cedar*, a lighthouse tender, and *King and Winge*, a fish boat, had arrived, the storm had risen again, making transfers too risky.[50]

As the passengers waited, some wrote letters to loved ones, while others wrote in their diaries. At least one wrote a will. The recovery of some of these items, along with other physical evidence, permits the reconstruction of the final hours of those on the ship. Moods vacillated between relatively calm and hopeful to despairing as the hours dragged on.[51]

At about 4:45 p.m. on Friday, October 25, the wind and waves rose, lifting the *Sophia*, pivoting the ship nearly 180 degrees, and thrusting it backward off the reef and into the water. The ship's wireless operator, David Robinson, sent out a plea for help at 4:50: "Ship Foundering on Reef. Come at Once."[52] At 5:20 Robinson's final plea reached Captain Miller of the *Cedar*, which was standing by: "For God's sake hurry, the water is coming in my room." His final words were indecipherable.[53] As the *Sophia* slid off the reef, a large gash opened in the bottom of the hull, and icy water rushed into the engine and boiler rooms. The boilers exploded, destroying the lower decks and killing passengers in the vicinity. The oil spewed into the sea, coating passengers and entering their lungs as they gasped for air. Not a single person aboard the ship survived. Most watches were stopped at 5:50, an hour after Robinson's first plea went out.[54]

When the *Cedar* and the *King and Winge* approached the reef at 8:30 a.m. on October 26, rescue crews were stunned to see just twenty feet of the ship's foremast above the water. They gaped at the incomprehensible sight. The vessel had sat so securely on the reef the day before.[55]

Alaska governor Thomas Riggs and Canadian Pacific representatives coordinated the rescue effort from Juneau. Hope of finding survivors quickly faded. By Sunday night nine search vessels had recovered more than one hundred bodies in the waters and on the shores of Lynn Canal.[56] Governor Riggs ordered flags in Alaska flown at half-staff on October 28.[57]

By the first days of November more than 180 bodies had been recovered. Of the first 162 brought to Juneau, nearly all appeared to have died from suffocation after inhaling oil, rather than drowning.[58] On November 20 Governor Riggs discontinued the official search. The previous weeks' search efforts had found only a few bodies. The governor declared the tragedy an "act of God," while assuring the public that Captain Locke and the captains of other vessels in the area had done everything possible to save the passengers and crew. Riggs praised Captain Locke as one of the region's "most competent mariners."[59]

On October 26 word reached Fort Yukon that the *Princess Sophia* had foundered in Lynn Canal and that all passengers and crew had perished. Mr. and Mrs. Walter Harper were listed among the dead. Stuck refused to believe the report, choosing to believe what seemed more likely—that the list included the names of survivors.[60] Two days later the news arrived that 187 bodies, all wearing life vests, had been recovered.[61]

Governor Riggs wired Stuck on October 31, telling him that Walter's body had been identified. The following day a telegraph from Juneau confirmed that Frances Wells Harper's body had been identified, based on Stuck's description of her. That evening residents of Fort Yukon gathered for a memorial service for all those who had perished on the *Princess Sophia*. Stuck wrote in his diary a simple statement: "I made an address on Walter's character."[62]

At Stuck's request, Guilliam Wells agreed to Frances's burial beside her husband in the Juneau cemetery.[63] Loved ones took some comfort in knowing that the two were not separated in death.[64] Guilliam Wells wrote his son John, "Frances and Walter rest side by side [in Juneau] as they should, having both lived most useful lives, daring all sorts of dangers and hardships in the service of others."[65]

Their single headstone reads, "Here Lie the Bodies of Walter Harper and Frances Wells, His Wife, Drowned on the Princess Sophia, 25th October 1918. May Light Perpetually Shine on Them. They were Lovely and Pleasant in Their Lives, And in Death They Were Not Divided."[66] Stuck chose the words, drawing from 2 Samuel 1:23.

The sinking of the *Princess Sophia* was the worst disaster in Alaska history.[67] The loss of all onboard after nearly two days had passed with so many rescuers eager to help shocked the world. Some forty bodies were never recovered, including that of Capt. Leonard Locke.[68] The Canadian government held an inquiry into the disaster, to determine where fault lay. The findings were inconclusive, but Captain Locke and the Canadian Pacific Railway were cleared of blame. Central questions were: (1) Could passengers have been removed from the *Sophia* early in the day of October 24? (2) Had CPR management pressured Locke into delaying the transfer of passengers from the ship until rescue ships sent by the CPR arrived? The report concluded that "peril at sea" had caused the sinking of the ship. It called claims that passengers might have been removed safely pure conjecture and found that the Canadian Pacific had in no way restrained the captain. Many family members of victims expressed dissatisfaction with the conclusion.[69]

Epilogue

Harper's Legacy

WALTER AND FRANCES Harper's deaths shook the community of Fort Yukon deeply. Clara Burke wrote that the two were "as close to us as our own kin."[1] According to Guilliam Wells's children, he bore the loss of his first-born child courageously, though he "aged greatly" in the following week. He had told family members many times that "he never expected to see Frances again."[2] Perhaps Alaska had seemed such a distant, mysterious, and wild place that her father feared Frances would fall victim to some menace there. Perhaps he anticipated that she would be swept off her feet by a rugged Alaskan man. Perhaps he thought she would dedicate her life to serving Alaska Natives. Perhaps his imagination simply fell short of a happy reunion with his first-born child during his lifetime. Guilliam Wells took comfort in believing that everything possible had been done to rescue the passengers on the *Princess Sophia*. He wrote his son John, "All the people at Juneau, from the Governor of Alaska down, unite in saying that no blame can attach to the Captain of the steamer."[3]

Frances's family established the Frances Wells Harper Memorial Fund to support the construction of a solarium at St. Stephen's Hospital. Happy Burke had had some success in using the "sunshine method" to treat Alaska Native patients with tuberculosis, and Frances had championed the idea of building a sun porch.[4] The structure was named the Frances Wells Harper Solarium.

Walter's death was a staggering blow to Hudson Stuck, the greatest sorrow he had ever known.[5] He hoped that Walter's memory would inspire young boys to follow in his footsteps. Already

Johnny Fredson, Moses Cruikshank, Esaias George, Paul Guinness, and many other boys had looked up to him. Stuck promised to support a youngster at St. Mark's who had known Walter, if the boy "made good" there. "Tell him I will stand by him and find a useful career for him," he wrote missionary Frederick Drane, adding, "I will send Sam a picture of Walter; no boy could have a finer model."[6]

By December Stuck had found a sense of purpose in beginning to write a book on his and Walter's last winter circuit. The narrative of their final journey would be "a memorial of my dear boy."[7] Scribner's published *A Winter Circuit of Our Arctic Coast* in April 1920. Despite his grief and the chronic pain in his shoulder, Stuck also wrote a history of the Episcopal Church's work in Alaska.[8] He traveled and lectured extensively to raise funds for the mission work. As a final gift to the Athabascan people, Stuck waged a valiant campaign against the salmon canneries that threatened the survival of the Native peoples of Alaska's northern Interior and Copper River Basin.[9] The 1919 salmon runs on the Yukon were disastrous. Subsistence fish wheels along the river caught barely enough salmon to feed the people and animals from day to day. Nothing was left to dry for the long winter.[10]

Stuck's persistent lobbying led to a Bureau of Fisheries study that recommended halting commercial fishing at the mouths of the Yukon and Copper Rivers.[11] In 1924 Congress passed the White Act, which required 50 percent escapement of fish into every stream. The law allowed the survival of sufficient numbers of fish to sustain the people who lived on these rivers. Equally important, it permitted enough fish to return upriver to spawn, ensuring future generations of fish. Hudson Stuck's influence on the White Act was evident in the final bill.[12]

Four years before the act's passage, Stuck had died of pneumonia, in October 1920 at the age of fifty-six. He was buried at Fort Yukon. According to the missionary Frederick Drane, Stuck never recovered from Walter's death.[13]

During an era of convulsive socioeconomic and cultural change, Walter Harper stands out as an exemplar of Athabascan manhood. In his first sixteen years, under his mother's guidance and immersed in her traditional lifeways, he developed a strong Athabascan identity and an ethic of excellence. In the last decade of his life, as he became increasingly immersed in his father's culture, he maintained his self-knowledge. He achieved mastery in subsistence and mechanical skills as he steadily advanced in his Western education. In his final years he committed to mastering Western medical science so that he could serve the Athabascan people in his native homeland.

Harper's brilliant performance on Denali helped secure not only the expedition's success but the legacies of team members. The renown they enjoyed following the summit advanced their careers and influence. Stuck's and Karstens's reputations extended nationally, especially owing to Stuck's several publications and speaking tours on the expedition. National acclaim contributed to Karstens's appointment as the first superintendent of Mount McKinley National Park. Publicity about the Denali ascent boosted Stuck's ability to raise funds for the Alaska mission work and his effectiveness in lobbying for Native interests. At home in Alaska, Stuck increasingly relied on Walter as he fulfilled his duties as archdeacon.

Walter's celebrity status in Interior Alaska grew, not only as the first person to stand atop Denali but as Archdeacon Stuck's right-hand man. People from all walks of life admired him. He represented excellence, integrity, and resilience. When the future of Alaska Natives looked grim, he demonstrated the potential of Native youth to withstand both cultural and personal assaults and to maintain their strength and dignity.

Harper's self-knowledge, purposefulness, and faith stand as a paradigm for resilience in the global society of the twenty-first century, just as they did a century ago in Alaska. The ethos that Walter Harper embodied transcends time and culture. His self-restraint and positive attitude would win admirers and promote success anywhere. As young people today search for meaning in life amid a bewildering array of signals, Walter Harper's experience offers guidance and wisdom. This legacy is all the more remarkable in that he lived but twenty-five years.

Notes

Preface

1. Stuck, *Winter Circuit*, dedication.

2. Native Americans never constituted more than a small percentage of the diverse student population, however.

3. Hudson Stuck to John Wood, November 24, 1917, Stuck Correspondence, PECUSA, in APRCA.

Introduction

1. For more than a century North America's tallest mountain was officially named Mount McKinley, after President William McKinley. In 2015 President Barack Obama restored the peak's traditional Athabascan name: Denali, the Great One.

2. Walter Harper's resilience in the face of rapid cultural change corresponds well with the Canadian psychologist John W. Berry's model of acculturation, which advances integration as the healthiest response to cultural change. Berry, "Acculturation among Circumpolar Peoples." Maintaining one's birth identity as one adjusts to the dominant culture produces the least stress in the individual. Berry's model identifies three less adaptive cross-cultural responses: assimilation (abandoning one's traditional identity through immersion in mainstream culture), separation (rejecting mainstream culture), and marginalization (alienation from both the birth culture and the dominant culture), all of which he finds to be more problematic. In Walter's case, two strong father figures—a highly regarded biological father whom he never knew, and a loving, if authoritative, surrogate father—eased his integration into mainstream society.

1. Childhood and Adolescence

1. A family tree created by Harper's sister, Margaret Burke, in September 1961 lists Walter Harper's birthdate as December 22, 1892. Arthur Harper and Family Folder, Box 2, Yvonne Mozée Collection, Mozée Family Papers, in APRCA.

Walter apparently was not certain of the exact date of his birth. He celebrated it January 1, 1918, at Point Hope, Alaska.

2. Harper-Haines, *Cold River Spirits*, 29.

3. Westerners have historically called the Iñupiat "Eskimos." The term is still commonly used in Alaska to refer to both Yup'ik and Iñupiat (some Iñupiat and Yup'ik prefer it, because it is inclusive of both groups). Iñupiat is the plural noun form of the term. Iñupiaq is used for a single individual, for the adjectival form of the word, and for the language.

4. Ben Mozée to Yvonne Mozée, August 5, 1951, Walter Harper Folder, Box 2, Yvonne Mozée Collection, Mozée Family Papers, in APRCA. Ben Mozée wrote to his daughter Yvonne that Archdeacon Stuck had learned of Jenny's mixed heritage after he had published his books. Yvonne Mozée was Arthur and Jenny Harper's granddaughter and the niece of Walter Harper.

5. Yvonne Mozée, "Walter Harper," B (this piece by Mozée is paginated A–L), in appendix to Stuck, *Ascent of Denali*; J. S. Harper, "Arthur Harper," 1, paper written in University of Alaska history class of Professor Cecil Robe, November 1, 1941, in Folder 8, Box 7, Cecil Robe Collection, APRCA. On the paper is a note, apparently written by Professor Robe: "Writer consulted his father and his uncle for information about his grandfather." However, Johanna Harper, a great-great-granddaughter of Arthur Harper, says that the author of the paper can only have been Flora Jane Harper, whom family members called Jane.

6. J. S. Harper, "Arthur Harper," 1.

7. Brooks, *Blazing Alaska's Trails*, 313.

8. Brooks, *Blazing Alaska's Trails*, 313.

9. Ogilvie, *Early Days on the Yukon*, 95.

10. Mercier, *Recollections of the Youkon*, 13–14. Non-natives mispronounced Nuchelawoya, where Walter Harper was born, as "Nukelakayet."

11. Stuck, *Voyages on the Yukon*, 139–40.

12. Koyukuk Station, located on the Yukon River in western Alaska, was so named because a telegraph station operated there.

13. Yvonne Mozée, address delivered at the dedication of the Harper Lodge at Denali, May 28, 1987; and Yvonne Mozée, interview by Katherine (Einar) Anderson, April 14, 1981, both in Conversations: Transcripts Folder, Box 2, Yvonne Mozée Collection, Mozée Family Papers, in APRCA.

14. Murphy and Haigh, *Gold Rush Women*, 24. Mozée writes that Jenny and Arthur met "perhaps in 1878" at Nulato. Mozée, "Walter Harper," B.

15. Russell, "Journey up the Yukon River," 153.

16. Murphy and Haigh, *Gold Rush Women*, 85.

17. Mozée, "Walter Harper," B.

18. Mozée, "Walter Harper," C; Ogilvie, *Early Days on the Yukon*, 64.

19. Ogilvie, *Early Days on the Yukon*, 267.

20. Murphy and Haigh, *Gold Rush Women*, 84–85.

21. Russell, "Journey up the Yukon River," 147.

22. Stuck, *Voyages on the Yukon*, 139–40; Osgood, *Han Indians*, 79.

23. Russell, "Journey up the Yukon River," 152.

24. Naske and Slotnick, *Alaska*, 27, 30.

25. Naske and Slotnick, *Alaska*, 36–37.

26. Naske and Slotnick, *Alaska*, 52. The explorer was Lt. Lavrenty Zagoskin.

27. Naske and Slotnick, *Alaska*, 48–49; Turck and Turck, "Trading Posts along the Yukon River," 53.

28. Naske and Slotnick, *Alaska*, 58–60.

29. Yarborough, introduction to *Recollections of the Youkon*, xi, 5.

30. Osgood, *Han Indians*, 6, 8.

31. Yarborough, introduction to *Recollections of the Youkon*, xii. Moise Mercier managed the Fort Yukon post until 1874, when he returned to Canada.

32. Osgood, *Han Indians*, 12; Ogilvie, *Early Days on the Yukon*, 69.

33. Russell, "Journey up the Yukon River," 148.

34. Russell, "Journey up the Yukon River," 154.

35. Russell, "Journey up the Yukon River," 152.

36. Schwatka, *Along Alaska's Great River*, 306, 313–14.

37. Mercier, *Recollections of the Youkon*, 28. Among these prospectors was Joseph Ladue, who later became a trading partner with Harper (32).

38. Wright, *Prelude to Bonanza*, 133.

39. Brooks, *Blazing Alaska's Trails*, 317–18.

40. Ogilvie, *Early Days on the Yukon*, 87.

41. Naske and Slotnick, *Alaska*, 73.

42. Russell, "Journey up the Yukon River," 152.

43. William Ogilvie relates a story of such a case, when a man with a reputation for violence stole the butter supply of Arthur Harper's trading post. The assemblage of miners condemned the thief to banishment, largely because of his well-known reputation for violence. Ogilvie, *Early Days on the Yukon*, 297–99.

44. Berton, *Klondike Fever*.

45. Brooks, *Blazing Alaska's Trails*, 328, 331. The Fortymile River was so named because it was about forty miles from Fort Reliance. Osgood, *Han Indians*, 10.

46. Russell, "Journey up the Yukon River," 153.

47. Russell, "Journey up the Yukon River," 154. Russell was a member of an expedition sent by President Grover Cleveland to survey the U.S.-Canadian border at the 141st meridian.

48. Yukon Register of Historic Places, Government of Yukon website.

49. Brooks, *Blazing Alaska's Trails*, 333.

50. Brooks, *Blazing Alaska's Trails*, 333–34.

51. A letter written by "Jane" to Yvonne Mozée states, "She got tired of Arthur Harper sending each young child away to be educated." Jane to Yvonne Mozée, November 22, 1972, Arthur Harper and Family Folder, Box 2, Yvonne Mozée Collection, Mozée Family Papers, APRCA.

52. Murphy and Haigh, *Gold Rush Women*, 24.

53. Harper-Haines, *Cold River Spirits*, 29–30.

54. Ogilvie, *Early Days on the Yukon*, 115–17.

55. Mozée, "Walter Harper," C.

56. Brooks, *Blazing Alaska's Trails*, 341; Spurr, *Geology of the Yukon Gold District*, 124. William Ogilvie had recommended naming the town Dawson after the Canadian geologist and surveyor who made the first report on the Yukon's resources in 1887. Brooks, *Blazing Alaska's Trails*, 341.

57. Berton, *Klondike Fever*, epilogue.

58. Wright, *Prelude to Bonanza*, 292.

59. "Arthur Harper," *Klondike News* (Dawson NWT), April 1, 1898, in Arthur Harper Folder, Box 2, Yvonne Mozée Collection, Mozée Family Papers, in APRCA; Ogilvie, *Early Days on the Yukon*, 101–2.

60. Ogilvie, *Early Days on the Yukon*, 223.

61. Brady, *Report of the Governor* (1905), 31.

62. Brady, *Report of the Governor* (1905), 29–30; House Committee on the Territories, *Conditions in Alaska*, 117. With trachoma, granulations formed on the eyelids, rubbing against the eye, eventually making the cornea opaque. The eyelids turned in and rubbed against the eye as well. Poor hygienic conditions were the greatest barrier to ridding the young people of this disease. Discharge from the eyes transferred to the hands and clothes and infected others. House Committee on the Territories, *Conditions in Alaska*, 110–12.

63. Swineford, *Report of the Governor* (1886), 28–29.

64. Strong, *Report of the Governor* (1914), 16.

65. Strong, *Report of the Governor* (1917), 71.

66. Waller, *Discovery of the Germ*, 25.

67. Waller, *Discovery of the Germ*, 1–2.

68. Strong, *Report of the Governor* (1914), 16; Strong, *Report of the Governor* (1916), 50.

69. Knapp, *Report of the Governor* (1894), 6.

70. Nichols, *Alaska*, 160–62.

71. Flora Jane Harper to Yvonne Mozée, November 22, 1972, Arthur Harper and Family Folder, Box 2, Yvonne Mozée Collection, Mozée Family Papers, APRCA.

72. Hudson Stuck, "Walter's Recollections," transcribed by Stuck at Black Jack's Place in late November 1917, while on the winter circuit with Harper, after Harper had told Stuck a great deal about his childhood. Stuck, *Winter Circuit*, 42. The transcribed recollections were placed in Stuck's diary (i.e., his ongoing series of general diaries) at the end of December 1917. Rev. Hudson Stuck diaries, Episcopal Diocese of Alaska Records, APRCA. (General diary entries are hereafter cited as follows: Stuck diary and date.)

73. Alton, "July 1915."

74. Stuck, "Walter's Recollections."

75. Stuck, *Winter Circuit*, 42.

76. Stuck diary, April 13, 1911.

77. Murphy and Haigh, *Gold Rush Women*, 85.

78. Stuck, "Walter's Recollections."

79. Stuck, "Walter's Recollections."

80. Harper-Haines, *Cold River Spirits*, 40, 53–54, 84.

81. Harper-Haines, *Cold River Spirits*, 35–36, 55.

82. Harper-Haines, *Cold River Spirits*, 40, 53.

83. Margaret O'Farrell to Eleanor Wells, January 19, 1919, Wells Clan website, http://www.wellsclan.us/History/frances/AF25.htm.

84. Quoted in Mozée, "Walter Harper," E.

85. Harper-Haines, *Cold River Spirits*, 30.

86. Hopkins, *Rise of the Social Gospel*, 3–6.

87. Donovan, *Different Call*, 11.

88. Dorsey, "Episcopal Women Missionaries."

89. Prucha, *Great Father*, 609–10.

90. Waggoner, *Missionaries in Alaska*, 63. As new denominations moved into the territory, the original 1880 agreement was amended. The Comity Agreement drew criticism for being rigid, arbitrary, and potentially self-serving, like earlier efforts by Western countries to colonize Africa and Asia. However, churches and mission societies generally followed it for several decades (65). New denominations entering the territory in the mid-twentieth century generally ignored the Comity Agreement, and it became less relevant as radio coverage and airplane travel increased. Nevertheless the influence of the denominations that built missions in the half century following Alaska's purchase continues.

91. Stuck, *Alaskan Missions of the Episcopal Church*, 13.

92. Mercier, *Recollections of the Youkon*, 50–51.

93. Stuck, *Alaskan Missions of the Episcopal Church*, 2–3.

94. Krauss, *Alaska Native Languages*, 21.

95. Stuck, *Alaskan Missions of the Episcopal Church*, 2–3.

96. Prevost traveled Outside in 1894, married, and brought his wife Louise back with him. Stuck, *Alaskan Missions of the Episcopal Church*, 42–44.

97. Stuck, *Alaskan Missions of the Episcopal Church*, 42–43; Krauss, *Alaska Native Languages*, 21.

98. Young, *Hall Young of Alaska*, 259 (original emphasis).

99. Krauss, *Alaska Native Languages*, 24.

100. Stuck, *Winter Circuit*, 8.

101. Dean, *Breaking Trail*, 32–33.

102. Dean, *Breaking Trail*, 171.

103. Stuck to Wood, February 27, 1917, Stuck Correspondence, PECUSA, in APRCA.

104. Dean, *Breaking Trail*, 184.

105. Stuck, "New Beginnings at Fort Yukon," third page (no visible page numbers).

106. Stuck diary, July 9, 1910.

107. Episcopal Diocese of Alaska, *Century of Faith*, 18, 27.

108. Dorsey, "Episcopal Women Missionaries," 253. By 1914 the missions at Chena Village, Rampart, and Circle City were vacant (254).

109. This pattern of Alaska Natives settling close to missions occurred throughout Alaska.

110. Dorsey, "Episcopal Women Missionaries," 308.

111. Stuck to Wood, December 28, 1910, Stuck Correspondence, PECUSA, in APRCA; Stuck, *Voyages on the Yukon*, 145.

112. Rowe, statement in *Hearings before the Committee on the Territories*, 7–8.

113. Simeone, *Rifles, Blankets, and Beads*, 28.

114. Simeone, *Rifles, Blankets, and Beads*, 24.

115. St. John's-in-the-Wilderness lay at the confluence of the Alatna and Koyukuk Rivers in northwestern Alaska.

116. Stuck, "Third Cruise of the Pelican," 400.

117. Stuck, *Winter Circuit*, 34.

118. Stuck to John Wood, January 1, 1910, Stuck Correspondence, PECUSA, in APRCA.

119. "Strategic Point," 11–12.

120. Stuck, *Alaskan Missions of the Episcopal Church*, 127.

121. "Strategic Point," 11–12; "Future," 2.

122. Betticher, "Tanana Valley Mission," 56; Stuck, *Alaskan Missions of the Episcopal Church*, 127.

123. Betticher, "Tanana Valley Mission," 56; "Annie Cragg Farthing," 10.

124. Betticher, "Tortella Hall," 12–13.

125. Stuck to Bishop Arthur S. Lloyd, November 16, 1918, Stuck Correspondence, PECUSA, in APRCA; Stuck diary, February 15, 1910.

126. Stuck diary, February 11, 1910.

127. Dorsey, "Episcopal Women Missionaries," 154. In other locations as well the Episcopal Church gave Alaska Natives windows and doors when they built cabins close to missions. Stuck, "Third Cruise of the Pelican," 399.

128. Grider, "St. Mark's Mission, Nenana," 41–43.

129. Grider, "St. Mark's Mission, Nenana," 42–44.

130. Cruikshank, *Life I've Been Living*, 22.

131. Cruikshank, *Life I've Been Living*, 23, 25.

132. Stuck, *Alaskan Missions of the Episcopal Church*, 128–29.

133. Stuck, *Alaskan Missions of the Episcopal Church*, 131–33.

134. Stuck, *Ten Thousand Miles*, 245.

135. Stuck, *Alaskan Missions of the Episcopal Church*, 133.

136. Stuck, *Ten Thousand Miles*, 315.

137. Stuck to Wood, December 28, 1910, Stuck Correspondence, PECUSA, in APRCA.

2. On the River and on the Trail

1. Cruikshank, *Life I've Been Living*, 26.
2. Drane, "Death of Archdeacon Stuck," 5.
3. Dean, *Breaking Trail*, 129.
4. Dean, *Breaking Trail*, 222–23.
5. Dean, *Breaking Trail*, 129–33.
6. Dean, *Breaking Trail*, 132.
7. Stuck diary, July 14, 1910.
8. Stuck diary, June 1, 1911.
9. Stuck, *Ten Thousand Miles*, 315–16.
10. Stuck diary, March 26, 1911.
11. Stuck diary, July 27, 1910.
12. Stuck to Wood, December 28, 1910, Stuck Correspondence, PECUSA, in APRCA.
13. Hudson Stuck, "Vale Walter Harper," *Fairbanks Daily News Miner*, December 4, 1918.
14. Stuck diary, June 27, 1911. The Episcopal mission society and specific churches in the states provided the doctors' salaries and medical supplies.
15. Stuck, *Alaskan Missions of the Episcopal Church*, 119–20.
16. Stuck, "Third Cruise of the Pelican," 401.
17. See Burke, *Doctor Hap*, for a rich account of the couple's thirty years of service in Fort Yukon.
18. Grafton Burke to Wood, October 30, 1917, Burke Correspondence, PECUSA, in APRCA.
19. Stuck, "Third Cruise of the Pelican," 402; Stuck diary, August 21, 1910.
20. Stuck diary, April 20, 1911.
21. Cole, "One Man's Purgatory," 86.
22. Stuck, *Voyages on the Yukon*, 121.
23. Stuck, *Voyages on the Yukon*, 121–22.
24. Stuck diary, August 31, 1910.
25. Stuck diary, May 26, 1909.
26. Stuck diary, April 10, 17, 1911.
27. Stuck diary, September 4, 22 (quotation), 1910.
28. Stuck, "Third Cruise of the Pelican," 397.
29. Stuck diary, March 6, 1910.
30. Stuck diary, May 27, 1911.
31. Stuck diary, February 6, 7, 1913.
32. Stuck diary, March 6, April 15, 1911.
33. Stuck diary, March 9, April 16, 1911.
34. Stuck diary, April 14, 1911.
35. Stuck diary, February 13, 1911.
36. Stuck diary, April 18, 1911.

37. Stuck diary, November 17, 1910.

38. Stuck diary, November 19, 1910.

39. Stuck diary, November 20–21, 29, 1910.

40. Stuck to John Wood, December 28, 1910, Stuck Correspondence, PECUSA, in APRCA.

41. Stuck diary, December 22, 1910.

42. Stuck to Wood, December 28, 1910.

43. Stuck diary, March 14, 19, 31, 1911.

44. Stuck diary, February 2, 1911. Stuck's final comment for the day was "But oh! how weary these road-house evenings are!" They were staying overnight at Fish Lake Roadhouse. On March 7, 1911, he wrote of the "wretched poor grub" at Berry's roadhouse: "We fare much better when we camp & I think this will be about our last roadhouse, for the expense is enormous."

45. Stuck diary, March 8, 9, 1911.

46. Stuck diary, February 24, 1911.

47. Stuck, *Ten Thousand Miles*, 299.

48. Stuck diary, February 21, 1911.

49. Stuck to Wood, December 28, 1910.

50. Stuck diary, April 14, 23, 1911.

51. Stuck, *Winter Circuit*, 9.

52. Butts, "Muscular Christianity and the Children's Story." Later readers would recognize the ethnocentrism in the books and the imperialistic values they endorsed. At the time, however, they reflected dominant mainstream views in Great Britain and North America. Henty and others who wrote in this genre presented these virtues as fundamentally British. They promoted the British Empire as ideally positioned to spread these values. The ethnocentric views expressed in some of them (e.g., British superiority and presumed inferiority of Africans, Natives, and other races) later generated controversy. PBS's online biography of Henty explains, "To the modern reader, Henty's books are notable for their hearty imperialism, undisguised racism, and jingoistic patriotism. To Henty's readers, though, devoted to his books in large numbers until World War II, British history was turned into adventure, and many boys learned that Great Britain became great and boys became men—to borrow from another of Henty's titles—'by sheer pluck.'" "G. A. Henty 1832–1902."

53. Stuck, *Winter Circuit*, 9–11, 17.

54. Stuck diary, April 25, May 1, 9, 1911.

55. Stuck diary, May 9–10, 1911.

56. Stuck diary, May 11, 12, 14–15, 1911.

57. Stuck diary, May 23, 1911.

58. Stuck diary, June 2, 1911.

59. Stuck, "Along Alaska's Great River," 638.

60. Stuck diary, June 6, 1911. On July 2, 1911, Stuck noted in his diary that Judge Overfield "seems to have sold out to the liquor men." A few weeks later

Stuck spoke at length with Overfield at Iditarod City, however, and he "came away with a much more favourable opinion of him than [he] had before." Stuck diary, July 27, 1911.

61. Stuck, "Along Alaska's Great River," 638–39.

62. Stuck diary, June 7, 13, 1911.

63. Stuck diary, June 21, 1911.

64. Stuck diary, August 8, 1912.

65. Stuck diary, June 25, 26, 1911.

66. Stuck, "Along Alaska's Great River," 641.

67. Stuck diary, January 1, 1912.

68. Stuck diary, July 17, 1911.

69. Walker, *Seventymile Kid*, 176.

70. Stuck diary, July 26, 30, August 4, 1911.

71. Stuck, "Along Alaska's Great River," 643–44.

72. Stuck, "Along Alaska's Great River," 640.

73. Stuck diary, August 26, 1911.

74. Stuck, "Along Alaska's Great River," 642.

75. Stuck diary, September 17, 1911.

76. Stuck, "Along Alaska's Great River," 644.

77. Stuck diary, January 16, 21, 1912.

78. Stuck diary, February 4, 1912.

79. Stuck diary, February 17, 1912.

80. Stuck diary, March 26, 1912.

81. Stuck diary, April 1, 2, 3, 1912.

82. Stuck diary, April 10, 14, 1912.

83. Stuck diary, April 24, May 10, 27, 1912.

84. Stuck diary, May 30, 1912.

85. Stuck, *Voyages on the Yukon*, 305–6; Stuck diary, June 25, 1912.

86. Stuck diary, June 26, 1912.

87. Stuck diary, July 1, 1912.

88. Stuck, *Alaskan Missions of the Episcopal Church*, 142–44. Bishop Rowe abandoned plans to build a hospital at Iditarod in the wake of the miners' exodus.

89. Stuck diary, July 21, 1912.

90. Stuck diary, August 7, 12, 13, 14, 1912.

91. Stuck diary, August 23, 1912.

92. Stuck diary, September 2–5, 1912.

93. Arthur Harper Family Record, compiled by Margaret Harper Burke, September 1961, Arthur Harper and Family Folder, Box 2, Yvonne Mozée Collection, Mozée Family Papers, APRCA.

94. Stuck, "Along Alaska's Great River," 642.

95. Stuck diary, September 19–20, 1912.

96. Stuck diary, September 20–22, 1912.

97. Stuck, *Alaskan Missions of the Episcopal Church*, 137–38.

98. Stuck diary, January 30–31, 1913.

99. Dorsey, "Episcopal Women Missionaries," 308.

100. Stuck diary, February 2, 1913, and Official Acts 1913 (at end of diary).

101. By 1920 Sam and Louise's financial difficulties forced them to send their four oldest children, ages ten, eight, six, and four, to a Catholic Church–run boarding school in Chemawa, Oregon. They remained there until 1929, when the school closed as the Great Depression began. Harper-Haines, *Cold River Spirits*, 85. Alaska Native children had been attending the Chemawa school and the Carlisle industrial school for Native Americans for decades. They had the same right to attend these schools as other Native American children. Memorandum for the Governor, prepared in the office of the secretary of the interior, published in Brady, *Report of the Governor* (1905), 37. It was later, in the 1930s and 1940s, that the U.S. Bureau of Education built numerous boarding schools in Alaska and began forcefully removing Native children from their homes to be educated and assimilated. The negative effects of this policy continue to be felt among Alaska Natives today, although the practice ended in the 1960s. La Belle and Smith, "Boarding School," 4.

102. Stuck diary, February 19, 1913.

103. Stuck, "Flying Visit to the Tanana Crossing," 84; Stuck diary, March 1, 3–9, 1913.

3. Ascent of Denali

1. Sheldon, *Wilderness of Denali*, 389.

2. Moore, *Mt. McKinley*, 1.

3. Moore, *Mt. McKinley*, 8; Stuck, *Ascent of Denali*, 157–58 (quote). The prospector William Dickey named the mountain for Ohio senator William McKinley, a candidate for president in 1896. Some years later a U.S. Army officer named its companion peak Mount Foraker in honor of Joseph Foraker, also an Ohio politician. Stuck, *Ascent of Denali*, viii. This pattern of explorers naming landmarks for notable individuals with no relation to the place dated from centuries earlier. When Congress created Mount McKinley National Park in 1917, it officially recognized the name Mount McKinley. Following a century-long effort to have the mountain's traditional name restored, President Barak Obama announced in August 2015 the renaming of the peak as Denali.

4. Wickersham, *Old Yukon*, 217.

5. Wickersham, *Old Yukon*, 186.

6. Mazel, *Pioneering Ascents*, 7, 9.

7. Stuck, *Ascent of Denali*, 4.

8. Stuck, *Ascent of Denali*, 83.

9. Wickersham, *Old Yukon*, 186.

10. Wickersham, *Old Yukon*, 224.

11. "Sourdough" was a term of respect for a crusty, experienced miner on the frontier.

12. Taylor's and McGonagall's accounts are cited in Moore, *Mt. McKinley*, 143–53 (Taylor's account), 188n (McGonagall's account).

13. Stuck, *Ascent of Denali*, 17–18.

14. Stuck, *Ascent of Denali*, 178.

15. Moore, *Mt. McKinley*, 107.

16. Stuck, *Ascent of Denali*, 3–4 (quotation on 3).

17. Stuck diary, March 23, 1911. Upon encountering Karstens and another man named Snowe on the trail on this date, Stuck wrote in his diary, "These are two of my best friends amongst the men of Alaska."

18. Stuck, *Ascent of Denali*, 5.

19. Walker, *Seventymile Kid*, 109. Sheldon collected thousands of wildlife specimens in the region and donated them to the Smithsonian Institution.

20. Harry P. Karstens to Mr. and Mrs. Sheldon, n.d. [but likely written in the fall or winter of 1913], Folder 2, Box 2, Charles Sheldon Papers, APRCA. "Sheldon 'O' Sheldon why dident [sic] you come in and make that trip as you suggested doing," Karstens wrote (1–2).

21. Walker, *Seventymile Kid*, 165.

22. Walker, *Seventymile Kid*, 174–75.

23. E. Karstens, "Mike Sfraga Talks with Eugene Karstens June 24, 1992."

24. Stuck, *Ascent of Denali*, 6.

25. Mackenzie, *Wolf Smeller*, 30, 34, 37.

26. Stuck diary, April 17, 1911.

27. Mackenzie, *Wolf Smeller*, 41–42. Esaias George's birthdate is given as January 20, 1896, at University of Alaska Museum of the North's *Denali Legacy* exhibit, in the "Finalizing the Team" panel, viewed June 3, 2013.

28. Mackenzie, *Wolf Smeller*, 3.

29. Stuck, *Ascent of Denali*, 7.

30. For instance, Robert Dunn's depiction of the 1903 climb led by Dr. Frederick Cook so openly related the bickering among the men that it caused a scandal. Dunn, *Shameless Diary of an Explorer*.

31. Stuck, *Ascent of Denali*, 6.

32. Stuck diary, December 2, 1917.

33. Karstens to Mr. and Mrs. Sheldon, n.d.

34. Stuck, *Ascent of Denali*, 11.

35. "Will Try to Scale M'Kinley's Heights," *Fairbanks Daily Times*, March 13, 1913.

36. Hudson Stuck Climbing Journal, March 24, 1913, Box 4, Hudson Stuck Papers 1902–20, APRCA. The American Geographical Society in New York City holds Stuck's original journal for 1913. (All of Stuck's other diaries are in the Episcopal Diocese of Alaska Records [MF 88, 91], APRCA.)

37. Stuck, *Ascent of Denali*, 12; Karstens to Mr. and Mrs. Sheldon, n.d., 4.

38. Walker, *Seventymile Kid*, 194–95. Walker writes that Karstens transported "forty-five hundred pounds" of supplies to Diamond City.

39. Stuck Climbing Journal, March 24, 1913.

40. Stuck, *Ascent of Denali*, 12.

41. Walker, *Seventymile Kid*, 193; Stuck, *Ascent of Denali*, 8–9, 13.

42. Stuck, *Ascent of Denali*, 15–16; Walker, *Seventymile Kid*, 209–11.

43. Stuck, *Ascent of Denali*, 17; Karstens to Mr. and Mrs. Sheldon, n.d., 9.

44. Stuck Climbing Journal, April 1, 1913.

45. Stuck Climbing Journal, April 8, 1913.

46. Stuck, *Ascent of Denali*, 18; Karstens to Mr. and Mrs. Sheldon, n.d., 9, 29.

47. Stuck, *Ascent of Denali*, 19. Stuck worked at cooking the meat, but he never hunted wild game.

48. Mackenzie, *Wolf Smeller*, 40; Stuck, *Ascent of Denali*, 18.

49. Walker, *Seventymile Kid*, 213; Stuck Climbing Journal, April 4, 1913.

50. Dean, *Breaking Trail*, 169–70.

51. Walker, *Seventymile Kid*, 110.

52. Karstens to Mr. and Mrs. Sheldon, n.d., 13. For instance, in his diary on April 23 and 25, 1913, and in Karstens's undated letter to Mr. and Mrs. Sheldon, he refers to Stuck as "deacon" or "the deacon."

53. Karstens to Mr. and Mrs. Sheldon, n.d., 12. This undated letter Karstens wrote to the Sheldons reveals far more than his diary; it includes his assessments of Stuck's failures. Though at thirty-four pages it is far less detailed than Stuck's *Ascent of Denali*, it marvelously complements Stuck's account in the book and the diaries of the men. He provides rich logistical detail, as well as a frank, in fact brutally honest, perspective on the tensions among the men during the ascent.

54. Walker, *Seventymile Kid*, 167.

55. U.S. Joint Federal-State Commission on Policies and Programs Affecting Alaska Natives, *Alaska Natives Commission Final Report*, 155–56. Not only Athabascans but Alaska Native peoples generally subscribe to the values of nonconfrontation and noninterference, which discourage individuals from confronting others about their behaviors, from meddling in others' business, and from giving others unsolicited advice.

56. Stuck, *Ascent of Denali*, 24.

57. Karstens to Mr. and Mrs. Sheldon, n.d., 15.

58. Walter Harper to Margaret Harper O'Farrell Burke, April 14, 1913, Walter Harper Folder, Box 2, Yvonne Mozée Collection, Mozée Family Papers, APRCA.

59. Mackenzie, *Wolf Smeller*, 44, 47.

60. Karstens to Mr. and Mrs. Sheldon, n.d., 15 (quotation).

61. Stuck Climbing Journal, April 19, 1913.

62. Tatum, 1913 Climbing Journal, April 19, 1913; Stuck Climbing Journal, April 25, 1913.

63. Karstens, 1913 Climbing Journal, April 20, 22, 1913.

64. Walter Harper 1913 Climbing Journal, April 26, 1913, in Walter Harper Diary Folder, Box 2, Yvonne Mozée Collection, Mozée Family Papers, APRCA.

65. Karstens, 1913 Climbing Journal, April 25, 1913. Karstens wrote this note on a "Memoranda" page at the end of the journal, indicating that it was writ-

ten on April 25. His writing is difficult to read, and I am not certain of the word *siwashy* nor is the final word clear, but the context suggests Karstens meant he would not receive the credit he deserved. "Siwash" was a term used in reference to mixed-race individuals in the north. As such it had negative connotations. The term also referred to camping out, in the manner of Alaska Natives. Exactly what Karstens meant in describing Stuck's photography as "siwashy" is uncertain, but the comment clearly expresses negative sentiment.

66. Stuck Climbing Journal, April 16, 1913.

67. Stuck Climbing Journal, April 26, 1913.

68. Stuck Climbing Journal, April 28, 1913.

69. Karstens, 1913 Climbing Journal, April 21, 1913; Stuck Climbing Journal, April 21, 1913.

70. Harper 1913 Climbing Journal, April 20, 27, May 7, 1913.

71. Stuck wrote in *Ascent of Denali* that the incident took place halfway up the glacier. Karstens related to Sheldon that it occurred at 11,500 feet at the head of Muldrow Glacier. Stuck, *Ascent of Denali*, 32; Karstens to Mr. and Mrs. Sheldon, 16.

72. H. Karstens, "Here's a Pioneer," interview in Fairbanks, 1950s.

73. Stuck, *Ascent of Denali*, 33–34.

74. Karstens to Mr. and Mrs. Sheldon, n.d., 16.

75. Mackenzie, *Wolf Smeller*, 47.

76. Karstens to Mr. and Mrs. Sheldon, n.d., 18.

77. Stuck, *Ascent of Denali*, 36, 37.

78. Karstens, 1913 Climbing Journal, May 9, 1913.

79. Browne, *Conquest of Mount McKinley*, 356–58.

80. Stuck Climbing Journal, May 9, 1913.

81. Stuck, *Ascent of Denali*, 42–43.

82. Karstens to Mr. and Mrs. Sheldon, n.d., 18–19.

83. Harper 1913 Climbing Journal, May 11, 1913.

84. Stuck, *Ascent of Denali*, 79.

85. Stuck, *Ascent of Denali*, 53, 79.

86. Stuck, *Ascent of Denali*, 26.

87. Stuck Climbing Journal, May 19, 1913.

88. Karstens to Mr. and Mrs. Sheldon, n.d., 11.

89. Stuck, *Ascent of Denali*, 34, 57.

90. Karstens to Mr. and Mrs. Sheldon, n.d., 17.

91. Tatum, 1913 Climbing Journal, May 18–19, 1913.

92. Stuck Climbing Journal, May 22, 1913; Tatum, 1913 Climbing Journal, May 22, 1913; Stuck, *Ascent of Denali*, 185.

93. Harper 1913 Climbing Journal, May 18, 1913; Stuck, *Ascent of Denali*, 44.

94. Harper 1913 Climbing Journal, May 25, 1913.

95. Stuck Climbing Journal, May 25, 26, 1913.

96. Tatum, 1913 Climbing Journal, May 27, 28, 1913.

97. Stuck Climbing Journal, May 27, 1913.

98. Karstens to Mr. and Mrs. Sheldon, n.d., 20.

99. Stuck Climbing Journal, May 27, 1913.

100. Harper 1913 Climbing Journal, May 29, 1913; Stuck, *Ascent of Denali*, 77.

101. Harper 1913 Climbing Journal, May 31, June 1, 1913.

102. Stuck, *Ascent of Denali*, 85.

103. Karstens to Mr. and Mrs. Sheldon, n.d., 24. Karstens wrote Sheldon that he was too angry to take a portion of Stuck's gear.

104. Stuck, *Ascent of Denali*, 85.

105. Stuck Climbing Journal, June 3, 1913.

106. Stuck, *Ascent of Denali*, 87.

107. Harper 1913 Climbing Journal, June 3, 1913.

108. Karstens, 1913 Climbing Journal, June 4, 1913.

109. Stuck Climbing Journal, June 4, 1913. Karstens reported, "Deacon having hard time breathing but we will get him there somehow." Karstens, 1913 Climbing Journal, June 4, 1913.

110. Stuck, *Ascent of Denali*, 93. The sourdough would not ferment at that altitude, and they had used all their baking powder.

111. Harper 1913 Climbing Journal, June 7, 1913.

112. Stuck, *Ascent of Denali*, 92–93; Karstens to Mr. and Mrs. Sheldon, n.d., 25.

113. Karstens, 1913 Climbing Journal, June 7, 1913.

114. Harper 1913 Climbing Journal, June 7, 1913.

115. Stuck, *Ascent of Denali*, 94.

116. Stuck, *Ascent of Denali*, 94–96.

117. Stuck, "On Denali (Mount McKinley)," 24.

118. Harper 1913 Climbing Journal, June 7, 1913.

119. Stuck, *Ascent of Denali*, 116.

120. Stuck, *Ascent of Denali*, 99.

121. Harper 1913 Climbing Journal, June 7, 1913.

122. Stuck, *Ascent of Denali*, 146–47.

123. Altitude chart, from Higher Peak Altitude Training, accessed September 1, 2014.

124. Coombs, *Denali's West Buttress*, 129.

125. Stuck, *Ascent of Denali*, 102.

126. Stuck, "On Denali (Mount McKinley)," 23, 25.

127. Stuck, *Ascent of Denali*, 105–6.

128. Harper 1913 Climbing Journal, June 7, 8, 1913.

129. Stuck, *Ascent of Denali*, 108–9.

130. John T. Moutoux, "Ascending the Steep Roof of the Continent Just to 'Look Out the Windows of Heaven,'" *Knoxville News-Sentinel*, May 22, 1932.

131. Stuck, *Ascent of Denali*, 119.

132. Stuck, *Ascent of Denali*, 125.

133. Stuck, *Ascent of Denali*, 123–25; Karstens to Mr. and Mrs. Sheldon, n.d. 29.

134. Stuck, *Ascent of Denali*, 126–28.

135. Mackenzie, *Wolf Smeller*, 47.

136. Stuck, *Ascent of Denali*, 128.

137. Mackenzie, *Wolf Smeller*, 56–57.

138. Campbell, "Granddaughter's Tale," 34–35.

139. Stuck, *Ascent of Denali*, 131; Stuck Climbing Journal, June 11, 1913.

140. Stuck, *Ascent of Denali*, 131–32.

141. Stuck Climbing Journal, June 12, 1913.

142. Karstens to Mr. and Mrs. Sheldon, n.d., 30.

143. Stuck, *Ascent of Denali*, 140.

144. "Alaska Churchman's Party Reaches Top of Mount McKinley," *Seattle Times*, June 20, 1913.

145. Tatum, 1913 Climbing Journal, June 7, 1913. Only the whereabouts of Karstens's pin is known. It lies in the Harry Karstens Collection with the American Alpine Club in Golden, Colorado.

146. "Communication," *Fairbanks Daily Times*, August 3, 1913.

147. Stuck, *Ascent of Denali*, 21–22.

148. Dean, *Breaking Trail*, 184.

149. Walker, *Seventymile Kid*, 284.

150. E. Karstens, "Mike Sfraga talks with Eugene Karstens June 24, 1992."

151. Dorsey, "Episcopal Women Missionaries," 273, citing *Alaskan Churchman* 10, no. 4 (August 1916): 102. Esaias George died in December 1920 at Stevens Village (death certificate number 941, Alaska Division of Vital Statistics).

152. John Wood to Grafton Burke, November 21, 1917, Burke Correspondence, PECUSA, in APRCA.

153. Tatum, 1913 Climbing Journal (note addressed to Archdeacon Stuck, placed at the back of the journal).

154. Tatum, Diary, June 7, 1922.

155. Tatum, Diary, September 11, 1922.

156. John Shearer, "Knoxvillian Robert Tatum Was among First to Climb Mt. McKinley," *Knoxville News-Sentinel*, June 11, 2013, http://www.knoxnews.com /news/local-news/knoxvillian-robert-tatum-was-among-first-to.

157. Stuck, *Ascent of Denali*, 186–87. In 1987 Princess Tours opened a hotel in Denali National Park. It named the facility Harper Lodge. A formal grand opening celebrated Walter Harper's life and accomplishments. His niece, Yvonne Mozée, the daughter of his beloved sister Jessie, presented a short life history of her uncle. Frank Riley, "Harper Lodge Opens in Denali Park," *Los Angeles Times*, June 28, 1987. In 2014 the National Park Service renamed its ranger station at Talkeetna the Walter Harper Talkeetna Ranger Station.

4. Mount Hermon School

1. Tatum, 1913 Climbing Journal, June 30, 1913.

2. Stuck Climbing Journal, July 26, 1913.

3. Stuck Climbing Journal, August 3, 1913.

4. Jessie had earned a diploma from San Francisco State Teachers College in December 1910. San Francisco State Teachers College statement, October 19, 1922, Aunt Margaret File, Box 2, Yvonne Mozée Collection, Mozée Family Papers, APRCA. I could find no indication of when Margaret earned her teaching credentials.

5. Yvonne Mozée, interview by Bill Schneider and Karen Brewster, September 11, 2003, Pioneering Women Oral History Project, Oral History #2000-07-14, APRCA. Both Jessie and Margaret divorced their first husbands and later remarried.

6. Harper-Haines, *Cold River Spirits*, 80, 82.

7. Stuck, *Ten Thousand Miles*, 316.

8. Stuck to Sheldon, September 22, 1913, Folder 14, Box 3, Charles Sheldon Papers, APRCA.

9. Hough, *Alaskans in the Far North*, 238.

10. Hough, *Alaskans in the Far North*, 214.

11. Stuck Climbing Journal, August 11, 1913.

12. Stuck Climbing Journal, August 21, 1913. Alaskans refer to the narrow strip of mountainous land and islands in southeastern Alaska that borders Canada as the "panhandle."

13. Coates and Morrison, *Sinking of the "Princess Sophia,"* 48.

14. Stuck Climbing Journal, August 21, 1913; "Alaska Steamer Sinks; 32 Drown," *New York Times*, August 19, 1913.

15. Lloyd, "Loss of the ss State of California."

16. Stuck Climbing Journal, August 25, 1913.

17. Stuck Climbing Journal, September 3, 1913.

18. Gatlin, "Interesting People," 38–39.

19. Stuck Climbing Journal, September 4, 1913.

20. Stuck Climbing Journal, September 5, 6, 1913; *The Hermonite*, 2 (from undated Mount Hermon publication in Walter Harper File, #7697MH, NMHA).

21. Application for Admission, Mount Hermon School, Walter Harper, Walter Harper File, #7697MH, NMHA.

22. Form dated November 26, 1913, Walter Harper File, #7697MH, NMHA.

23. Stuck to Charles Sheldon, Folder 14, Box 3, Charles Sheldon Papers, APRCA.

24. Hamilton, *Lift Thine Eyes*, 40.

25. Catalog of Mount Hermon School 1913–14, no. 81 (January 17, 1914), 24, 39, Walter Harper Folder, Box 2, Yvonne Mozée Collection, Mozée Family Papers, APRCA.

26. Carter, *So Much to Learn*, 21.

27. Catalog of Mount Hermon School 1913–14, 23; Askins, "Bridging Cultures," 104, 106.

28. Hamilton, *Lift Thine Eyes*, 31.

29. Prucha, *Great Father*, 695–96.

30. Pratt, "Advantages of Mingling Indians with Whites," 260–61.

31. Prucha, *Great Father*, 697, 699.

32. Askins, "Bridging Cultures," 111–12, 114, 116.

33. Askins, "Bridging Cultures," xii, 14–15.

34. Askins, "Bridging Cultures," 128–30.

35. Mackenzie, *Wolf Smeller*, 85.

36. Moses Cruikshank, interview by William Schneider; Askins, "Bridging Cultures," 116. "John Fredson" was actually Johnny Fred. In the process of applying for the youth's admission to Mount Hermon, Hudson Stuck changed his last name to Fredson, which he thought would ease his adjustment at Mount Hermon.

37. Stuck to John Wood, December 28, 1910, Stuck Correspondence, PECUSA, in APRCA.

38. Catalog of Mount Hermon School 1913–14, 7, 20.

39. Stuck to Cutler, January 15, 1916, Walter Harper File, #7697MH, NMHA.

40. Stuck to Cutler, December 6, 1913, Walter Harper File, #7697MH, NMHA.

41. Hamilton, *Lift Thine Eyes*, 101.

42. Catalog of Mount Hermon School 1913–14, 59–60.

43. Mackenzie, *Wolf Smeller*, 81.

44. Application for Admission, Mount Hermon School.

45. Walter Harper to Jessie Harper Mozée, September 28, 1913, Walter Harper Folder, Box 2, Yvonne Mozée Collection, Mozée Family Papers, APRCA. Stuck paid for music lessons for Walter and for Arthur Wright. Stuck to Cutler, September 13, 1913, Walter Harper File, #7697MH, NMHA.

46. Harper to Mozée, February 13, 1914, Walter Harper Folder, Box 2, Yvonne Mozée Collection, Mozée Family Papers, APRCA; Moses Cruikshank, interview by William Schneider.

47. Mackenzie, *Wolf Smeller*, 86.

48. Hamilton, *Lift Thine Eyes*, 30–31.

49. Harper to Mozée, September 28, 1913.

50. Carter, *So Much to Learn*, 85.

51. Carter, *So Much to Learn*, 131.

52. Carter, *So Much to Learn*, 167–68.

53. Carter, *So Much to Learn*, 123.

54. Hamilton, *Lift Thine Eyes*, 122; Carter, *So Much to Learn*, 131.

55. Hamilton, *Lift Thine Eyes*, 117.

56. Copy of *Hermonite*, n.d., 2, in Walter Harper File, #7697MH, NMHA.

57. Harper to Mozée, November 9, 1913, Walter Harper Folder, Box 2, Yvonne Mozée Collection, Mozée Family Papers, APRCA.

58. Sheldon to Cutler, October 20, 1913, Walter Harper File, #7697MH, NMHA.

59. Harper to Mozée, November 9, 1913.

60. Hamilton, *Lift Thine Eyes*, 204.

61. Hamilton, *Lift Thine Eyes*, 147.

62. Thomas Reed to John Chapman, November 13, 1913, Thomas Reed File, #7822, NMHA.

63. Dean, *Breaking Trail*, 223. Wright, along with his wife Myrtle, a mission-

ary nurse whom he married in 1922, remained in church service for decades. Al Wright, interviewed by Bill Schneider, June 15, 2012, Oral History Recording #2012-08-03 pt. 2, APRCA.

64. Harper to Mozée, February 13, 1914.

65. Harper to Mozée, February 13, 1914. "Deuce" would have been strong language for Harper, as it meant "devil." By anyone else's definition this would not have been strong language, but Harper never used foul language.

66. Harper to Mozée, April 18, 1914, Walter Harper Folder, Box 2, Yvonne Mozée Collection, Mozée Family Papers, APRCA.

67. Harper to Mozée, April 18, 1914.

68. Harper to Mozée, July 5, 1914, Walter Harper Folder, Box 2, Yvonne Mozée Collection, Mozée Family Papers, APRCA.

69. Harper to Mozée, February 13, 1914.

70. Harper to Mozée, November 9, 1913.

71. Harper to Mozée, April 18, 1914.

72. Stuck to Cutler, February 25, 1914, Walter Harper File, #7697MH, NMHA.

73. Stuck to Cutler, February 17, 1914, Walter Harper File, #7697MH, NMHA.

74. Hudson Stuck, "Vale Walter Harper," *Fairbanks Daily News Miner*, December 4, 1918.

75. Harper to Mozée, April 18, 1914.

76. Harper to Mozée, July 5, 1914; Stuck to Cutler, December 24, 1914, Walter Harper File, #7697MH, NMHA; Stuck to L. L. Norton, May 15, 1915, Walter Harper File, #7697MH, NMHA.

77. Stuck to Cutler, May 27, 1914, Walter Harper File, #7697MH, NMHA.

78. "Yukon Indian Opens Coney Island Eyes," *New York Times*, June 1, 1914, http://denali2013.org/wp-content/uploads/2013/02/Walter-Harper-in-Coney-Island.pdf.

79. "Yukon Indian Opens Coney Island Eyes," *Fairbanks Daily Times*, July 8, 1914.

80. Stuck to Cutler, June 2, 1914, Walter Harper File, #7697MH, NMHA.

81. Stuck, *Winter Circuit*, 170.

82. Harper to Mozée, July 5, 1914.

83. Stuck to Cutler, February 23, 1916, Walter Harper File, #7697MH, NMHA.

84. Stuck to Cutler, December 17, 1915, Walter Harper File, #7697MH, NMHA.

85. Stuck to Cutler, February 23, 1916.

86. Harper to Stuck, February 24, 1916, Walter Harper File, #7697MH, NMHA.

87. Stuck to Cutler, February 25, 1916, Walter Harper File, #7697MH, NMHA.

88. Stuck, *Winter Circuit*, 338.

89. Harper to Stuck, February 24, 1916.

90. Harper to Stuck, February 24, 1916.

91. Harper to Stuck, February 24, 1916 (original emphasis).

92. Stuck to Cutler, April 17, 1916, Walter Harper File, #7697MH, NMHA.

93. Stuck to Cutler, June 28, 1916, Walter Harper File, #7697MH, NMHA.

94. Lester P. White, Secretary, Mount Hermon Alumni Association, to Bradford Washburn, April 20, 1951, Walter Harper Folder, Box 2, Yvonne Mozée Collection, Mozée Family Papers, APRCA.

95. Cutler to Stuck, June 30, 1916, Walter Harper File, #7697, NMHA.

96. John Chapman, undated article clipping from *Spirit of Missions*, 1918, 247, Thomas Reed File, #7822, NMHA. During his time at Mount Hermon, Reed spent a week at Columbia University in New York working with Professors Franz Boas and P. E. Goddard, the foremost linguists of the time working with Athabascan languages. Episcopal missionary John Chapman, who had spent many years recording the Athabascan dialect at Anvik, was meeting with the linguists as well, and they sought Tommy's assistance. Chapman to Cutler, January 20, 1915, and February 2, 1915, Thomas Reed File, #7822, NMHA.

97. Mackenzie, *Wolf Smeller*, 84–85, 140.

98. Burke, *Doctor Hap*, 290.

99. Mackenzie, *Wolf Smeller*, 184.

100. Mackenzie, *Wolf Smeller*, 120.

101. Multiple documents in Moses Cruikshank File, #10926, NMHA. Tatum's brother, E. R. Tatum, as well as others contributed to Cruikshank's tuition and other expenses at the school.

5. Return to Alaska

1. Biographical note in William A. Thomas Collection, APRCA.

2. W. A. Thomas diary, July 8, 1916, Thomas Collection, APRCA (hereafter Thomas diary and date).

3. Thomas diary, July 9, 1916.

4. Baldwin, *Enchanted Enclosure*, chap. 6, "Grand Loop," https://www.nps.gov/parkhistory/online_books/baldwin/chap6.htm/.

5. Baldwin, *Enchanted Enclosure*, chap. 1, "Introduction," https://www.nps.gov/parkhistory/online_books/baldwin/chap1.htm/.

6. Thomas diary, July 10, 1916.

7. Thomas diary, July 12, 1916.

8. Thomas diary, July 16 (quotation), 17, 1916.

9. Thomas diary, July 15, 1916.

10. Thomas diary, July 18–20, 1916.

11. Thomas diary, July 21–23, 1916 (quotation from July 23).

12. Thomas diary, July 25, 1916.

13. Fortuine, *Chills and Fever*, 317.

14. They could not travel from Seattle to Skagway on a Canadian ship. U.S. law forbid the transfer of passengers and goods between U.S. ports on foreign-owned ships. Travelers to and from Alaska on foreign-owned ships typically transferred in Vancouver.

15. Thomas diary, July 29, 1916.

16. Thomas diary, August 2, 1916.

17. Thomas diary, August 4, 6, 1916.

18. Stuck diary, August 6, 1916; Thomas diary, August 8, 1916.

19. Harper-Haines, *Cold River Spirits*, 178.

20. Thomas diary, August 13, 18, 1916.

21. Thomas diary, August 19, 1916.

22. Bradner, *1916 Alaska Diary*, 61.

23. Bradner, *1916 Alaska Diary*, 63.

24. Thomas diary, September 10, 17 (quotation), 1916.

25. Harper to Mount Hermon Cashier, November 18, 1916, Walter Harper File, #7697MH, NMHA.

26. Stuck to Wood, April 13, 1917, Stuck Correspondence, PECUSA, in APRCA; Stuck diary, October 6, 10, 1916; Stuck to Wood, February 27, 1917, Stuck Correspondence, PECUSA, in APRCA.

27. Burke, *Doctor Hap*, 226.

28. Stuck, "New Beginnings at Fort Yukon," 5, 7.

29. Dean, *Breaking Trail*, 206.

30. Stuck to Wood, April 13, 1917.

31. Stuck, "Arctic Hospital," 38.

32. Clara Heintz Burke to Lindley, September 8, 1917, C. Burke Correspondence, PECUSA, in APRCA.

33. Stuck to Wood, April 13, 1917.

34. C. Burke to Lindley, September 8, 1917.

35. Stuck diary, October 19, 1916.

36. Stuck diary, December 10, 12, 1916.

37. Stuck, *Voyages on the Yukon*, 145.

38. Stuck diary, November 30, December 1, 2, 4, 1916.

39. Stuck to Wood, February 27, 1917, Stuck Correspondence, PECUSA, in APRCA.

40. Frances Wells to All, July 15, 1917, 3–5, Wells Clan website, http://www.wellsclan.us/History/frances/AF15.htm; Burke, *Doctor Hap*, 221, 226.

41. F. Wells to J. Wells, June 6, 1917, Wells Clan website, http://www.wellsclan.us/History/frances/AF12.htm; Dean, *Breaking Trail*, 233.

42. George Gordon King to F. Wells, August 21, 1917; and King to F. Wells, August 22, 1917, both in Wells Correspondence, PECUSA, in APRCA.

43. Third Generation, biographical sketches of Guilliam and Margaretta Wells, Wells Clan website, http://www.wellsclan.us/History/generatn/d3.htm#P15.

44. "Victims of Sea Disaster: Miss Wells, of Germantown, on Ill-Fated Alaskan Steamship," *Germantown Pennsylvania Guide*, November 2, 1918.

45. "In Memoriam," 18.

46. Dorsey, "Episcopal Women Missionaries," 241.

47. F. Wells to J. Wells, February 23, 1917, Wells Clan website, http://www.wellsclan.us/History/frances/AF05.htm.

48. F. Wells to J. Wells, May 11, 1917, Wells Clan website, http://www.wellsclan.us/History/frances/AF10.htm.

49. F. Wells to Wood, April 27, 1917, Wells Correspondence, PECUSA, in APRCA.

50. F. Wells to J. Wells, June 6, 1917.

51. Wood to F. Wells, June 5, 1917, Wells Correspondence, PECUSA, in APRCA.

52. F. Wells to All, July 15, 1917.

53. F. Wells to All, July 15, 1917.

54. Stuck to Arthur Selden Lloyd, July 4, 1917, Stuck Correspondence, PECUSA, in APRCA.

55. F. Wells to All, July 15, 1917.

56. F. Wells to All, July 15, 1917.

57. F. Wells to All, July 15, 1917.

58. F. Wells to All, July 15, 1917.

59. Stuck to Lloyd, July 3, 1917.

60. Cruikshank, *Life I've Been Living*, 26–27.

61. Cruikshank, *Life I've Been Living*, 27.

62. Cruikshank, *Life I've Been Living*, 28; Stuck to Lloyd, July 3, 1917.

63. Cruikshank, *Life I've Been Living*, 28.

64. Cruikshank, *Life I've Been Living*, 28.

65. Dean, *Breaking Trail*, 232–33; Stuck diary, August 11, 1917.

66. Wood to C. Burke, June 29, 1918, Burke Correspondence, PECUSA, in APRCA.

67. Stuck diary, September 13, 29, 1917; Stuck, *Winter Circuit*, 6.

68. Stuck to Wood, February 27, 1917.

69. Stuck diary, October 14, 1917.

70. Stuck, *Winter Circuit*, 4–5.

71. Burke, *Doctor Hap*, 226.

72. Fortuine, *Chills and Fever*, 173.

73. Waller, *Discovery of the Germ*, esp. chap. 16.

74. Burke, *Doctor Hap*, 221–22.

75. M. Wood to C. Burke, September 5, 1918, Burke Correspondence, PECUSA, in APRCA. Mrs. John Wood wrote Clara Burke that the Mission Society had not been able to send one nurse to the foreign missions that year because all nurses willing to travel were going "over there."

76. Dean, *Breaking Trail*, 254.

77. Stuck to Wood, November 24, 1917, Stuck Correspondence, PECUSA, in APRCA. Stuck wrote, "During all these years he has never even smoked notwithstanding my constant smoking, and knows the taste and smell of liquor only enough to detest both."

78. Stuck diary, October 19, 23, 30, 1917.

79. Grafton Burke to Wood, October 30, 1917, Burke Correspondence, PECUSA, in APRCA.

80. Stuck diary October 30, November 4, 1917; Stuck, *Winter Circuit*, 4–5.

81. Burke, *Doctor Hap*, 226.

82. Margaret O'Farrell to Eleanor Wells, January 19, 1919.

6. The Winter Circuit

1. Stuck, *Winter Circuit*, 9.
2. Hudson Stuck, "Vale Walter Harper," *Fairbanks Daily News Miner*, December 4, 1918.
3. Stuck diary, November 8, 1917.
4. Stuck, *Winter Circuit*, 18.
5. Stuck, *Winter Circuit*, 25.
6. Stuck, *Winter Circuit*, 24.
7. Stuck to John Wood, November 24, 1917, Stuck Correspondence, PECUSA, in APRCA.
8. Stuck, *Winter Circuit*, 23–24.
9. Stuck to Wood, November 24, 1917.
10. Stuck, *Winter Circuit*, 26.
11. Stuck, *Winter Circuit*, 26.
12. Stuck diary, November 20, 1917; Stuck, *Winter Circuit*, 29.
13. Stuck to Wood, November 20, 24, 1917, Stuck Correspondence, PECUSA, in APRCA.
14. Stuck used the expression coined by Grafton Burke when he was a young boy—that his assistants worked while Stuck "stood around and made remarks." It seems that this expression became a running joke among Stuck and his admirers, as Harper used the expression when they were at Point Hope.
15. Stuck to Wood, November 24, 1917.
16. Dean, *Breaking Trail*, 227–29.
17. Stuck, *Winter Circuit*, 173.
18. Stuck, *Winter Circuit*, 66.
19. Stuck diary, November 21, 27, 1917.
20. Stuck, *Winter Circuit*, 31, 41.
21. Stuck, *Winter Circuit*, 38.
22. Stuck, *Winter Circuit*, 338.
23. Stuck to Wood, November 24, 1917.
24. Stuck, *Winter Circuit*, 34.
25. Stuck, *Winter Circuit*, 39–42. Stuck sat up long into the night recording Harper's words in his diary.
26. Stuck diary, December 18, 1917.
27. Stuck, *Winter Circuit*, 78.
28. Burch, "Inupiat and the Christianization of Arctic Alaska."
29. Burch, "Inupiat and the Christianization of Arctic Alaska," 81. Uyarak had been the first convert of Axel Karlsson, a Swedish Evangelical Covenant missionary who arrived in Unalakleet in 1887. Regarding the rapid spread of Christianity in the area, the anthropologist Ernest Burch identified a number of conditions that contributed to the surge, including the effectiveness of Iñupiaq evangelists and the timing of the movement. Iñupiaq communities had been effectively under siege at the time by destructive Western influences, includ-

ing deadly diseases that had killed many of their leaders. Their shamans were powerless against these diseases. Missionaries' remedies, on the other hand, often seemed to work miracles. Moreover Alaska Native spiritual beliefs were not exclusive, and many traditional beliefs did not conflict directly with Christianity. Thus one could maintain much of one's traditional spirituality while embracing the Christian message.

30. Stuck, *Winter Circuit*, 84–85.

31. Stuck, *Winter Circuit*, 85.

32. Hudson Stuck, "Vale Walter Harper," *Fairbanks Daily News Miner*, December 4, 1918.

33. Stuck, *Winter Circuit*, 146–48 (quotations on 147).

34. Stuck, *Winter Circuit*, 84–85.

35. Stuck, *Winter Circuit*, 323.

36. Stuck, *Winter Circuit*, 93.

37. Stuck, *Winter Circuit*, 94.

38. Stuck, *Winter Circuit*, 107.

39. Lowenstein, *Ultimate Americans*, 4–6, 9.

40. Captain Beechey named Cape Thompson for Deas Thomson, commissioner of the British Navy, but on his map he inserted a *p* in the name. Stuck, *Winter Circuit*, 94. Since then the place is referred to as either Cape Thomson or Cape Thompson.

41. Lowenstein, *Ultimate Americans*, 63–67.

42. Stuck, *Winter Circuit*, 103–5.

43. Lowenstein, *Ultimate Americans*, 118.

44. Average weather for Point Hope, Alaska, from WeatherSpark Beta, accessed August 7, 2013, https://weatherspark.com/averages/33039/Point-Hope-Alaska -United-States. Point Hope experienced "polar day" from May 24 to July 17, when the sun was continuously above the horizon.

45. "Christmas at Point Hope."

46. Stuck, *Winter Circuit*, 112–13; "Christmas at Point Hope," 77–78. Some missionaries, such as those of the Swedish Evangelical Covenant Church, opposed all forms of dancing. Other missionaries opposed Alaska Native dancing, owing to its association with traditional spiritual beliefs.

47. Stuck, *Winter Circuit*, 113, 125–26; Stuck diary, January 10, 1918.

48. Stuck diary, January 1, 1918.

49. Stuck, *Winter Circuit*, 114.

50. Stuck, *Winter Circuit*, 106, 115–16. Thomas was rationing the dwindling coal supply.

51. Stuck diary, January 7, 1918.

52. Stuck, *Winter Circuit*, 123.

53. Stuck, *Winter Circuit*, 117–19.

54. Stuck diary, January 10, 19, 1918.

55. Stuck wrote in *A Winter Circuit* that there would be "no opportunity

whatever of receiving any" mail along the route (8), but this was in the context of explaining that he looked forward to the break from his professional correspondence. At Kotzebue, Stuck received communications from both Barrow and Point Hope, telling him that he was expected. The communications may have been telegrams (83).

56. Both quotes from Stuck, *Winter Circuit*, 123.

57. Stuck, *Winter Circuit*, 126, 131.

58. Stuck, *Winter Circuit*, 246.

59. Stuck, *Winter Circuit*, 185.

60. Stuck, *Winter Circuit*, 158–59.

61. Stuck, *Winter Circuit*, 160; Stuck diary, February 10, 1918.

62. Stuck, *Winter Circuit*, 164.

63. Stuck, *Winter Circuit*, 176.

64. Stuck diary, February 18–20, 1918.

65. Stuck diary, February 20, 1918.

66. Stuck, *Winter Circuit*, 178.

67. Stuck, *Winter Circuit*, 192.

68. Stuck, *Winter Circuit*, 184–85; Stuck diary, February 14, 1918.

69. Stuck, *Winter Circuit*, 205, 209–10.

70. Stuck, *Winter Circuit*, 213.

71. Brower, with Farrelly and Anson, *Fifty Years below Zero*, 253.

72. Stuck, *Winter Circuit*, 214.

73. Brower, with Farrelly and Anson, *Fifty Years below Zero*, 253.

74. Stuck, *Winter Circuit*, 227.

75. Stuck, *Winter Circuit*, 215.

76. Stuck, *Winter Circuit*, 215, 217.

77. Stuck, *Winter Circuit*, 218–19 (quotation on both pages).

78. Brower, with Farrelly and Anson, *Fifty Years below Zero*, 257.

79. Stuck, *Winter Circuit*, 284–85.

80. Stuck, *Winter Circuit*, 284,

81. Stuck diary, April 4, 1918.

82. Stuck diary, April 5, 1918.

83. Stuck, *Winter Circuit*, 314.

84. Stuck, *Winter Circuit*, 283–84.

85. Usher, "Canadian Western Arctic," 171, 175.

86. Stuck, *Winter Circuit*, 321. Usher explains that five distinct groups of inland and coastal Inuit, including Iñupiat from the Arctic coastal region of Alaska, had been attracted to the region by the whaling activity and had formed an integrated and acculturated population in the region. Usher, "Canadian Western Arctic," 169–71.

87. Zaslow, *Opening of the Canadian North*, 272–73. Controversy developed after the expedition's main ship, the *Karluk*, became locked in ice in September 1913. Stefansson and five others left the ship to go hunting and never returned.

Four months after their departure the ship was crushed in the ice. Of the twenty-eight men aboard the *Karluk,* only twelve survived.

88. Stefansson, *Friendly Arctic,* 680–82.

89. Stuck to Wood, May 18, 1918, Stuck Correspondence, PECUSA, in APRCA.

90. Stuck, *Winter Circuit,* 334–36.

91. Stuck, *Winter Circuit,* 228; Riggs, *Report of the Governor of Alaska* (1918), 12–13. Governor Thomas Riggs wrote in his annual report that year, "It has been very gratifying to hear the numerous expressions of regret by natives throughout the Territory that they should have been exempted from the operations of the draft law" (12). Riggs expressed hope that the government would allow Natives to serve. The policy had been changed by the time the report was published.

92. Stuck, *Winter Circuit,* 338.

93. Stuck, *Winter Circuit,* 338.

94. Stuck, *Winter Circuit,* 338–39.

95. Stuck, *Winter Circuit,* 344.

96. Stefansson, *Discovery,* 210.

97. Stuck, *Winter Circuit,* 347.

98. Wood to Frances Wells, May 16, 1918, Wells Correspondence, PECUSA, in APRCA.

99. Stuck to Wood, May 18, 1918.

100. F. Wells to Wood, March 2, 1918, Wells Correspondence, PECUSA, in APRCA.

101. Dean, *Breaking Trail,* 234.

102. Hopkins, *Rise of the Social Gospel,* 327.

103. In a letter to Bishop Arthur Lloyd, Stuck wrote, "Now that, thank God, the war is done, there will, I suppose, be no dearth of nurses." Stuck to Lloyd, November 26, 1918, Stuck Correspondence, PECUSA, in APRCA.

104. Wells, "Good Argument."

105. F. Wells to Guilliam A. Wells, April 30, 1918, Wells Clan website, http://www.wellsclan.us/History/frances/af16-1.htm.

106. F. Wells to Guilliam A. Wells, April 30, 1918.

107. F. Wells to Guilliam A. Wells, May 27, 1918, Wells Clan website, http://www.wellsclan.us/History/frances/af16-2.htm.

108. F. Wells to Guilliam A. Wells, May 27, 1918.

109. F. Wells to G. A. Wells, June 2, 1918, Wells Clan website, http://www.wellsclan.us/History/frances/af16.htm.

110. Stuck diary, May 24, 1918.

7. Summer and Fall 1918

1. Frances Wells to Guilliam A. Wells, May 26, 1918 (postmarked June 2, 1918), Wells Clan website, http://www.wellsclan.us/History/frances/af16.htm.

2. F. Wells to Guilliam A. Wells, May 26, 1918.

3. F. Wells to Guilliam A. Wells, May 26, 1918.

4. Stuck diary, June 1, 1918.

5. F. Wells to John Wood, June 18, 1918, Wells Correspondence, PECUSA, in APRCA.

6. M. Wood to Clara Burke, September 5, 1918, Burke Correspondence, PECUSA, in APRCA.

7. Dean, *Breaking Trail*, 255.

8. G. A. Wells to J. Wood, July 31, 1918, Wells Correspondence, PECUSA, in APRCA.

9. Stuck diary, July 12, 16, 17, 18, 1918.

10. Stuck diary, July 18, 20, 23, 1918.

11. Stuck diary, July 21, 1918.

12. Stuck diary, July 25, 27, 28, 29, 30, 1918.

13. Stuck diary, August 27, 1918.

14. Dean, *Breaking Trail*, 268.

15. Bradner, *1916 Alaska Diary*, 63.

16. Stuck diary, May 24, 1918.

17. Stuck diary, August 8, 10, 11, 1918.

18. Stuck diary, August 16, 1918.

19. Stuck diary, August 23, 1918.

20. Stuck diary, August 23, 1918.

21. Stuck diary, November 7, 1918.

22. Stuck diary, August 24, 1918.

23. Stuck, "Wild Ride," 743.

24. Stuck diary, August 25, 1918.

25. Stuck, "Wild Ride," 744.

26. Brief biography of Jessie Harper Mozée Milligan, written to Yvonne Mozée, Mother Folder, Box 2, Yvonne Mozée Collection, Mozée Family Papers, APRCA.

27. Stuck, "Wild Ride," 744.

28. Frances Wells Harper to Margaret Harper O'Farrell, September 28, 1918, Wells Clan website, http://www.wellsclan.us/History/frances/AF18.htm.

29. Wells Harper to O'Farrell, September 28, 1918.

30. Frances Wells Harper to Jessie Harper Mozée, September 27, 1918, Walter Harper Folder, Box 2, Yvonne Mozée Collection, Mozée Family Papers, APRCA.

31. Stuck diary, September 4, 1918.

32. Wells Harper to Mozée, September 27, 1918.

33. Wells Harper to Mozée, September 27, 1918.

34. Wells Harper to O'Farrell, September 28, 1918.

35. Wells Harper to Mozée, September 27, 1918.

36. Wells Harper to O'Farrell, September 28, 1918.

37. Wells Harper to O'Farrell, September 28, 1918.

38. Stuck diary, October 10, 1918.

39. Stuck diary, September 4, 1918; Dean, *Breaking Trail*, 255. Stuck wrote

that the sum was "some $10,000." Stuck to Bishop Arthur Lloyd, November 16, 1918, Stuck Correspondence, PECUSA, in APRCA.

40. Stuck, "Advertisement," n.d., inserted at end of Stuck diary of 1918.

41. Wells Harper to Mozée, September 27, 1918.

42. Coates and Morrison, *Sinking of the "Princess Sophia,"* 48–49.

43. Coates and Morrison, *Sinking of the "Princess Sophia,"* 50–51.

44. Coates and Morrison, *Sinking of the Princess Sophia,"* 63.

45. O'Keefe and Macdonald, *Final Voyage,* 52.

46. Coates and Morrison, *Sinking of the "Princess Sophia,"* 68; O'Keefe and Macdonald, *Final Voyage,* 66.

47. Coates and Morrison, *Sinking of the "Princess Sophia,"* 66.

48. Coates and Morrison, *Sinking of the "Princess Sophia,"* 69.

49. Coates and Morrison, *Sinking of the "Princess Sophia,"* 85–87.

50. O'Keefe and Macdonald, *Final Voyage,* 69.

51. Coates and Morrison, *Sinking of the "Princess Sophia,"* 86, 202n45.

52. Coates and Morrison, *Sinking of the "Princess Sophia,"* 91.

53. Coates and Morrison, *Sinking of the "Princess Sophia,"* 92.

54. Coates and Morrison, *Sinking of the "Princess Sophia,"* 94–95.

55. O'Keefe and Macdonald, *Final Voyage,* 75.

56. O'Keefe and Macdonald, *Final Voyage,* 78–79.

57. "In Memoriam," 828.

58. O'Keefe and Macdonald, *Final Voyage,* 83.

59. Coates and Morrison, *Sinking of the "Princess Sophia,"* 117 (quotation), 119.

60. Stuck diary, October 26, 1918.

61. Stuck diary, October 28, 1918.

62. Stuck diary, October 31, November 1, 1918 (quotation).

63. Stuck diary, November 1, 3, 1918.

64. From the Wells Clan website: Aunt Jeannie to John Wells, November 17, 1918, http://www.wellsclan.us/History/frances/AF23.htm; George Wells to John Wells, November 2, 1918, http://www.wellsclan.us/History/frances/af21.htm; Eleanor Wells to John Wells, October 28, 1918, http://www.wellsclan.us/History/frances/af19.htm.

65. G. A. Wells to J. Wells, December 4, 1918, Wells Clan website, http://www.wellsclan.us/History/frances/af24.htm.

66. O'Keefe and Macdonald, *Final Voyage,* 60.

67. Stuck diary, November 7, 1918.

68. O'Keefe and Macdonald, *Final Voyage,* 81, 178.

69. O'Keefe and Macdonald, *Final Voyage,* 160–61.

Epilogue

1. Burke, *Doctor Hap,* 234.

2. George A. Wells to J. Wells, November 2, 1918, Wells Clan website, http://www.wellsclan.us/History/frances/af21.htm.

3. G. A. Wells to J. Wells, December 4, 1918.

4. Stuck to Bishop Arthur S. Lloyd, December 12, 1918, Stuck Correspondence, PECUSA, in APRCA.

5. Stuck to Bishop Arthur Lloyd, November 16, 1918, Stuck Correspondence, PECUSA, in APRCA; Drane, "Death of Archdeacon Stuck," 5.

6. Stuck to Frederick Drane, October 31, 1918, Folder 2, Box 1, Frederick Drane Correspondence, PECUSA, in APRCA.

7. Stuck to Lloyd, December 30, 1918, Stuck Correspondence, PECUSA, in APRCA.

8. Stuck, *Alaskan Missions of the Episcopal Church*.

9. Dean, *Breaking Trail*, 275–76.

10. Dean, *Breaking Trail*, 278–79.

11. Dan Sutherland to Grafton Burke, January 26, 1921, Burke Correspondence, PECUSA, in APRCA.

12. Dean, *Breaking Trail*, 290.

13. Drane, "Death of Archdeacon Stuck," 5.

Bibliography

Archival Collections

APRCA. Alaska and Polar Regions Collections and Archives. Rasmuson Library, University of Alaska Fairbanks

    Episcopal Diocese of Alaska Records (MF 88, 91)

        Rev. Hudson Stuck Diaries

MF 88, reel 1, contains 1904, 1905, 1910.

MF 91, reel 1, contains 1909, 1911, 1912; reel 2 contains 1914, 1915, 1916; reel 3 contains 1917–18.

    Hudson Stuck Papers 1902–20

Box 4 contains a copy of the Hudson Stuck Climbing Journal from the 1913 ascent of Denali; the American Geographical Society, in New York City, holds the original.

    PECUSA. Protestant Episcopal Church in the USA. National Council (Domestic and Foreign Missionary Society). Alaska Records. 1884–1952 (MF 142) (Originals in Domestic and Foreign Society Alaska Papers 1889–1939, Archives of the Episcopal Church, Austin TX)

        Grafton Burke Correspondence, reels 3 and 4

        Frederick Drane Correspondence, reels 8 and 9

        Hudson Stuck Correspondence, reels 25–27

        Frances Wells Correspondence, reel 28

    Harper, J. S. "Arthur Harper: The Grand Old Man of the Yukon," November 1, 1941. Cecil Robe Collection.

    Mozée Family Papers.

        Yvonne Mozée Collection. Box 2.

Walter Harper 1913 Climbing Journal, in Walter Harper Diary Folder.

    Mozée, Yvonne. Interview by Bill Schneider and Karen Brewster, recorded September 11, 2003, Fairbanks AK. Oral History Recording #2000-07-14.

Sheldon, Charles. Papers.

Thomas, William A. Collection.

Wright, Al. Interview by Bill Schneider, recorded June 15, 2012. Oral History Recording #2012-08-03 pt. 2.

NMHA. Northfield Mount Hermon Archives, Mount Hermon MA

Cruikshank, Moses. File #10926.

Harper, Walter. File #7697MH.

Reed, Thomas. File #7822.

Published Sources

Alton, Thomas. "July 1915: Wickersham Meets the Tanana Chiefs." Paper delivered at Alaska Statewide Phi Alpha Theta meeting, University of Alaska Fairbanks, March 2010.

"Annie Cragg Farthing." *Alaskan Churchman* 5, no. 2 (February 1911): 10.

Askins, Kathryn. "Bridging Cultures: American Indian Students at the Northfield Mount Hermon School." PhD diss., University of New Hampshire, 2009.

Baldwin, Kenneth H. *Enchanted Enclosure: The Army Engineers and Yellowstone National Park; A Documentary History*. Washington DC: U.S. Army Office of the Chief of Engineers, Historical Division, 1976. Accessed February 1, 2015. https://www.nps.gov/parkhistory/online_books/baldwin/.

"Bear, 1885." U.S. Coast Guard website. Accessed February 15, 2015. http://www.uscg.mil/history/cutters/Bear/Bear1885.asp.

Berry, J. W. "Acculturation among Circumpolar Peoples—Implications for Health Status." *Arctic Medical Research* 40 (1985): 21–27.

Berton, Pierre. *The Klondike Fever: The Life and Death of the Last Great Gold Rush.* New York: Carroll & Graf, 1958.

Betticher, Charles. "Tortella Hall." *Alaskan Churchman* 3, no. 1 (November 1908): 12–13.

———. "The Tanana Valley Mission." *Alaskan Churchman* 2, no. 4 (August 1908): 52–57.

Bradner, Lester. *A 1916 Alaska Diary.* [Saunderstown RI]: Robert Bradner Publications, 2008.

Brady, John. *Report of the Governor of Alaska to the Secretary of the Interior.* Washington DC: GPO, 1905.

Brooks, Alfred. *Blazing Alaska's Trails.* Fairbanks: University of Alaska and the Arctic Institute of North America, 1953.

Brower, Charles, in collaboration with Philip Farrelly and Lyman Anson. *Fifty Years below Zero: A Lifetime of Adventure in the Far North.* New York: Dodd, Mead, 1943.

Browne, Belmore. *The Conquest of Mount McKinley: The story of three expeditions through the Alaskan wilderness to Mount McKinley, North America's highest and most inaccessible mountain.* New York: G. P. Putnam's Sons, 1913.

Burch, Ernest. "The Inupiat and the Christianization of Arctic Alaska." *Etudes/Inuit/Studies* 18, no. 1–2 (1994): 81–108.

Burke, Clara Heintz. *Doctor Hap.* As told to Adele Comandini. New York: Coward-McCann, 1961.

Butts, Dennis. "Muscular Christianity and the Children's Story." In *Children's Literature and Social Change: Some Case Studies from Barbara Hofland to Philip Pullman,* 23–35. Cambridge: Luttsworth Press, 2010. Accessed July 28, 2014. http://www.lutterworth.com/pub/childrens%20literature%20ch3.pdf.

Campbell, Diane. "A Granddaughter's Tale: Native Alaskans, Including a Teenage Boy, Played a Major Role in Historic First Climb to Denali's Summit; The Stuck-Karstens Expedition." *Alaska Magazine* 79, no. 1 (February 2013): 34–35.

Carter, Burnham. *So Much to Learn: The History of Northfield Mount Hermon School in Commemoration of the 100th Anniversary 1980.* Northfield MA: Northfield Mount Hermon School, 1976.

"Christmas at Point Hope." *Alaskan Churchman* 12, no. 3 (May 1918): 76–77.

Clark, Walter. *Report of the Governor of Alaska to the Secretary of the Interior.* Washington DC: GPO, 1910.

———. *Report of the Governor of Alaska to the Secretary of the Interior.* Washington DC: GPO, 1911.

Coates, Ken, and Bill Morrison. *The Sinking of the "Princess Sophia": Taking the North Down with Her.* Fairbanks: University of Alaska Press, 1991.

Cole, Terrence. "One Man's Purgatory." *Alaska Journal* 9, no. 3 (Summer 1979): 85–90.

Cook, Harold. "From the Scientific Revolution to the Germ Theory." In *Western Medicine: An Illustrated History,* 80–101. New York: Oxford University Press, 1997.

Coombs, Colby. *Denali's West Buttress: A Climber's Guide to Mount McKinley's Classic Route.* Seattle: Mountaineers, 1997.

Cruikshank, Moses. Interview by William Schneider. Project Jukebox, Alaska and Polar Regions Department, Rasmuson Library, University of Alaska Fairbanks. http://jukebox.uaf.edu/site/akmushing/content/interviews.

———. *The Life I've Been Living.* Recorded and compiled by William Schneider. Fairbanks: Alaska and Polar Regions Department, Elmer Rasmuson Library, University of Alaska, 1986.

Dean, David. *Breaking Trail: Hudson Stuck of Texas and Alaska.* Athens: Ohio University Press, 1988.

"Denali Legacy: 100 Years on the Mountain." University of Alaska Museum of the North. Accessed October 20, 2014. http://www.uaf.edu/museum/exhibits/special-exhibits/past-exhibits/denali-legacy/.

Donovan, Mary Sudman. *A Different Call: Women's Ministries in the Episcopal Church, 1850–1920.* Peabody MA: Morehouse Publishing, 1986.

Dorsey, Janine. "Episcopal Women Missionaries as Cultural Intermediaries in Interior Alaska Native Villages, 1894–1932." PhD diss., University of New Mexico, 2008.

Drane, Frederick B. "The Death of Archdeacon Stuck." *Alaskan Churchman* 15, no. 1 (November 1920): 5.

Dunham, Samuel. *The Alaskan Gold Fields and the Opportunities They Offer for Capital and Labor.* Department of Labor Bulletin No. 14. Washington DC: U.S. Department of Labor, 1898.

Dunn, Robert. *The Shameless Diary of an Explorer: A Story of Failure on Mt. McKinley.* 1907. New York: Modern Library, 2001.

Episcopal Diocese of Alaska. *A Century of Faith: Centennial Commemorative, 1895–1995, Episcopal Diocese of Alaska.* Fairbanks: Centennial Press and Episcopal Diocese of Alaska, 1995.

Fortuine, Robert. *Chills and Fever: Health and Disease in the Early History of Alaska.* Fairbanks: University of Alaska Press, 1989.

"The Future." *Alaskan Churchman* 2, no. 1 (November 1907): 2.

"G. A. Henty 1832–1902." The First Golden Age, PBS.org. Accessed June 1, 2013. http://www.pbs.org/wgbh/masterpiece/ railway/age/henty_bio.html.

Gatlin, Dana. "Interesting People: Arthur Voegtlin." *American Magazine,* August 1913, 38–39.

Grider, M. S. "St. Mark's Mission, Nenana." *Alaskan Churchman* 6, no. 2 (May 1912): 41–44.

Hamilton, Sally Atwood, ed. *Lift Thine Eyes: The Landscape, the Buildings, the Heritage of Northfield Mount Hermon School.* Mount Hermon MA: Northfield Mount Herman, 2010.

Harper-Haines, Jan. *Cold River Spirits: Whispers from a Family's Forgotten Past.* Kenmore WA: Epicenter Press, 2000.

Higher Peak Altitude Training. Altitude chart. Accessed September 1, 2014. http://www.higherpeak.com/altitudechart.html.

Hoggatt, Wilford B. *Report of the Governor of Alaska to the Secretary of the Interior.* Washington DC: GPO, 1909.

Hopkins, Charles Howard. *The Rise of the Social Gospel in American Protestantism, 1865–1915.* New Haven: Yale University Press, 1940.

Hough, Emerson. *Alaskans in the Far North.* New York: Harper and Brothers, 1918. Accessed March 1, 2015. http://www.gutenberg.org/files/28694/28694 -h/28694-h.htm#XIV.

House Committee on the Territories. *Conditions in Alaska: Statement of M. H. Foster, February 15, 1912.* Washington DC: GPO: 1912.

"In Memoriam." *Spirit of Missions,* December 1918, 18.

Karstens, Eugene. "Mike Sfraga Talks with Eugene Karstens, June 24, 1992." Denali, National Park Service website. Accessed August 28, 2014. http:// www.nps.gov/dena/historyculture/1913.htm.

Karstens, Harry. "Here's a Pioneer." Interview with Harry Karstens, Fairbanks,

1950s. Edited and transcribed in February 2013 by Jay Elhard, Denali National Park and Preserve. Accessed August 28, 2014. https://www.nps.gov/media /video/view.htm?id=C78BE689–1DD8-B71C-0743C108D6B6C560.

———. 1913 Climbing Journal. Harry P. Karstens Collection. Henry S. Hall Jr. American Alpine Club Library, Golden CO. Accessed March 20, 2016. http://explore.americanalpineclub.org/ index.php/Detail/Object/Show /object_id/5408.

Knapp, Lyman E. *Report of the Governor of the District of Alaska to the Secretary of the Interior 1894*. Washington DC: GPO, 1894.

Krauss, Michael. *Alaska Native Languages: Past, Present, and Future*. Alaska Native Language Center Research Papers No. 4. Fairbanks: Alaska Native Language Center, 1980.

La Belle, Jim, and Stacy M. Smith. "Boarding School: Historical Trauma among Alaska's Native People." National Resource Center for American Indian, Alaska Native, and Native Hawaiian Elders, October 2005. https://www.uaa .alaska.edu/academics/college-of-health/nrc-alaska-native-elders/_documents /yr2_2boarding-school.pdf.

Lloyd, Steve. "The Loss of the SS State of California, Gambier Bay, Alaska, August 1913." *The Sea Chest*, September 2009, 14–24. http://nebula.wsimg.com /5120a55a28c90347a82402c2fc8eccf4?AccessKeyId=49438a3d51eeaba12898 &disposition=0&alloworigin=1.

Lowenstein, Tom. *Ultimate Americans: Point Hope, Alaska: 1826–1909*. Fairbanks: University of Alaska Press, 2008.

Mackenzie, Clara Childs. *Wolf Smeller (Zhoh Gwatson): A Biography of John Fredson, Native Alaskan*. Anchorage: Alaska Pacific University Press, 1985.

Mazel, David. *Pioneering Ascents: The Origins of Climbing in America, 1642–1873*. Vienna VA: Potomac Appalachian Trail Club, 1991.

Mercier, François Xavier. *Recollections of the Youkon: Memoires from the Years 1868–1885*. Translated, edited, and annotated by Linda Finn Yarborough. Anchorage: Alaska Historical Society, 1986.

Mining and Engineering World. Vol. 44, January 1–June 24, 1916. Chicago: Mining World, 1916.

Moore, Terris. *Mt. McKinley: The Pioneer Climbs*. 2nd ed. Seattle: Mountaineers for the University of Alaska, 1981.

Mozée, Yvonne. "Walter Harper." Appendix to *Ascent of Denali: First complete ascent of Mt. McKinley, highest peak in North America, containing the original diary of Walter Harper, first man to achieve Denali's true summit*, by Hudson Stuck. New York: Charles Scribner's Sons, 1914. Reprint, Seattle: Mountaineers, 1977.

Murphy, Claire Rudolf, and Jane G. Haigh. *Gold Rush Women*. Portland OR: Alaska Northwest Books, 1997.

Naske, Claus-M., and Herman E. Slotnick. *Alaska: A History of the 49th State*. 2nd ed. Norman: University of Oklahoma Press, 1987.

Nichols, Jeannette Paddock. *Alaska: A History of Its Administration, Exploitation, and Industrial Development during Its First Half Century under the Rule of the United States.* Cleveland: Arthur H. Clark, 1924.

Noble, Dennis L., and Truman R. Strobridge. *Captain "Hell Roaring" Mike Healy: From American Slave to Arctic Hero.* Gainesville: University Press of Florida, 2009.

Ogilvie, William. *Early Days on the Yukon & the Story of Its Gold Finds.* Ottawa: Thorburn & Abbott, 1913.

O'Keefe, Betty, and Ian Macdonald. *The Final Voyage of the "Princess Sophia": Did They All Have to Die?* Surrey BC: Heritage House, 1998.

Osgood, Cornelius. *The Han Indians: A Compilation of Ethnographic and Historical Data on the Alaska-Yukon Boundary Area.* New Haven: Yale University Department of Anthropology, 1971.

Pratt, Richard H. "The Advantages of Mingling Indians with Whites." In *Americanizing the American Indians: Writings by the "Friends of the Indian" 1890–1900*, edited by Francis Paul Prucha, 260–71. Cambridge MA: Harvard University Press, 1973.

Prucha, Francis Paul. *The Great Father: The United States Government and the American Indians.* Vol. 2. Lincoln: University of Nebraska Press, 1984.

Riggs, Thomas. *Report of the Governor of Alaska 1918.* Washington DC: GPO, 1918.

Rowe, Peter T. Statement in *Hearings before the Committee on the Territories of the House of Representatives on Conditions in Alaska*, January 16, 1912. Washington DC: GPO, 1912.

Russell, Israel. "A Journey up the Yukon River." *Journal of the American Geographical Society* 28, no. 2 (1895).

Schwatka, Frederick. *Along Alaska's Great River: A popular account of the travels of an Alaska exploring expedition along the great Yukon River, from its source to its mouth, in the British Northwest Territory, and in the Territory of Alaska.* New York: George M. Hill Company, 1898.

Sheldon, Charles. *The Wilderness of Denali: Explorations of a Hunter-Naturalist in Northern Alaska.* New York: Charles Scribner's Sons, 1930.

Simeone, William E. *Rifles, Blankets, and Beads: Identity, History, and the Northern Athapaskan Potlatch.* Norman: University of Oklahoma Press, 1995.

Spurr, Josiah. *Geology of the Yukon Gold District, Alaska.* U.S. Geological Survey 18th Annual Report, part III. Washington DC: GPO, 1898.

Stefansson, Vilhjalmur. *Discovery: The Autobiography of Vilhjalmur Stefansson.* New York: McGraw-Hill, 1964.

———. *The Friendly Arctic: The Story of Five Years in the Polar Regions.* New York: Macmillan, 1921.

Strong, J. F. A. *Report of the Governor of Alaska 1916.* Washington DC: GPO, 1916.

———. *Report of the Governor of the Territory of Alaska to the Secretary of the Interior.* Washington DC: GPO, 1914.

———. *Report of the Governor of the Territory of Alaska to the Secretary of the Interior*. Washington DC: GPO, 1917.

Stuck, Hudson. *The Alaskan Missions of the Episcopal Church*. New York: Domestic and Foreign Missionary Society, 1920.

———. "Along Alaska's Great River." *Spirit of Missions*, September 1912.

———. "The Arctic Hospital." *Scribner's Magazine* 76, no. 1 (July 1919): 37–44.

———. *Ascent of Denali: First complete ascent of Mt. McKinley, highest peak in North America, containing the original diary of Walter Harper, first man to achieve Denali's true summit*. New York: Charles Scriber's Sons, 1914. Reprint, Seattle: Mountaineers, 1977.

———. "A Flying Visit to the Tanana Crossing." *Alaskan Churchman* 7, no. 3 (May 1913): 84.

———. "New Beginnings at Fort Yukon." *Spirit of Missions*, July 1909.

———. "On Denali (Mount McKinley)." *Spirit of Missions*, January 1914.

———. "St. Stephen's Hospital, Fort Yukon, Alaska." *Alaskan Churchman* 13, no. 3 (May 1919): 73–77.

———. *Ten Thousand Miles with a Dog Sled: A Narrative of Winter Travel in Interior Alaska*. Introduction by Terrence Cole. New York: Charles Scribner's Sons, 1914. Reprint, Lincoln: University of Nebraska Press, 1988.

———. "The Third Cruise of the Pelican." *Spirit of Missions*, May 1911.

———. *Voyages on the Yukon and Its Tributaries: A Narrative of Summer Travel in the Interior of Alaska*. New York: Charles Scribner's Sons, 1917.

———. "A Wild Ride." *Spirit of Missions*, November 1918, 741–44.

———. *A Winter Circuit of Our Arctic Coast: A Narrative of a Journey with Dog-Sleds around the Entire Arctic Coast of Alaska*. New York: Charles Scribner's Sons, 1920.

Swineford, A. P. *Report of the Governor of the District of Alaska to the Secretary of the Interior*. Washington DC: GPO, 1886.

"A Strategic Point." *Alaskan Churchman* 1, no. 4 (August 1907): 11–12.

Tatum, Robert. 1913 Climbing Journal. Robert G. Tatum Papers, MS 0774, University of Tennessee Knoxville Libraries Scout Special Collections Online. http://dlc.lib.utk.edu/ spc/view?docId=tei/0012_003086_000201_0000/0012 _003086_000201 _0000.xml;query=;brand=default.

———. Diary, 1922 January 1–December 23. Robert G. Tatum Papers, MS 0774, University of Tennessee Knoxville Libraries Scout Special Collections Online. http://dlc.lib.utk.edu/spc/view?docId=tei/0012_003086_000202_0000/0012 _003086_000202_0000.xml;query=Robert%20G.%20Tatum;brand=default.

Turck, Thomas J., and Diane L. Lehman Turck. "Trading Posts along the Yukon River: Noochuloghoyet Trading Post in Historical Context." *Arctic* 45, no. 1 (March 1992): 51–61.

United States. Joint Federal-State Commission on Policies and Programs Affecting Alaska Natives. *Alaska Natives Commission Final Report*. Vol. 2. Anchorage: Joint Federal-State Commission on Policies and Programs Affecting Alaska Natives, 1994.

Usher, Peter. "The Canadian Western Arctic: A Century of Change." *Anthropologica*, n.s., 13, no. 1–2, Special Issue: Pilot, Not Commander—Essays in Memory of Diamond Jenness (1971): 169–83.

Waggoner, Michael. *Missionaries in Alaska: A Historical Survey to 1920*. Anchorage: Alaska Historical Commission, 1980.

Walker, Tom. *The Seventymile Kid: The Lost Legacy of Harry Karstens and the First Ascent of Mount McKinley*. Seattle: Mountaineers Books, 2013.

Waller, John. *The Discovery of the Germ: Twenty Years That Transformed the Way We Think about Disease*. New York: Columbia University Press, 2003.

Washburn, Brad. "A Brief History of the West Buttress Route's Origins." In *Denali's West Buttress: A Climber's Guide to Mount McKinley's Classic Route*, edited by Colby Coombs, 18–26. Seattle: Mountaineers, 1997.

Wells Clan website. http://www.wellsclan.us/History/.

WeatherSpark Beta. Average weather for Point Hope, Alaska, usa. Accessed August 7, 2013. https://weatherspark.com/ averages/33039/Point-Hope -Alaska-United-States.

Wells, Frances. "A Good Argument." *Alaskan Churchman* 13, no. 3 (May 1918): 77–79.

Wickersham, James. *Old Yukon: Tales, Trails, and Trials*. Edited by Terrence Cole. Fairbanks: University of Alaska Press, 2009.

Wright, Allen A. *Prelude to Bonanza: The Discovery and Exploration of the Yukon*. Sidney bc: Gray's Publishing, 1976.

Yarborough, Linda Finn. Introduction to *Recollections of the Youkon: Memoires from the Years 1868–1865*, by François Xavier Mercier. Anchorage: Alaska Historical Society, 1986.

Yeend, Warren. *Gold Placers of the Historical Fortymile River Region, Alaska*. U.S. Geological Survey Bulletin No. 2125. Washington dc: gpo, 1996.

Young, S. Hall. *Hall Young of Alaska: The Mushing Parson*. New York: Gleming H. Revel Company, 1927.

Yukon Register of Historic Places. Government of Yukon website. Accessed November 16, 2014. http://register.yukonhistoricplaces.ca/Place/1170.

Zaslow, Morris. *The Opening of the Canadian North, 1870–1914*. Toronto: McClelland and Stewart, 1971.

Index

social gospel, 17, 137
Spence, Frank, 131
State of California, 82
Stefansson, Vilhjalmur, 133, 135–35, *136*
Stevens Village, 48
St. John's in-the-Wilderness, 24, 30, 32, 119, 121, 160n115
St. Mark's Mission, 25–28, 29, 55, 78, 105
Stringer, Isaac, 40
Strong, J. F. A., 12
St. Stephen's Hospital, 105, 106–8, 133, 140, 142
Stuck, Hudson:
—as archdeacon: on Farthing, 28; agitates for Barrow hospital, 131–32; appeals for support for mission, 112, 152; arrival in Alaska, 21, 23; campaign against alcohol, 40, 43, 107–8; chooses Walter Harper as his guide/interpreter, 28; death, 152; feelings for Clara Burke, 32–33; feels his age, 118; friendship with Wood, xiv, 111; on importance of subsistence skills, 121; keeps diary, 121; meets Stefansson, 136–37; picture, *22*; planned trip to Point Hope mission, 114; protests Alaskan canneries, 142, 152; publishes books, 113, 152; rescues badly burned boy, 143–44; and smallpox, 41, 42; and St. Stephen's Hospital, 105, 107; on summer mission trail with Walter Harper, 39–42, 44–48, 81, 106, 112, 141–44; as traveling missionary, 29–31; and *A Winter Circuit of Our Arctic Coast*, xi, 121, 134–35, 152; on winter mission trail with Walter Harper, 34–38, 42–44, 48–49, 109, 115, *116*, 117–38
—Denali climb: at base camp, 58, 60; bestowing of place names during, 79; and descent, 76; earlier climbing experience, 51–52; funding of, 54–55; idea of, 41, 45; Karsten's difficulty with Stuck on, 56, 60, 62, 77, 166n53, 166n65; lectures on, 83; physical ills during, xiv, 60, 68, 70, 71; picking team for, 54–55; pictures, *58*, *63*; planning for, 46–47, 48, 49; reaches peak, 72; reaction to fire, 64; receives plaudits for, 77; reminisces

about, 132; use of to help mission, 78; work on ascent, 60–61, 65, 67, 68
—relationship with Walter Harper: beginning of, 25; and book dedications, xi, 113; compensation for labor in, ix–xiii; and diary keeping, 121, 134; effect of Walter Harper's death on, 149, 150, 151–52; father-son relationship develops in, 115; growing trust in, xiv, xix–xx, 122, 134–35; legacy of seen through, 120; love for Walter Harper, 28, 34, 79, 115, 119; during Mount Hermon years, 84, 92, 94, 95–96, 97; nature of, 120; pictures, *103*, *108*; and planned trip to Point Hope, 114; praise for Walter Harper, 56, 68, 70, 117, 119, 131, 135, 144; scolding of Walter Harper, 40; sense of owing to Walter Harper, xiv, 119; travel to NYC in, 82–84; trip from Mount Hermon to Alaska in, 99–102; as tutor in, 28, 39, 67, 94, 97, 115, 120–21, 125, 132, 135; view of Walter Harper's faith, 31–32; view of Walter Harper's plans for marriage and army, 115, 134, 140; Walter Harper achieves independence from, xix–xx; Walter Harper as interpreter for, 31, 43, 142; Walter Harper as riverboat guide for, 28, 30–31, 34, 39, 42, 44–45, 143–44; and Walter Harper's father, 90, 119; at Walter Harper's wedding, 144; Walter Harper works as assistant for, 31, 33, 40–41, 81, 106; worry over Walter Harper's future prospects, 38, 81–82, 119, 146
Sulzer, Charles, 142
Swineford, A. P., 12

Tanana, 23–24, 25, 46, 49, 82, 142
Tatum, Robert: chosen for expedition, 55; inexperience as climber, xx; life after Denali, 78–79; mission work, 81; at Mount Hermon, 94; part in Denali ascent, 56, 59, 60, 64, 65, 66, 67, 68, 70, 71; pays Cruikshank's tuition, 98; reaches peak of Denali, 72, 73
Taylor, William, 53
Thomas, Chief, 105

Thomas, William, 99–102, *103, 104,* 105–6, 123, 124–27

United States, 6, 11–12, 17–18, 85

Veniaminov, Ivan, 18
Voegtlin, Arthur, 83

Wainwright, 128–29
Watson, Richard, 89
Wells, Frances: arrives in Alaska, 109–12; boards *Princess Sophia,* 146; bonds with sisters-in-law, 115, 144, 145–46; commitment to mission work, 137, 138; corresponds with Wood, 111, 136, 137, 140; death of, 149, 150, 151; falls in love with Walter Harper, 114–15, 127; and Jenny's slippers, 144, 146; marries Walter Harper, 144–45; nurses Walter Harper, 114; picture, *110;* prepares her family for marriage, 139–40; reunion with Walter Harper, 137, 138; work at St. Stephen's Hospital, 140, 151
Wells, Guilliam, 109, 139–40, 150, 151

Wells, John, 150, 151
whaling, commercial, 132–33
White Act, 152
Wickersham, James, 13, *15,* 51, 52–53, 78
William, Alexander, 13, *14,* 16
William, Robert, 13
A Winter Circuit of Our Arctic Coast (Stuck), xi, 121, 134–35, 152
Wood, John: corresponds with Hudson Stuck, xiv, 38, 119; and Frances Wells, 111, 136, 137, 140; on summer mission with Stuck, 112; view of Walter Harper, 113
World War I, 115, 118, 130, 142, 146
Wright, Arthur: and Episcopal mission, 23; at Mount Hermon, 84, 86, 91; Stuck dedicates book to, 113; as Stuck's assistant, 29, 30–31

Yanert, Bill, 33
Yanert, Herman, 33
Yellowstone Park, 99–101
Young, S. Hall, 20